Advance Praise
for
THE NEW ENTREPRENEURS

"The New Entrepreneurs is provocative and fresh. The authors' diverse views of the future are filled with insight and challenge."

> David Altany
> Features Editor
> *Industry Week*

"A compelling collection of essays! Each communicates riveting entrepreneurial ideas for all leaders in business, government, medicine, education, religion, and technology. A 'must implement' book for men and women who yearn to create responsible-oriented'transformation out of our current chaotic business, political and social environments. A rich resource for the 21st century, today."

> Pamela R. Monroe
> President, San Francisco Chapter
> National Association of Women Business Owners

"In a world defined by rapid change, *The New Entrepreneurs* captures the leading thinking that is creating the new business paradigm. Yet it transcends the usual intellectual verbiage that often surrounds these discussions by providing entrepreneurs with a useful, real-life framework for managing the rapid change taking place in their own lives and organizations.

> Darrell J. Brown
> President & Executive Editor
> *Leaders* magazine

"In an age of unprecedented change, the need for creative entrepreneurship could not be greater. This book blazes with the passion, drive, vision, brilliance, and rebelliousness of a new breed of entrepreneurs. It offers the essence of their special talent we must all cultivate today."

William E. Halal
Professor of Management
George Washington University
author, *Internal Markets: Bringing the Power of Free Enterprise Inside Your Organization*

"If you've ever asked yourself what makes the difference between an entrepreneur and a corporate manager (and who in business hasn't?), read *The New Entrepreneurs* and you will find the key—ATTITUDE!"

Rolf Österberg
author, *Corporate Renaissance*
former Chairman, Swedish Newspapers Association

"New people, new motivation, new objectives—the emphasis in this book is really on the word 'new.' From the entrepreneurs themselves you learn how they have employed spirit and passion in ways that take us well beyond traditional concepts of entrepreneurship. A high point is the section on what entrepreneurs of the future will do to invent the entrepreneurial organization itself."

Perry Pascarella
Vice President
Penton Publishing Inc.

"A practical guide for inventing the future. We can all learn from these pioneers how to get what we want and make the world a better place."

Jonathan Dana
President & CEO
Triton Pictures

"This book offers lots of state-of-the-art advice and personal inspiration for anyone with an entrepreneurial bent. Turn to any page and get absorbed in the wit and insight that make this book a powerful resource for today's leaders."

Ann Morrison
author, *The New Leaders: Guidelines on Leadership Diversity in America*
co-author, *Breaking the Glass Ceiling*

"The 'new entrepreneurship' is a felicitous term for describing both a new kind of businessperson and a restructuring of business as we have known it. Large corporations are downsizing and dematerializing before our eyes. In many cases the organizational fragments and discarded persons create 'new paradigm' entities with new operative values and a new sense of the true mission of business. The individual who seeks to understand this momentous development would do well to start with this book."

Willis Harman
President, Institute of Noetic Sciences
co-founder, World Business Academy

"The New Entrepreneurs: Business Visionaries for the 21st Century is eminently readable and both practical and inspiring."

Hardy Jones, filmmaker
co-owner, Hardy Jones/Julia Whitty Productions

"Someone once said, 'An entrepreneur is someone who works 60-80 hours a week to avoid having to work 40.' *The New Entrepreneurs* dispels the myth that entrepreneurs choose that way of work because something is *wrong* with corporate life. They choose it because something is *right* with putting our values and visions to work as fully as we can, by any means. The authors demonstrate clearly that we all can do this! Perhaps we've just been waiting for the inspirational gifts that the authors shower on us in *The New Entrepreneurs!*"

William Miller
author, *Quantum Quality*

"If you have ever wondered what qualities one must 'really' possess to be an entrepreneur—you will find them clearly defined in this book. *The New Entrepreneurs* offers a fabulous insight into the consciousness of an entrepreneur."

Shirley Nelson
CEO and chairman
Summit Bank

"Many 'think tanks' agree that 'our world is in an accelerating and fundamental change requiring new solutions' (Paul Hwoschinsky). This book goes further: It puts us in contact with the forerunners of the business—women and men of the post-industrial age. It shows concretely how they try to adapt creatively to a new type of uncertainty and complexity. Strikingly enough, the psychology of the new entrepreneur is described largely by women. Is this an indication that the key actors in this changing period could be mostly women?"

Marc Luyckx
member, Forward Studies Unit
European Commission, Brussels

"A fiercely good book—it gets to the heart of it: The new entrepreneur is a social change agent more than he or she is a businessperson. To the new entrepreneur, making a difference is more important than making a fortune. As the book's varied and exciting insights unfold, it becomes clear that the new entrepreneur is following a 'calling' and not just a career—and is doing it with passion. In truth, there is no choice but to change the world. It goes with the franchise, and the DNA, of being a new entrepreneur."

Bob Schwarz, author, lecturer
founder, Tarrytown School of Entrepreneurship

THE NEW ENTREPRENEURS

BUSINESS VISIONARIES FOR THE 21st CENTURY

Featuring essays by:

Anita Roddick • Peggy Pepper

Betsy Burton • Greg Steltenpohl • Ron Kovach

Jeff Sholl • Jacqueline Haessly

David P. Jasper • Richard B. Brooke

Sharon Gadberry • John H. Stearns

Cheryl Alexander • Marjorie Kelly • Chris Manning

Paul Hwoschinsky • William B. Sechrest

Nicholas P. LiVolsi • Bill Veltrop

Edited by

MICHAEL RAY AND JOHN RENESCH

STERLING
& STONE, INC.
New Leaders Press
San Francisco

New Leaders Press
Sterling & Stone, Inc.
1000 Chestnut Street, Suite 14C
San Francisco, CA 94109
415/928-1473

Credits

The editors and publisher wish to acknowledge the following sources:

Marjorie Kelly's essay was adapted from an original article published in the May/June 1993 issue of *Business Ethics* magazine entitled "Dangerous Vision: Social mission can't substitute for business basics" and is reprinted with permission from the publisher.

Graph of the hero's journey ©1991 Lorna Catford and Michael Ray from *The Path of the Everyday Hero*, used with permission of authors.

Photo Credits: Sharon Gadberry photo by *San Francisco Chronicle;* Marjorie Kelly photo by *Business Ethics* magazine; Peggy Pepper photo by The Houston Post Co.; Michael Ray photo by Stanford University; Bill Veltrop photo by Sara G. Gist of Elizabeth's.

 Printed in the United States of America on recycled paper.

The New Entrepreneurs: Business Visionaries for the 21st Century. Michael Ray and John Renesch, editors.

ISBN 0-9630390-2-4

First Edition
First Printing 1994

This book is dedicated to those entrepreneurs who are making things happen with a commitment to new values—to those men and women who are on the path of the "hero's journey"

ENTREPRENEUR
(an tre pre noor)

" A person who organizes, manages, and assumes responsibility for a business or other enterprise."

—Random House Dictionary

"Person of enterprise, beginning or running a business (or acting as intermediary) with chance of loss or profit."

—A Concise Dictionary of Foreign Expressions

"A person who organizes and manages an enterprise, especially a business, usually with considerable initiative and risk."

—Webster's College Dictionary

"Person in effective control of commercial undertaking."

—The Concise Oxford Dictionary

"A person who manages a commercial undertaking, especially one involving commercial risk."

—Oxford American Dictionary

"A person who organizes, operates, and assumes the risk for business ventures, especially an impresario."

—American Heritage Dictionary

Table of Contents

Preface

This book was a lot of work for a lot of people. But, it was worth it!

Seldom do you have the opportunity to receive business wisdom first hand—directly from those people who make things happen every day in the business world.

Most business people are too busy to write and very few consider themselves skilled at writing books. As a result, most books about business are written by academics and consultants who may be intimately aware of some real case histories but they are none-theless observers of the business experience.

Entrepreneurs are less likely to write for the benefit of others since they are typically very involved in their businesses and are usually preoccupied with the day-to-day dynamics of their enter-prises.

When New Leaders Press embarked on putting together this collection of writings by entrepreneurs, we knew it would be diffi-cult to interest them in writing anything very lengthy. Therefore, we asked them to create the essence—the "nuggets"—that they would include in a book if they ever wrote one.

While we found it more difficult than we had planned, we feel the reader of this book is the beneficiary. Here are eighteen entre-preneurs sharing their innermost experiences as self-employed men and women with visions for a very different world in the future.

We are thrilled with the variety of businesses represented, the multiple perspectives shared by these courageous men and women, and the potpourri of entrepreneurial applications contained in this book.

The reader is receiving first hand wisdom from the real world of enterprise, handed down by people engaged in the dilemmas and challenges facing good-hearted, visionary entrepreneurs about to enter the 21st century. Never have conditions been so uncertain; never has change been so constant and drastic.

Virtually, none of these authors are professional writers. None of them are writing from the ivory towers of academia, where so many business books originate. All of them are deeply engaged in the world of commerce as it has never been before.

We trust that each reader will recognize the value of hearing directly from the visionary, the warrior, the implementer of purpose—those men and women who are making things happen in the world.

Now that this book has been completed—tough as it was for the authors (many of whom had never written before), our editing staff, and many others involved in the creation of this collection—we are thrilled with the outcome. Hand in hand with this feeling of gratification and pride, however, there is a feeling of sadness or loss. In many ways creating a collection like this is much like having a baby. Conception, gestation, labor and delivery—each phase comes with its own emotions.

Everyone associated with this book hopes you enjoy our "baby" and find inspiration and much value from reading it.

Michael Ray and
John Renesch, the editors

Acknowledgements

Several of the authors wish to thank those people who were particularly supportive of their efforts to generate essays for this book.

Cheryl Alexander would like to thank Barbara Shipka for her encouragment and energetic spirit, Jeanne Barker-Nunn for her review, feedback, and comments on the manuscript, and her husband and partner, Douglas Hawkinson, for his entrepreneurial drive, un-ending support, unconventional thinking, and vision.

Richard Brooke acknowledges Wayne Packnit of Foster Farms in Livingston, California, for instilling a mental and emotional toughness, a clear sense of responsibility, and introducing him to the realities of business. He thanks Kurt Robb for "teaching me the beliefs and methodologies for success and inspiring me to pursue them with a grand purpose." To Carol McCall and Mike Smith, of the World Institute for Life Planning Group, Brooke acknowledges them "for coaching me to do what I'm not willing to do, thus saving my life of no regrets."

Sharon Gadberry wishes to thank editor Kristen Anundsen for her assistance in putting her ideas and thoughts into complete sentences. She also thanks her partners, clients, and family for their continuing challenge and inspiration.

Jacqueline Haessly acknowedges Pat and Gerry Mische for sharing a vision and those parents, educators, volunteers and friends whose continued support for peacemaking help make a difference in the lives of children and families across the globe. With heartfelt gratitude, she also thanks her daughter Kris, her sons Fran, Randy, Ernie, and Mike, and her life-partner Dan Di Domizio whose unconditional love, belief in peacemaking, and on-going help has made her work a joy.

David Jasper says every entrepreneur learns sooner or later that their spouse is *the* foundation ahead of money, ideas, or talent. In that light he thanks his supportive, patient, and loving wife, Sharon.

Nicholas P. LiVolsi acknowledges his two colleagues, Jane Bell and Ronnie Butler, who collaborated with him in writing his essay as well as serving with him as co-directors of the World Trust.

Anita Roddick wishes to thank Jeremy Sherman who helped her with her book, *Body & Soul,* while he was in the U.K.

Jeff Sholl acknowledges Barbara Shipka, who persuaded him to "write" instead of just "read." He also thanks Richard Fischer, Elizabeth Sloan, and Arthur Davis "for their ideas, editing, assistance, and critique." He offers a special acknowledgment to his fellow teammates with Green Giant Fresh, the subjects of his essay.

John Stearns would like to thank Barbara Shipka for proposing that he write this essay and acknowledges the excellent editing work and suggestions provided by Jeanne Barker-Nunn. He would also like to thank the many associates who have been a part of his entrepreneurial adventures.

Greg Steltenpohl wishes to thank his wife Bonnie, and all of the Freshness entrepreneurs at Odwalla whose dedication has allowed him to spread the vision.

Bill Veltrop wishes to thank Kim Krisco and Barbara Vogl for their strong support and editing contribution. He is particularly grateful to Geoffrey Hulin, who not only provided the flint in sparking the idea for creating this fable but also played a masterful co-creative role in helping to shape the story itself. He credits Hulin with putting on his cosmetic surgeon robes and transforming a grossly overweight manuscript into an easily embraceable chapter.

New Leaders Press wishes to thank all the authors for contributing their ideas, experience, wisdom, and their hearts to this work. Each contributor has provided a perspective of a larger collective vision for how business can serve society in a sustainable and energizing way.

We would also like to thank all the authors of our previous books, *New Traditions in Business: Spirit & Leadership in the 21st Century* and *When the Canary Stops Singing: Women's Perspectives on Transforming Business,* for what we've learned from working with each of them.

The following vendors have been particularly supportive over the past several years and we thank them with great appreciation: Barrentine & Associates; InfoCom Group; Jensen & Roye, CPA's; and Sherbank Corporation.

For those vendors involved in the production of this collection, we offer our very sincere thanks. This team includes Amy Kahn, Rick and Carolynn Crandall and their team at Select Press, Lisa Sanford of Sanford-Miller Graphics, and Lyle Mumford and his team at Publishers Press.

John Renesch wishes to personally thank Pat Barrentine for all her help in past book projects and wishes her well in her new career. He also wants to individually thank Barbara Shipka, a significant supporter of this project and other New Leaders Press projects that are underway. To Michele Scott, he is grateful for those wonderful days in La Quinta, where he did some of his best editing. He also expresses sincere appreciation for his co-editor, Michael Ray, for his year-round support as a colleague and friend. For his colleague Steven Piersanti, founder of Berrett-Koehler Publishers, he is particularly grateful for the unselfish sharing of his "self-ness" as well as his years of experience in the publishing business.

Sincere gratitude is felt for a group of friends who have supported him for the past five years in a very special and private way: Earl & Sheila Babbie; Donna Balsamo; Diane Behling; George Fritz; Bettina Herbert; Ben Hidalgo; Jim Hodge and his partners at Sheppard, Mullin, Richter & Hampton; Tom Jackson, Alice

Jensen and her partners at Jensen & Roye, CPA's; Kris Knight; Carol Lerner; Diane Levine; Barbara Musser; Alan Parisse and Bettina Herbert; Jim and Muriel Ray; Jerry Richardson; Bob and Fran Ruebel; Mac Suzuki; Peter Turla; and Donald Weck.

Renesch also wants to thank Willis Harman for his friendship and inspiration, Dr. David Berenson for his personal availability as a friend, guide, and fellow entrepreneur, Sheila Woodworth for her suggestion for the title "The Calling" for the Introduction, Cyril Morong for his blending the worlds of economics and mythology (scc the Introduction), and Lazaris and the people at Concept Synergy for all the lessons and growth he has gained over the past ten years.

Michael Ray wishes to thank John Renesch not only for inviting him to co-edit this book but also for being a beacon lighting the path of the new paradigm. He also acknowledges his brother, Richard Ray, who started Michael on the entrepreneurial path, is one of the most creative business people he has ever known, and an exemplary human being. Finally, he thanks the nearly two hundred visitors to his classes, the vast majority of them entrepreneurs, as well as his key collaborators in course development entrepreneuring: Rochelle Myers, Lorna Catford, Sandhya McCracken, and Kazimierz Gozdz.

For those people who took the time to review early drafts of this collection and provide their feedback and comments, verbal and written, everyone involved with this book thanks you all. This includes David Altany, Earl Bakken, Danell Brown, Jonathon Dana, William Halal, Willis Harman, Hardy Jones, Marc Luyckx, William Miller, Pamela Monroe, Ann Morrison, Shirley Nelson, Rolf Osterberg, Perry Pascarella, and Bob Schwarz.

Finally, the advisory board of New Leaders Press/Sterling & Stone, Inc. has been invaluable as a resource and we wish to acknowledge each of them: Pat Barrentine, David Berenson, William Halal, Willis Harman, Paul Hwoschinsky, Jim Liebig, William Miller, Shirley Nelson, Christine Oster, Steven Piersanti, Catherine Pyke, James O'Toole, Michael Ray, Stephen Roulac, Jeremy Tarcher, Peggy Umanzio, and Dennis White.

John Renesch
is editor and publisher of *The New Leaders* business newsletter and managing director of Sterling & Stone, Inc. He also serves as publisher for New Leaders Press, producers of collective works such as *New Traditions in Business,* which he also edited, and *When the Canary Stops Singing.*

He has been an entrepreneur since the early 1960s. His career includes a wide variety of business experiences: real estate, financial services, event promotion, public relations, and publishing. He served as managing director for a real estate investment firm he co-founded and was the founding CEO for a secondary market real estate securities brokerage firm in the mid 1980s.

Renesch was a founding trustee of the World Business Academy, served as its managing director (1990–1992), and received its Willis Harman Award in 1990. He is a member of the advisory board for the World Future Society's World 2000 project and speaks publicly on transformative leadership in business.

Introduction

The Calling

John Renesch

Many modern business scholars have recently concluded that the short-term future holds the promise of a significant rise in entrepreneurship. This increased activity will be many times greater than the large increases we've seen recently—like a tidal wave!

There are two significant contributing factors to this mammoth increase—one representing an *inner* drive for self-fulfillment by growing numbers of individuals and another representing *external* circumstances whereby organizations will be in increasing need of entrepreneurial talent both inside the company (intrapreneurs and entrepreneurial-managers) and as outside contractors (outplaced services or vendors).

This means a concurrent increase in both supply and demand of entrepreneurs in the upcoming years as we slide into the new millennium. This is particularly encouraging when you consider the growing numbers of "new thinkers" who possess an entrepreneurial spirit—who have a personal mission or inner drive to organize or launch a commercial activity that creates value in the world.

These factors combine to promise very exciting times ahead for business—times that certainly include even more changes than we've become accustomed to. As a long-time entrepreneur myself, I look forward to this growing fellowship, particularly the increased number of colleagues who share my values and my vision for our future together.

The Passion

I invented my first product in 1955, based on my interest in motorsports. At the tender age of eighteen, I sunk every nickel I had (about $300) into prototypes based upon a promise of additional capital from a local businessman. He reneged. I was disappointed.

Eventually I recovered my passion, my pride, and some of my money. I was now an "entrepreneur" as well as a teenager.

Through the years, I have adventured down many exciting trails of entrepreneurship, having been a partner, owner, or founder of several dozen enterprises. For me, there is no feeling in the world like creating something out of an idea—something that will bring value to people.

I've been engaged in a wide variety of activities—design, development, investing, marketing, promotion, publishing, event production, public relations, and training, to name some. I've owned or co-owned business in industries that included investment securities, real estate, construction, motorsports, advertising, golf, and personal development, as examples.

I've lived the exciting life of an entrepreneur for nearly forty years, and I love it. Yes, even the heartache of failure, the rage of betrayal, and the disappointment upon recognizing one's limitations are worth the effort when there is also the elation of a success, the joy of seeing an idea turn into something of value, and the fulfillment of a job well done.

The Spirit

When I announced plans to create this book as a collection of entrepreneurs' writings, I was asked to describe the personality trait of this breed of business person who can be so-labeled "entrepreneur."

As I attempted to respond, I realized that there are no clear lines of distinction that define an entrepreneur. You cannot recognize an entrepreneur solely from what he or she is doing. There's a *spirit* of entrepreneurship that is like a fire in the gut for some people.

I see significant distinctions between *entrepreneurs* who live to create businesses, products and services of value to society and *entrepreneurial activities* which are engaged in by a wide assortment of people. These activities are sharply defined and are certainly indicative of some entrepreneurial behavior.

Owning a business—whether it was purchased, started from scratch, or developed from a franchise—is an entrepreneurial activity. *But a business owner is not necessarily an entrepreneur.* Taking a risk in business is not necessarily an indication that a person has that entrepreneurial fire burning in his or her belly. A good many successful business owners who once took a chance in starting their enterprises did not willingly take the risk. Some were "laid off" from career-path jobs and found a lack of opportunities for getting re-hired. As a result, they started getting fee jobs wherever they could and subsequently discovered that they were building a base of regular customers.

The quintessential entrepreneur, in contrast, knows that his or her mission is to create enterprise—which includes producing value for society or some segment of society and creating jobs so that others may find fulfillment in their work.

By now, many of you are familiar with Joseph Campbell's writings or his popular PBS television series with Bill Moyers. Campbell has popularized the mythology of the "hero's journey" in following one's "bliss." In a 1992 article in *The New Leaders* business newsletter, Arkansas economist Cyril Morong compared Campbell's mythological hero with the entrepreneur who is seeking his or her bliss—a sort of modern-day version of those who sought the Holy Grail—living in a constant quest.

Sheila Woodworth, an entrepreneur who started her own hairstyling salon in San Francisco in the late 1980's, was cutting my hair one day while I was conceiving this book. I was recounting Morong's comparison of Campbell's mythological hero and the modern entrepreneur—citing the passion I felt for business when I was merely twelve or thirteen. Sheila suggested a name to describe this feeling, this yearning from within. She asked, "How about 'The Calling'?"

"That's it!" I responded. "That is just how it felt to me!"

Yes, I knew in my early adolescent years that I would always work for myself. I didn't have a clue about what the word "entrepreneur" meant—not even how to pronounce it! But I knew the *feeling*. The fire within was already burning.

The Past

In the past couple of generations, entrepreneurs have been publicly associated with opportunistic action, the exploitation of the market for individual financial gain. However, in the earliest days of merchandising—and up until the heyday of the Industrial Age— artisans and craftsmen met the needs of the community, supplying them with items and services they preferred to purchase rather than to build or perform themselves. They didn't "create demand" or convince the public that they "needed" their products. Then came the powerful forces of marketeering, promotion, and advertising in its myriad of forms. The definition of "need" started changing within the context of the marketplace.

"Need" is now a relative term—do we really *need* two hundred varieties of breakfast cereal or six hundred makes and models of new cars to select from? Do we really *need* all those items we buy that end up in garage sales one year later?

The Vision

New entrepreneurs are coming on to the business scene, carrying with them a whole new set of values. This new breed of entrepreneur is not the exploitive opportunist who sees a way to make a fast buck packaging the ashes of some disaster and selling them as memorabilia. While this new entrepreneur possesses the passion I wrote about earlier, he or she also possesses a deep sense of "rightness"—to be socially responsible, to honor the human spirit, and to do the right thing for all of his or her stakeholders— everyone they impact.

These new entrepreneurs are visionaries—men and women who can see the need for business being done very differently than in the past.

They recognize that business has become the most dominant

social institution on this earth. As a result, they see that business has a fiduciary relationship with society and all of its support systems.

A fiduciary is someone who looks out for the best interests of the other. So, instead of telling customers the *least* amount about their products, a fiduciary would disclose everything the customer might want to know. This context-shift in relationship is historic and has already begun—not by governmental regulation or decree, but by new entrepreneurs with values that reflect caring, sustainability, and responsibility.

These new entrepreneurs believe that people will have more fun, be more creative, work harder, and therefore be better employees or co-workers if they are treated with respect and dignity, not as machines that need to be "tuned up" periodically.

We are in the very early phases of seeing these new entrepreneurs in action. Only a relative handful of them have surfaced publicly at this time. Those we read about are definitely the "early editions."

These early pioneers are bucking the established way of doing things and deserve our applause. But, they are not models to be copied exactly or mentored forever. They are early versions of new entrepreneurs and, as pioneers, they have a lot of trailblazing to do. They are still considered "alternative" or newsworthy because of their values.

The Future

The new entrepreneurs of the future will stand on the shoulders of these courageous pioneers and build a whole new consensus about how business is to be done so that these new values become the "norm"—the basis for good, sound business practice.

In the times ahead, we will see degrees of change that will make the present chaos look like child's play. The climate for business will continue to intensify, contributing greater and greater uncertainty in the global marketplace. If you believe, as many of us do, that society is in the midst of one of the most significant paradigm shifts of all time, we'll need a critical mass of population who can function effectively in such a transition.

Since entrepreneurs are generally far more comfortable with

uncertainty and complexity, who better to serve society as leaders and visionaries, finding comfort and challenge in the tumultuous times ahead?

I'm reminded of a metaphor that was spontaneously used in a conversation with Carlos Siffert, then incoming CEO of Promon Technolgia SA, a Brazilian engineering and consulting company. A group of us were asking him about doing business in such a volatile economy as Brazil's was in 1991 with annual inflation rates in the hundreds! He told us that, "Doing business in Brazil these days is like playing badminton in a hurricane."

Siffert's metaphor is a harbinger for business in the 21st Century, and the visionaries contributing to this book can prepare us for what's ahead.

The Authors

Part One contains several essays that describe the making of the entrepreneur. One of the highest profile entrepreneurs in the world, Anita Roddick, co-founder of The Body Shop, examines real, heartfelt commitment in business, sharing some of her own stories and values in the process. She writes like she speaks—frankly and directly—about responsible business practices. Peggy Pepper addresses the value of passionate involvement, considering it to be the "real" quality the entrepreneur has to sell. Former Supercuts and PIP Printing CEO Betsy Burton shares her valuable experience as she recognizes the need for more entrepreneurial qualities in managers of the future. Finally, in a conversational format, Greg Steltenpohl visits a class at Stanford Business School, revealing his own perspectives on founding his company, Odwalla Juices. Co-editor Michael Ray, professor of the class, moderated the dialogue between the students and this successful entrepreneur.

Part Two consists of anecdotes—real-life examples of entre-preneurship, spanning a wide variety of applications. Ron Kovach relays the real-life drama of converting South Central Los Angeles gang members into post-1992-riot entrepreneurs. Jeff Sholl shares his own experience as part of an intrapreneurial team inside the Green Giant food organization. Jacqueline Haessly portrays an unusual entrepreneurial application—her business of peace education, structured as a for-profit enterprise. David Jasper, whose principle business is an incubator for high-tech/scientific ventures, reports on his own efforts to take over an OMNIMAX theater business and make it profitable.

The third portion of this collection contains six essays that echo a similar theme—*personal responsibility*. OxyFresh USA, Inc. CEO Richard Brooke shares his own personal climb from life in a chicken factory to running a marketing network of over 13,000 people. His essay focuses on living "where the buck stops," taking personal "response-ability." Sharon Gadberry examines entrepreneurship from two perspectives—that of her clients, outplaced executives, and that of an owner of her own successful business. John Stearns stresses execution—or implementation—as a key to succeeding in the entrepreneurial adventure. Cheryl Alexander suggests that new attitudes by outplaced executives will turn crisis into opportunity and, in some cases, awaken the entrepreneur in many corporate veterans. *Business Ethics* magazine publisher and co-founder Marjorie Kelly describes her own lessons in pragmatics gained from her efforts to establish a socially responsible publishing company. Professor Chris Manning shares his own entrepreneurial adventure as he strives to create an emotionally healthy workplace for his Denver-based consulting practice.

In Part Four, venture capitalist Paul Hwoschinsky paints a picture of the 21st Century entrepreneur who recognizes the asset value of relationships, experience, and other non-financial balance sheet items. Texas lawyer Bill Sechrest shows us how our present economic system—the most powerful of all social systems in the Western world—is obsolete. Like Einstein, he sees solutions coming from a change in the way we think about money and what it means. Former American Express executive and World Trust founder Nicholas P. LiVolsi envisions the new entrepreneur as a collaborator, working in union with the local community for the collective good. Finally, Bill Veltrop tells a fictitious tale of Arthur, who imagines a future headline in a newspaper he plans to start that provides great hope for the future.

In our conclusion, my co-editor Michael Ray compares modern entrepreneurs with heroes. As the co-author of *The Path of the*

Everyday Hero and the holder of an endowed chair at Stanford Business School, Ray possesses a unique perspective on the business founder/owner/risk-taker as a 21st Century "hero." He is one of the most entrepreneurial academics in the world, launching three innovative and visionary courses at the School at times when others considered them to be "very far out" on the fringe. These were "Creativity in Business" (in 1979), "New Paradigm Business" (1990), and "The Enneagram and Leadership" (1994).

As you read the essays of these visionary entrepreneurs, I invite you to be inspired and challenged, to be excited and concerned, to be joyous and frustrated. Whatever your reaction, I urge you to become part of the dialogue for new values in business.

Part One

The Soul of the New Entrepreneur

Making It Worth It
Anita Roddick

Passion: The Entrepreneur's Real Business
Peggy Pepper

Transformations in the Workplace:
The Emergence of the Entrepreneurial Manager
Betsy Burton

Vision, Mission, Values, and the Environment:
A Conversation at the
Stanford Graduate School of Business
Greg Steltenpohl

Entrepreneurs are seldom born. They learn how to deal with risk, to operate independently, and manage multiple priorities—usually early in their lives. The attitudes they develop allow them to accept and work with the hazards and complexities of starting and managing their own enterprises. As the world evolves, new attitudes will be necessary if the entrepreneurs of tomorrow are going to thrive.

In this portion of the book, four authors examine the need for new attitudes from entrepreneurs who wish to succeed in the next century.

Anita Roddick, co-founder of The Body Shop, writes about her learnings as an entrepreneur committed to being socially responsible while succeeding in growing her chain of stores to over 1,000 in forty-five countries.

Based upon her own experience as a founder of a $1.3 billion company, Peggy Pepper suggests that the entrepreneur's true product is his or her passion—whether he or she is raising capital or selling products or services.

Betsy Burton, former head of Supercuts and PIP Printing, has now started a new company and anticipates the need for all managers to become more entrepreneurial in the turbulent times ahead.

Finally, Greg Steltenpohl reveals his philosophy and the culture of his company, Odwalla, Inc., during a conversation with MBA students at Stanford University.

Anita Roddick
is founder and group managing director of The Body Shop International, a chain of retail stores supplying natural personal-care products in forty-five countries, through over 1,000 franchises and company–owned outlets. She has been featured in *Time, Newsweek,* and numerous other publications for her outspoken attitudes for socially responsible activism. *Inc.* magazine called her the single force that has "changed business forever." Her husband, Gordon, serves as chairman for the company while she is an active public spokesperson for the business and socially responsible practices.

She is the author of *Body and Soul,* her autobiography and the story of The Body Shop, and a founding member of Business for Social Responsibility. Over the past ten years, she has received honorary degrees from five British institutions of higher learning and has been the recipient of numerous awards, including the Veuve Cliquot Business Woman of the Year Award; the Order of the British Empire in the Queen's New Year Honours List, the World Vision Award, plus several environmental awards including the National Audubon Society Medal, the International Banksia Environmental Award, and the UN Global 500 Environmental Award.

1

Making It Worth It

Anita Roddick

The world is full of a number of things.
I'm sure we should all be as happy as kings.
— Robert Louis Stevenson

You get about seventy-five years here on earth if you are lucky. Stevenson got only forty-four. Every one of us has things we yearn to devote our precious, limited hours on earth to, but few of us consider work one of them. Most employees find their work boring and insufferable.

It is a shame—though in a way it's understandable. Work is what you have to do to pay for the bare necessities and a few frills: the drink at the bar with your friends, the electricity to run your home entertainment center, the tennis racket that will double the power of your serve. It has been more or less that way for employees since before the Dark Ages.

But things are changing—and they should change even more. Increasingly, people expect their work to be fulfilling. In the past, employee motivation wasn't important. The serfs, slaves, and peasants didn't expect much from work. As long as you could suppress uprisings, you could rely on a basic level of productive output.

13

Nowadays it's different. People dream bigger dreams. They expect more from life and are comforted less by the notion of bliss in the hereafter (heaven or retirement).

At The Body Shop, we have tried to make work fulfilling for our employees. This essay details the many ideas we've tried and found successful. Some of this new approach to work has to do with the concepts everyone is bandying about these days: flextime, continuing education, childcare. Much has to do with taking on a mission that extends beyond "business as usual." Absolutely none of it is a fait accompli. What you won't get here is one of those business checklists in which the answer to all of your company's problems appears perfectly clear and obvious—on paper. It is all a scramble. We decide we want to try out some social invention within the company. We gradually get it implemented, warts and all. We are constantly tweaking.

I am writing this primarily for you managers or business leaders who—given your company's culture—can't begin to imagine baring your soul at work. Perhaps it's because you are a scrap metal dealer and your customers are all rednecks. Perhaps it's because your shareholders or board directors are a nose-to-the-grindstone bunch and you worry they will think you a complete fool if you suddenly start talking about New Age concepts at work.

Since its inception, The Body Shop has been headquartered in a small British town whose population was once described by someone as "a holiday resort for the newly-wed and nearly-dead." In the last elections, the overwhelming majority voted Conservative. We've got our culture to contend with too. British subjects are generally tolerant of eccentrics but we have had to work hard at making soulful outlandishness prevail in an environment steeped in stuffy tradition. So even though we operate in what some may perceive as a "soft and friendly" retail industry, and you don't, you may still find our experiences relevant.

15 Requirements for Fulfilment at Work

Fulfillment at work is:
- Earning a good salary.
- Feeling challenged by your work.

- Variety in your tasks.
- Having responsibility and control over a particular area.
- Being able to see the direct results of your work in your company's finished product, especially your creative work.
- Knowing that the company's profits aren't wasted on the undeserving (e.g., another Mercedes for the boss).
- Being honored for your opinion.
- Being respected for your talents.
- Not having your work wasted.
- Not being forced to do things that you know won't work.
- Knowing the company is basically healthy.
- Knowing your job is relatively secure.
- Enjoying the good companionship of your colleagues and teammates.
- A chance to address some of the world's tougher problems in collaboration with your co-workers.
- A little controversy for stimulation.

Who Wants The Change?

Start by asking these questions:
- Who in the company seriously wants to make work more fulfilling? Just you? Management? The employees?
- Who sets the tone and culture in your company?

There are two routes to go. If management wants to make the company a more interesting and exciting place to work, then read on. There are countless things they can do to pull the company in that direction.

If they don't, or are ambivalent, ask yourself this question:
- Is there anything I can do to help management see the value of making work more fulfilling for more employees?

What excites these leaders in their private lives? Is there a way to make the company an expression of the things they find personally fulfilling so that eventually they will see the merit in doing the same for employees?

If you can't answer these questions, the most your company's employees can do is "guerrilla warming." That is, they can try to inject as much employee-initiated fun into the workplace as they can get away with.

If the bosses in your company realize that work needs to be fulfilling, you're half-way there. Gordon and I are very informal people. We would have been climbing the walls in search of an escape route long ago if we had to operate in a stifling traditional business culture. So it was easy for us to send a clear, direct signal to our employees that we encourage free expression, a search for meaning outside the narrow confines of our business and industry, and a relatively playful attitude towards work. We are accessible and loose with our staff, not because it is a good strategy, but because we couldn't have it any other way. We are not afraid to look fallible.

Yet we still have employees who are afraid to speak their minds to us. We accept that some of it is inevitable, though we do all we can to make employees feel at home. As Tom Peters says, "It takes time for employees to overcome life-long learning to follow orders and not initiate or innovate."

But even if you are "loose" primarily because it makes strategic sense, sending a clear consistent message is important. Employees expend a lot of energy trying to determine what the boss really wants. To them, your actions speak louder than your words. If you say you are for empowerment, but maintain tight control over them, they will know you don't really mean to empower them. Likewise, if one of your company's several bosses seems genuinely supportive of programs to make work life more fulfilling, while another boss of equal or greater power seems reluctant, your company's employees will err on the side of safety and assume that fulfillment at work can't be had. Ambiguity from the top always breeds cynicism and detachment. This is especially true when you try to change old patterns and get the employees more invested in their work.

Above All, Make It Human

We were searching for employees but people showed up instead.

Business does not have to be drudgery. It doesn't have to be just the science of making money. It is something that people (employees, customers, suppliers, franchisees) can genuinely feel great about—but only on one condition: the company must never let itself become anything other than a human enterprise.

How do you do this? What is the secret?

When Franklin Roosevelt was elected president, he told his staff of several thousand to "Do something. If it works, do it some more. If it doesn't work, do something else." The art of making work fulfilling is really just trying things that you and the other human beings in your office would really like, and doing more of those things that are well reviewed. It is that simple. The only real trick is making sure that fun, excitement, and passion are truly valued in the company. If your business operations consume everybody's time and the culture demands that employees confine themselves to the things that get dropped into their in-tray, work will not become a more humanizing experience. Expend energy to break patterns.

Put Heart Into Your Physical Environment

You can find beauty in anything, but some things are more conducive to finding it than others. Bring beauty, excitement, and style into the very furnishings of your company's office and plant and distribute them evenly throughout the facilities.

In our warehouse we have eight life-size men flying about near the ceiling on twelve-foot long bottles and bananas. In the gardens outside the offices there's a full-scale fiberglass replica of Seurat's Dejeuner sur l'Herbe. It's funny and charming. And we hang art not just in the boardroom but everywhere. If you can't afford to do that, you can still afford to make your premises homey and human. Invest in the best facilities you can afford, clean bathrooms, a canteen [cafeteria] with atmosphere. Most employees spend more time at work than they do awake at home.

- If your environment is squalid, you are promoting mental squalor.

- If your environment is sterile, you are promoting mental sterility.
- If your environment is threadbare, you are promoting the limitation of creativity.

Any modern "homemakers" magazine will tell you how to create atmosphere on a tight budget. However, we are talking about something more.

Never underestimate the power of a surprise and the power to delight the eye. Nothing is as surprising as human expression out of context. People come into your offices expecting to find sterility. If you invest in any kind of bold, audacious exhibition of something human and interesting, it will pay for itself in corporate culture, not to mention publicity. Are you in the iron trade? Then why not commission a low-budget iron sculpture by one of your more creative welders?

There's a neon light manufacturer in Austin, Texas who created a 25-foot square neon mural out of spare parts on his frontage in an industrial park. It not only exhibits the dramatic power of neon, it depicts life threatened by nuclear war. It is controversial, but it is definitely human. It turned a lowly neon light-maker's shop into an expression of his humanity and a significant local landmark.

We have Oscar Wilde quotes about nature painted in two-foot-high letters on walls, and exhibitions about human rights issues in our hallways. We want to know what's on everyone's mind so we've installed twelve "ideas boards" throughout the company. A selection of these ideas is passed on to a board member who may respond in the Q & A section of our internal newsletter, or even reply directly. This builds a dialogue which adds to our humanity.

One of the hardest barriers to break down is between the office and plant workers. We work away at it by making no areas off limits to anyone. Anyone from tea ladies to senior management can use our executive board room for their regular meetings.

Put Heart In Your Corporate Culture

The old boring way of running a business is to not mix it with pleasure. That's out. You have to discover ways that you and your fellow employees can mean more to each other than "business associates." This may include, but should definitely not be limited to, chatting at large office parties. It means occasionally having the kind of profound late-night, mind-blowing conversations with them that you haven't had since your old college days. It means disrupting the hierarchy with audacity, capers, and pranks. It means subverting this dominant paradigm, breaking down the barriers between boss and employees, abandoning the taboos that limit who can talk to whom about what.

You cannot rely on your employees to initiate change. The boss must take the lead. Robert Townsend talks about management by creating chaos. The master manager says, "I'm the person responsible for making a mess of this place. All companies tend toward sluggishness and bureaucracy. My job is to keep everybody here a little off balance." The president is the chief dis-organizer.

But what if your company can barely keep its head above water just covering the basics? You might say: "It's easy for Anita to talk about recklessness. She can afford to. She's got a successful company with a healthy profit margin."

True but irrelevant. We've invested in mischief-making since our founding. And size is no panacea either. We find that the larger you get—the greater the pressures. Our company's tendency to calcify, bureaucratize, and succumb to the demands of our in-boxes has only grown. We say "Do it Now!" If your business fails, at least you'll have fond memories of good times to keep forever. We can assure you it won't fail as a result of any investment you make in humanizing the corporate culture.

The main point is to remove the barriers between work life (seen as boring) and real life (seen as fun). Make work fun by making it real. 'Real' for human beings means growing, and growth is only nurtured by freedom. Treat your employees like adults. Give them freedom commensurate with their responsibilities for making the company a success. Eventually, if you give them enough freedom, they will begin to demand changes in the company. Listen to them for God's sake. They are closer to the workings of the company than most managers and bosses can afford to be. Encourage change. Develop in yourself a ravenous appetite for new ways of approaching old problems.

There are countless sources of good information about things you can do to instigate pleasure in the business environment. One key is to integrate the various levels of the company. Meetings to discuss company values encourage direct communication between, say, a forkhoist [forklift] driver and a director. Put that combination in a social setting, such as a dinner, and it becomes even more interesting. The Body Shop runs Family Days and Company Days at Head Office, which help familiarize staff not just with co-workers, but with activities in other areas of the company. Ben and Jerry's Homemade has regular appreciation days for each of its departments where office workers will wear trucker uniforms on Trucker Appreciation Day. We make a point of getting drunk with new franchisees because we really want to bond with them better than we can by just reading their résumé and interviewing them.

All of the above ideas are fairly standard. But, in 1989, we really expanded on the concept of humanity in the workplace. After the fall of the Berlin Wall and the repressive regime of Nicolae Ceausescu, in Romania, we adopted several orphanages that were in an appalling state. We sent "love teams" of The Body Shop employees bringing medical and food supplies—but above all else, affection, to children who had barely been touched in their entire lives. This isn't charity. This is employee training and a damned better training course than any high-priced simulation, experiential weekend we could send our staff on. Working together under such stress and serving people with such need, teaches humble service and empathy like nothing else can. It opens our hearts. It fills us with a sense of urgency and appreciation and takes us beyond our very limited, comfortable Western sense of reality. Beyond that, it is a great equalizer and communion for us all.

Put Heart In Your Employee Policy

None of the ideas above will do much to build rapport and sense of purpose in the workplace if you don't also concentrate on developing an enlightened personnel policy. Again, there is plenty of good literature on how it's done. They key principle is to encourage a sense of ownership. Nothing will do this better than giving your employees real ownership (duh!) in the form of stock options and stock as bonuses.

Looking after the needs of staff may seem obvious, but how many workplace nurseries are there? We provide subsidized places to the children of staff at our headquarters in Littlehampton in a purpose-built crèche [daycare center]. This is a necessity, but we have taken no half-measures. We have turned a pressing need into a real benefit for staff.

We provide choice regarding the whole benefits package available to staff. Employees can choose from a range of options according to their particular needs. Staff without children have different needs than those with children. You are not only dealing with your employees but also their families. Your employee policy can embrace your employees' lifestyles.

But don't stop there. Townsend says being a manager is like being a partner to a very productive money-maker. Your job is to make the money-maker's job as productive as possible. You remove obstacles, you provide a sounding board, you intervene on their behalf. The manager should be in the service of his or her employees.

We apply this concept in our employee policy. All of our management is interviewed, and to a large extent chosen, by the people they will manage. And integral to our manager's job is the responsibility for knowing and helping employees with non-work-related problems. We have an occupational health advisor and a confidential counselor to offer specialized help.

Some matters relate to both work and home. The company's healthcare policy embraces our stance on HTV and AIDS. Our headquarters staff have attended HIV and AIDS compulsory education seminars so that the policy is thoroughly understood.

We put a premium on personal experiences one can gain through service to society. The Body Shop's employment policy's most unusual element is our community projects. We allow all employees to devote one-half day a month (on salary) to any volunteer activity they choose.

The company also actively encourages and supports our subsidiaries and shops world-wide to do the same. We organize community action trade fairs, where volunteer organizations can promote their causes to our staff and 'recruit' new volunteers. Again, this is not about charity. It's about learning how to be an active citizen in your community and how to conduct your business in a way in which everybody wins—the company, your staff, and the community.

The Body Shop believes that it is immoral for business to trade in the heart of a community and then ignore the existence of the community, its needs and problems.

It all comes full-circle. Business is exciting to us when it becomes a vehicle by which we can do greater things than simply making a profit. But, you won't be able to do greater things through your business unless it is strong and healthy. To be strong and healthy, your business needs staff who find work exciting, engaging, and even thrilling sometimes.

Some companies allocate a percentage of profits to charitable giving, but how much input do employees have in this? Perhaps companies enable staff to give through the payroll, but when it comes to doing bigger things with company money, do your employees have a say in where it goes? We set up The Body Shop Foundation in 1989 as a registered charity. Its purpose was to gather moneys from company fund-raising initiatives and donations from directors, franchisees, employees, and friendly outsiders, for social, environmental and human rights causes. Since 1989, over £1.4 million [approximately $2.1 million (U.S.)] has been allocated to various causes. Staff are encouraged to come forward with ideas. If they do not want to concern themselves with the larger national and international issues that can be supported through the Foundation, there is a Local Charities Working Group at our headquarters site. The Body Shop's old or damaged stock is sold to staff and the proceeds allocated to a committee to donate to local causes.

There are many ways to encourage staff to view their working lives as directly contributing to the communities in which they live and the world at large. This is not about handouts. It is about involving your staff in choices about their own and other people's environment.

But remember, it they don't feel that they can effect change in the work place, they sure as hell won't feel like they can change anything outside of work.

Peggy Pepper
at the age of 28, created Osborne Energy Corporation, an oil-energy company in Houston, Texas which reported revenues of $1.3 billion less than five years later with fewer than one hundred employees. After selling the company in 1983, she formed First Concept Corporation, specializing in strategic marketing, to champion the success of other entrepreneurs.

Her clients have included members of the Fortune 500 and emerging growth companies in the U.S., Canada, England, Mexico, and Japan. She is a graduate of Rider College in Business Communications. Pepper is co-executive producer of "The American Business Chronicle" television show and a member of the National Association of Female Executives, World Business Academy, Who's Who in American Business, and Outstanding Young Women in America.

2

Passion:
The Entrepreneur's Real Business

Peggy Pepper

The essence of entrepreneurship is passion. It's the *passion* for the product and not the product itself that turns the entrepreneurial dream into reality. The entrepreneur who conveys his/her passion, who blends personality with product, will be guaranteed success.

Sounds great, you say? But, what about the numbers? Aren't they important? Yes, they are; they can make or break a deal in the *final* analysis. But first comes passion.

For years, "the numbers" have been given entirely too much clout. We have inappropriately placed top priority on the numbers. We, as a business collective, have been out of order for a very long time. The effect is finally beginning to surface everywhere in corporate America.

Downsizing continues to put the numbers first. "If we cut people, we can make the numbers work—by cutting overhead, we can appear to show greater profits." The "empowerment" we hear so much about in corporate life seems, in reality, to be a cloak for the numbers as well. This is evidenced by the corporate question: "How can we get one person to do the work of the three we just let go?"

All of this makes it a terrific time to be an entrepreneur in America! Those coming straight out of corporate life know how *not* to operate! This is a chance for individuals to discover the truth about what works—for them.

Numbers only provide support, which is secondary to the *idea* and to you, the idea-maker. Before any projections can be generated, the *idea* has to be in place. *You,* not the numbers, are in the driver's seat. Your passion, your drive, your idea will spark someone else to say, "Let's run the numbers!" The numbers are merely the analytical details. Details do not create businesses. People do.

The elements of passion are firepower, enthusiasm, and excitement. These are the driving forces of any business —the intangible, yet obvious, qualities which make potential customers and investors take notice—and place orders.

During the last twenty years, as both an entrepreneur and a consultant to entrepreneurs, I have heard many excited investors say, "I think this is a winner of an idea. We will find a way to make the numbers work!"

People do business with people—not numbers, not extended warranties. The greater the regard in the marketplace for the *who* selling the *what,* the greater the chances for success.

For years, Wendy's sold hamburgers. Thousands of places sell hamburgers. But, when Wendy's started using founder Dave Thomas in their television commercials, sales shot up. Requests for franchises dramatically increased. People identified with this man who was a "regular Joe," a family guy who even named his business after his own daughter. Hamburgers are actually the by-product of Wendy's—of a relationship the public has developed with this man. As our world becomes more and more technologically driven, it is even more necessary to focus business on people and the relationships to be developed on both sides of the equation.

Spreadsheets, spewing three feet of rosy projections, will not open doors, let alone minds and hearts. The power of the product is in the passion—and the compassion—of its creator.

The greatest challenge for the entrepreneur is this: Discover how to grab people right in the gut. Engage their hearts, *then* make sense to their heads. Their pocketbooks will follow.

Look at the huge sums we are willing to pay entertainers, actors, and athletes—the people who can arouse our own passion for living, who have the ability to give us a reason to feel deeply about something. We routinely shower these people with hundreds of millions of dollars in exchange for their ability to instill us with passion.

We become engaged in their "personhood"—in their own passion for what they do. The "numbers" in this case may be the yards rushing or runs batted in or box office receipts. It is clear that we, as fans, are capable of rewarding our heroes with our loyalty *and* our money. This does not pertain only to entertainment. The entrepreneur has the same opportunity.

Yet, a perturbing statistic continues to lurk on the landscape for new businesses in America. Companies still fail at the same rate—within the first two to three years of inception. Most often, undercapitalization gets the blame. We are giving "numbers" the power again. The problem has nothing to do with some worldwide shortage of funds. The problem *is* about the absence of passion. The person with the money to invest *must* be motivated with enough *desire* to take the time to get involved in the first place. Investors, and then customers, must be taken on an internal journey from "Gee, that's nice to know" all the way to "I must have this!" Here is the bottom line: No desire, no dollars.

Passion will attract the people who will bring the power of both capital and contacts to your deal. An entrepreneur and former client, who became a tremendously wealthy, nationally-known fitness guru, is a great example. Formerly an extremely fat person who got fit, Susan began an exercise studio catering to people who were too obese to attend regular exercise classes. She was passionate about helping others get healthy without being subjected to the ridicule usually encountered by people who are grossly overweight.

Susan had no personal wealth and admitted to having no "numbers sense" whatsoever. But she did have two things. First, she possessed a passionate commitment to her cause. Secondly, she identified a niche that had not been "pretty enough" for the fitness industry to pay attention to before. Her idea to "Stop The Insanity" of crash dieting created the desire in an investor to loan her $10,000, half of which she used just to pay off a stack of past-due bills.

With the remaining money, she convinced a television producer to create a promotional video. He got so caught up in her intense desire to succeed that he produced the video for considerably less than his usual fee. Using the video, Susan filled others with passion for her idea.

Within less than a year, an investor came forward to take her vision skyward. The investor *wanted* to take care of the numbers for her. He saw that, since he was providing the funding, it truly was to his advantage to also handle the projections and the accounting.

Sales from her products and fitness program topped $70,000,000 in 1993, her third year in business, with no end in sight! A good idea, fueled by passion, made it happen.

Susan's story does not have to be unique. It is not necessary to have evangelical skills to make your dream come true. Chances are, you won't aspire to star in television infomercials, as she did. But sharing your own passion about your dream, in your own unique way, will drive your success too.

After more than twenty years of participating in every conceivable facet of the entrepreneurial experience, I have developed guidelines—important things to know and key things to do in making your idea the success it can be. The guidelines have to do with putting things in the right order: Operating from the inside out. What needs "to be" before we determine what we need "to do."

So first, focus on the human *being*—or, as I call it, *powering your passion* with reality. Secondly, look at the human *doing*—or *packaging your passion* with personality.

Powering your Passion with Reality

The key to keeping passion for your dream alive is to know what's real—what you can expect, what you are really getting into, and what you are up against when you enter the entrepreneurial arena. Most often, loss of firepower comes from lack of clarity, not lack of stamina.

Operating from "Yes, this is what I expected," "I knew this would happen," and "I planned for it" is considerably more powerful than "Why didn't somebody tell me it would be this way? —I had no idea!" The vision must be seen clearly—with 20/20 clarity and focus.

The crucial difference between debilitating self-sabotage and powerful success is understanding the important subtlety between what's *true* and what's *real*. It may sound like I'm saying the same thing. I am not. But, isn't what's *true* also real? Not necessarily. This is what gets most entrepreneurs into trouble *before* they ever get started. They base their new lives on a truth—but not on total reality.

The Pitfalls and the Paradoxes

Making it successfully through the pitfalls of entrepreneurship involves being clear about these perpetual paradoxes. Understanding them will eliminate most of the anguish experienced by new entrepreneurs. Even more importantly, this understanding allows better, more pro-active planning to take place—for both manpower and money.

Knowledge of these paradoxes is power over them. *Knowing* that you know what you know instead of *thinking* you know what you know is the key to real self-confidence. Self-confidence fuels passion. It is a powerful magnet for success. So, let's get clear on these "truths" that usually end up not being the "reality."

1. I AM THE EXPERT: Statistics show that most entrepreneurial ventures are started by people who are considered by their peers and themselves to be experts in their field. They have consistently excelled at their craft and have received many kudos and rewards for their outstanding achievements.

For example, Tom was a highly successful inventor of preschooler educational toys. He had built a solid reputation for creating world-renowned, multi-million-dollar revenue producers for nearly twenty years at a large computer company.

There was no reason for him to believe he couldn't do the same thing on his own. Yet, after nearly a year of presenting his carefully-thought-out prototypes, he had no takers. Deflated and dazed with defeat, he asked, "If I am such an expert, what am I doing wrong?" Like every disillusioned expert I've worked with, Tom was doing two things which sabotaged his firepower and enthusiasm:

FIRST, he had let the *truth* of his real expertise in his industry niche skew his overall image of himself as an expert in all things. Tom's dedicated brilliance in design and engineering had actually left him unprepared for other skills he now needed, like putting together his formal presentation, or getting a crucial appointment with someone he did not know. He did not know how to manage a production line, how to negotiate his own contracts, and so on.

What experts often forget is that their mastery of a certain niche has usually required an intense and prolonged focus. It took a certain amount of "life with the blinders on" to get to the *expert* status. The paradox for the expert to confront is that the development of his/her expertise actually causes "blind spots" in other realms—with each area equally critical to his/her success.

SECOND, these blind spots contribute heavily to the entrepreneur's inability to accurately project what, who, and how much will be needed. Why?

What we humans don't fully understand, we tend to discount, or dismiss as simpler and easier than it really is. It's hard to see the time, labor and experience it takes to make something look effortless. You would think that someone who has achieved expert status at *anything* would be aware of this. What I have found in working with "experts" is this: The degree to which the person has let the development of his/her talent consume his/her life is the degree to which he/she possesses an equal blind spot in other areas. In most cases, the accomplishment took an all-consuming effort. Therefore, when the "expert" status is reached, there is an all-consuming sense of mastery. The premise of expertise is the *truth*. The *reality*, however, is that this skewed sense of mastery puts a veil of simplicity on everything else.

Then there is the matter of the well-developed ego. People who spend the majority of their lives developing themselves as experts are going to have a tremendously difficult time admitting to feeling inept. Everyone else has come to rely on them as experts, too. They are then trapped, to some degree, in a set of expectations, both internally and externally, that they are supposed to know everything.

The nature of entrepreneurship—the adventure of it—is to live with the treachery of all the things you *thought* you knew. The rush of adrenaline comes from finding both the inner resources and the right people to help solve problems you have never encountered before. The problem with most experts is they fail to ask for help, in advance, from other experts.

2. I HAVE COME UP WITH SOMETHING SO GREAT, IT WILL SELL ITSELF: Most of the people we see have come up with some interesting twists on a familiar product, or they have become experts in a particular arena which appears to be ready for growth. What they have done is *truly* innovative and terrific. In some cases, near genius. They have every reason to be tremendously excited about what they are doing.

But, here again, is the reality. Even Coca Cola increases its advertising budget every year. They are selling the best-known consumer product, perhaps of all time. Yet they keep pushing their message harder than ever, all the time!

Don't diminish your energy and set yourself up for disillusionment with the thought that "if you build it, they will come." That only happens in the movies. The promotional budget for *A Field of Dreams*—the movie that the "you build it" line comes from—was in the multi-millions. The movie makers knew it wasn't true, either.

You must know a couple of things very well. Who is your customer, and who is your competition?

Tom, the toy inventor, saw his customer as the child for whom he was creating the toys. We repositioned his thinking to see his customer as the parent—or more specifically—the child who the parent once was. He saw the need to position his presentation and his product. He got excited again, too. His is not an uncommon mistake. Often, the user, the one the product was created for, is not the buyer.

Diamond rings are a good example. Diamond rings are purchased by men but worn by women. Self-help books are another example. Even the ones written about men are predominantly purchased by women. (They are also, sometimes, later hurled at men—hence, the importance of the paperback format.)

Understanding who is actually making the buying decision can be tricky. Just as an actor will "get in character" to portray a role effectively, the visionary entrepreneur will develop a mindset of the person he or she sees buying the product or needing the service.

Often, people we counsel will tell us that what they are doing is so unique that no one else is doing it. They claim there is "no competition." The unique part may be absolutely true. But, again, we have a blind spot to contend with.

Anyone who is in a business or manufactures a product that is remotely close to yours will see *themselves* as your competition, even when you don't. When you build it, they will be the ones who will come—to check you out. So, even if you think not, it is wise to find out everything you can about anyone who thinks they are your competitors.

3. I AM FINALLY IN CONTROL OF MY OWN LIFE: True. You *are* the company. It's your ball game—you pitch, catch, and field all the fly balls. This paradox is the single biggest hat pin in the entrepreneurial bubble. So, what's really "real" here?

The only thing you are really in control of is your own choices. You cannot *control* the outcome of anything. And, here's the real kicker. You still will be held *responsible* for the outcome of everything!

You can control where your workspace will be. You may start your business, like many entrepreneurs, at home. You cannot control when the roof leaks, when the power may go off, when the dog begins to bark at a deafening level right through a deal making/deal breaking conversation, or when the spilled orange juice seeps its way through every page of your latest proposal. Home offices have their distractions.

You can also control the selection of company office hours. If you have employees, that's when *they* work. You, on the other hand, with your new-found freedom from the corporate clock, will find yourself working twenty-four hours a day. It is an entrepreneurial reality that, for the first two years at least, your entire being will be "on the job" no matter where you are. Not only will your "brainstorm" control your time, it will control your mind!

You can control the selection of your staff. You cannot control what they do. When the "garden lasagna" flies from the hands of your best waiter and oozes down the cashmere-clad back of a new customer, you will get the cleaning bill and the opportunity to apologize.

You have no control over what I call "Acts of God and the President." When President Bush declared the Persian Gulf War to be official, it dealt a devastating blow to most businesses in America for months. Consumers were consumed with only one thing—the desire to stay home. Yet, for the entrepreneur, the rent and employees still had to be paid.

"At least my business is all mine—nobody owns me." This, too, is true. But the most successful people I have seen have been the ones willing to give up part of their businesses, to take in investors for a piece of the ownership. There is nothing like having other people believe in you enough that they are willing to put their money where their mouth is. When you accept an investor's money, you have someone else who is as committed to your success as you are.

Again, Susan, the fitness guru, is a great example of this philosophy. She presently owns less than 30% of her business. But 30% of $70 million is considerably better than 100% ownership of a stack of bills, which is where she started.

Investors who make their living providing equity capital can also be tremendous business advisors. Chances are, they know the trends surrounding your business and they have done their home-work on your business—in many cases, maybe even better than you have. They have usually "seen it all" and can steer a business in the right direction. In getting a good investor, you also gain access to their rolodexes which contain networks of people whose experience and skills can contribute to the success of the business.

Many new entrepreneurs with whom we work start out view-ing an investor as a "necessary evil"—someone who is taking a piece of their dream. They see it as losing control. Again, there is truth in the feeling. Some control *is* lost, but you no longer shoulder 100% of the risk. What is gained is a potential coach, a sounding board, a committed ally, and a pocketbook to add power to the passion.

The realities of entrepreneurship can be very exciting. Even the problems—and there will be many—are part of the adventure. The nature of the adventure is to welcome the unknown—to have the self-confidence to handle whatever comes your way. When what seems to be "the worst," at the moment, actually does get handled, it serves to build an increasing inner confidence. A confi-dence that is also reality-based.

Entrepreneurship provides a powerful means of knowing many truths about what it takes to run and grow a business, about human nature, and about what it takes to motivate employees and customers. Most importantly, you will know yourself like never before. Your strengths and weaknesses will be dramatically played out in the form of profit and loss statements, paychecks, and parking lots full of cars. If a life of learning and growing, both personally and professionally, is your desire, then entrepreneurship provides the perfect vehicle of perpetual motion to see your desires take shape.

Packaging Your Passion—With Personality

Passion creates urgency. Anything else gets passed over.

Passion creates the ring of truth and the voice of authority that says "I ardently believe that what I am doing is important. You shouldn't miss this. This is important for you, too!" Passion has an unmistakable clarity which is a tremendous magnet for the leaderless, uncertain masses who are about to "channel surf" through life like never before.

The advent of the 500-channel world requires *anyone* entering the marketplace with *any* product or service to be even more conscious of what will motivate the new consumer, overwhelmed with choices, to chose you. "Hundreds of choices" are forever affecting the mentality of a consumer collective.

Even now, consumers claim exhaustion from too much information, "option overload," too much to think about, too many catalogs weighing down the mail and the mind. Added to this overload is the speed at which all forms of information come pouring in. There is already a sense of too much, too fast, all the time. The cup is no longer "half empty" *or* "half full." It is overflowing—spilling out everywhere, making a mess of our self-esteem. We can't keep up. Everyone else seems to be "getting it." What's wrong with me?

Human nature dictates an ardent desire "not to miss anything." Part of every highway car accident is the slow-down of the rubberneckers on the other side. Television news consistently remains in the "Top Ten" in the viewer ratings. A recent survey showed that the average American keeps his/her television on a channel less than a minute at a time before moving on to all the other channels available. So, what is the answer when you want to be heard above the cacophony? I suggest three things:

1. Be Clear
2. Make a Promise—Keep it Simple
3. Consistently Keep your Promise

1. BE CLEAR. How many times have you met someone at a cocktail party and your opening question is "What do you do?" After hearing a lengthy explanation, don't you often still wonder what the person does for a living? As the listener, don't you find it at least slightly irritating that this person could not be more concise and articulate?

A person who is not clear makes others feel uncomfortable and impatient. It also makes them wonder if the lack of clarity has something to do with their own ability to comprehend. This results in a diminished sense of self. People who are feeling diminished will not be interested in becoming friends. This same scenario, played out in business, will not get customers, either. People buy products and commit to contracts that they understand and they feel have a promise of a life-enhancing experience.

All too often, when new entrepreneurs make their initial "pitch," the same thing happens. People listen politely to what they have to say. But, if they don't "get it," they won't say so. They just walk the entrepreneur to the door—with no order in hand. Rarely, will they give out second chances.

Clarity and brevity help the entrepreneur make a better presentation. If it takes less time to present, there is a greater level of energy available. How often have you sat through a presentation that had you fascinated the first three minutes and daydreaming the last twenty? Momentum and passion for buying go out the window when the energy level of the presenter diminishes. Clarity and brevity also send a message of confidence from the presenter to the audience. It says, "I'm in charge here. I know my stuff and I am excited about it!"

Most of the time, entrepreneurs find themselves wearing all the hats—that of creator, manufacturer, and marketer. A great danger in being "so close" to the product is the inability to see what someone with *no* knowledge would find necessary to know. Even people familiar with the industry may still have a need to learn something which you have overlooked as being too obvious or elementary. While either the technology or experience required to develop your product or service might be a source of well-founded pride, much of that information becomes irrelevant to a customer or an investor. So, here are the three key elements in making the perfect pitch to a potential customer or investor:

A. How will it enhance my life?

B. Why is it better than all the things like it? (How will I tout my decision to buy if someone questions my judgment?)

C. What does it cost?

The first two questions are the most important because when people decide they want something badly enough, they will find a way to pay for it—no matter what. Selling something based merely on its facts, features, and figures will never be enough. In most buying decisions, the facts are the servants to the feelings. If you must chose between two equally matched people to hire or two equally outfitted products, like in the purchase of a car, for example, you will go with the one you have the best "feeling" about.

The job of the entrepreneur is to create an indelible perception of life enhancement in the mind of the consumer, along with the motivation to have it. The success of Ralph Lauren is an example. Some retailers might tell you about the durability of a zipper or the color-fastness of the cotton construction—the features. But Ralph Lauren brilliantly creates a passion for a certain way of life. Through his image advertising and *then* through his products he has made the entire world want to be part of it. He has shown an active understanding that consumers do not merely buy a "pitch" or a product. They are developing a relationship—a relationship based on a dream of a better, more aesthetic, more grand and yet genteel way of seeing themselves. They are investing in a better vision for their own personal world. Hopefully, your own vision will be one they can see themselves in as well.

The most highly planned, well-thought-out product or service will fall like the metaphorical tree in the uninhabited forest without the passion that makes the vision a complete picture. I call it the "living element" of the product.

Take the example of Ivory Soap. Like Coca Cola, Ivory has become an All-American icon. When it was originally created in the lab, the experts sent this suggested copy to explain their new product to the public:

> The alkaline elements and vegetable fats in the product are blended in such a way as to secure the highest quality of saponification, along with a specific gravity that keeps it on top of the water, relieving the bather of the trouble and annoyance of fishing around for it in the bottom of the tub during the bather's bathing!

Pretty exciting stuff, right? Makes you want to rush to the store for some, no? No, indeed. We would have never heard of Ivory Soap if someone had not come along, after reading the copy, and penciled in the margin, "I think this means—it floats!"

Now that *was* exciting. At the time, no one had ever heard of such a thing. Suddenly, bathing became something with a novelty twist. "It floats" became the tag line synonymous with good, clean fun. Clear and simple.

Later, Ivory used the slogan "It's 99 $^{44}/_{100}$ percent pure!"—another simple, yet strong subliminal message that said, "You cannot get cleaner (and, therefore, better) than this!" Ivory made a clear promise and kept it. It has never been the least expensive soap on the market.

2. MAKE A PROMISE—KEEP IT SIMPLE. The promise is developed by being clear about the end result. What is your ultimate goal for the customer? In developing this, you can also create your mission statement because, in reality, they are the same thing.

For many companies, I suggest using the "promise" as their "tag line." The tag line is the phrase used immediately after the name of the company, such as "7-UP, the Un-Cola," or "United Airlines—Fly the Friendly Skies." Here is an example of a company I worked with recently in developing the promise/mission statement/ tag line.

The company makes rubber fittings, millions of them. Not the things most people get too excited about, or even think about for that matter. Their mission statement said something about making the "best fittings in the world." I know a client is in trouble when they have the word "best" in their mission statement. "Best" is supposed to somehow connote commitment and passion. It doesn't.

The passion comes from what you are proud of. What sets you apart? Something was there or you wouldn't have started the business in the first place. Something about what you do made you decide that you had an edge on the competition. Something got you excited about doing your business in the first place. These are the things which need to be communicated to the public.

In the case of the rubber fittings company, their elements were made with a special compound they had developed which made the fittings both more pliable and longer-lasting. They also had developed design techniques which allowed the fittings to be used in multiple applications. This is what the owner was proud of.

When you consider that there is not a car, boat or plane that does not use fittings of this type, you suddenly comprehend the importance of the broad-based impact this company had throughout the world. This perspective shifts rubber fittings from mere widgets to a product with a world-view. Our new promise/mission statement/tag line became this:

Together longer in a changing world

This phrase speaks about the relationship a customer could expect as well as the actual benefits of buying their product.

Once the passion is put into words, then, and only then, is it time to add the graphic design. It is after going through the process of seeing your company as the world might see it and identifying the words that a clear sense of "that's it!" will happen when looking at various graphic designs to choose from.

So often, new entrepreneurs come to me thinking that marketing is merely putting a brochure together. Brochures and collateral pieces are the *last* piece of the marketing puzzle.

The way you will achieve the best possible result is by doing things in the right order. Brochures and ancillary items, like videos, direct mail pieces and promotional pieces, *support* the passion. They are merely the visual wrapper.

The rubber fittings company had the picture of their best selling rubber connector of the front cover on their original brochure. They had spent a fortune using a four-color format and a very expensive photographer.

By becoming clear themselves about the importance of the

work they did in making the world move better, they decided to project this feeling visually. Their brochure took on a cleaner, more sophisticated look. They used photographs of their people working in the company and printed testimonials from customers. The photographs showed the end users—like cruise ships and airplanes (showing the thousands of fittings used in a caption under each photo)—in order to drive home the message of the magnitude of their work. The actual widget pictures weren't even used in their new brochure. The widgets showed up where they belonged—in a parts catalog.

What they ended up with was a powerful new impact for a fraction of the price. The company owners credited the new imaging with substantially increasing employee morale. A new sense of pride permeated the work force. Sales increased substantially during the course of the next year.

This philosophy does not have to be limited to companies which have tangible products to sell. The same principles can work just as well for service businesses.

The key is to clearly state the end result of what your customer stands to gain from doing business with you. If you are an accountant, for example, you can say something like "XYZ Accounting—infinite peace of mind in a finite world." If that is what you want for your customers—give it to them. Let them know, immediately, what you want to promise them. Then live up to it.

Which brings us to our third answer.

3. CONSISTENTLY KEEP YOUR PROMISE. The best salesman in the world is a satisfied customer. People who have purchased something that has worked well for them, something that has enhanced their lives, their self-esteem, and their overall sense of well-being are eager to share their success. People who have consulted with someone and have not only enjoyed the process, but achieved spectacular results—results they could not have gotten on their own—are passionate about their good fortune.

In twenty years, I have never seen anyone who was not consistently proud of *themselves* for selecting what they thought to be the best and having it work out. To get back to human nature again, people who are excited about something or someone, naturally want to share their enthusiasm. Enthusiasm is contagious.

The best packaging for your product—better than brightly colored boxes and brochures—is the *person* who has proudly bought it from you. That is why it is critical to keep satisfied customers once you have them. As mentioned earlier, your customers have begun a relationship with you, with your vision. Do not give them a reason to see things differently.

So, again, we must look at the "order of things." And it is the same. The inside must drive the outside.

Before any marketing plan can be developed for a client, it is necessary, first, to take a look at the inner structure of the company. We must evaluate its inner workings to make certain that external growth can be supported. All the great ad campaigns, brochures and promises in the world will fall flat if orders come in and are poorly handled, the product lacks consistent quality controls, there is no stock, or customers are put on hold indefinitely.

So often, companies spend hundreds of thousands of dollars on new, glitzy packaging, trade shows, and television commercials. But they will fail to handle some of the simplest logistics, like adding the extra phone lines to handle the new business. Employees are often left out of the loop in being informed about new products or new promotions, leaving enthusiastic customers to get the cold shoulder because of misinformation. When the insides of the company do not match the outsides, it makes customers crazy and angry. It also makes them go away.

The perfect pitch with no support can create a serious U-turn in the road to success. A concerned consultant can quickly look like a con-man if he/she cannot back up what he/she says. I have seen many truly honest, intelligent new businessmen and women trying to retrieve their dreams from the disaster of a bad impression. A bone heals faster than a bad impression.

Here's a story that illustrates the value of consistency. Think of yourself at an elegant, black-tie dinner-dance. From a distance, you see a woman, dressed in a stunning gown, gliding through the room. Impressed, you move toward her for a closer look, expecting the pleasure of the full view of a "knock out." As she turns toward you, it becomes apparent that the woman has neglected to comb her hair or apply some much needed make-up. Not only are you jolted by the discordant image, but shocked at the incongruity. How could someone who appeared to be so regal, so "together" be incapable of following through with these equally important details? She has spoiled everything. Her looks and your trust.

When you add consistency to the equation of entrepreneurship, you are setting your success in concrete.

Conclusion

After taking clients through the processes outlined in this chapter, some decide that the entrepreneurial life is not for them. I applaud them for making the decision sooner rather than later. Entrepreneurship is tough. Entrepreneurship requires so much more soul searching and so much more time and energy than appears on the surface. That's why merely escaping a bad boss or the politics of corporate life is not reason enough to take the leap.

Passion is the key. Passion for life. Passion for work. Passion for a dream. Choosing entrepreneurship is a choice for championing our dreams. Living our dreams is a critical component of a healthy life and a healthy, hopeful society. A Harvard study was conducted a few years ago on the importance of dreaming. Test subjects were allowed to go to sleep and, as they hit REM, the stage in sleep where dreaming begins, they were awakened. This process continued throughout the night. The subjects actually got an appropriate number of hours of sleep—they were just kept from dreaming. Within three nights, every subject was diagnosed as clinically depressed, with some approaching catatonia.

Dreams generate ideas. Ideas mixed with energy create passion. People are attracted to passionate people in every arena, including work. There is a reason why some people call their work "livelihood." For some, entrepreneurship will provide the greatest way to be alive. People who feel passionate about who they are and what they do—people who dare to turn their dreams into reality—provide an important example for the rest of us to follow. When we buy their products, when we use their services, when we pay the price of admission, we are also saying "yes" to passion.

Betsy Burton
is President and Chief Executive
Officer of Supertans, a Canoga
Park, California-based chain of
tanning salons, which she co-founded in 1992 with her husband, Robert
Harvey. This start–up follows an impressive career in the retail franchise
business. In 1987, Burton partnered with Knightsbridge (an investment
banking firm) in the acquisition of Supercuts, a nation-wide hair-care
franchise. During her four-year tenure as president and CEO, profits more
than doubled and the system grew by over 200 units. Supercuts became
a publicly traded company and she sold her interest. Prior to starting
Supertans, she served as Chairman and CEO of PIP Printing, the nation's
leading business printing franchise.

Burton received an MBA from the University of Chicago Graduate
School of Business. In 1986, she was honored by President Reagan as one
of the top fifty women entrepreneurs in the United States.

3

Transformations in the Workplace: The Emergence of the Entrepreneurial Manager

Betsy Burton

According to conventional wisdom, the entrepreneur is the inventor, the creative genius, the risk-taker who embarks upon a new enterprise. This person is stereotyped as impulsive, somewhat eccentric, and almost always a *terrible* manager.

On the other hand, the corporate manager is seen as trained, professional, and skillfully diplomatic. This person is typically cautious and reserved in decision making, and believes the "creative guys" are further down the ranks .

The two are a veritable contradiction.

I might also add that the manager has historically been rewarded for actions which are consistent with the corporate culture, including of course, office politics. Mistakes are rarely made by the "trained" professional and, if they are, they are either not acknowledged or they are blamed on someone else.

Furthermore, any creativity or entrepreneurial spirit displayed by a professional manager is stifled by corporate bureaucracy, red tape, and a tendency toward *inaction*. Even though no one can find anything wrong with an idea, too many good ideas get left on the table or filed away for future reference simply because no one wanted to make a decision.

The Old Rules Are No Longer Working

The new marketplace is dynamic. Situations are constantly changing. Take a look at the number of companies that have grown complacent and lost market share to competitors, not because the competitors are smarter than they are, but because they failed to change. Why is this? Because many managers are unable to buy into change. The very rationale used to hire these professionals is the very basis for it no longer working.

Unfortunately, it often takes a crisis for an organization to recognize the need to "unlearn" the old rules. Some companies have tried, or have given lip service to "intrapreneurism" within the corporate environment. The problem is, they have failed to understand that this change must start at the top.

The Entrepreneurial Manager

The CEO of the future will be the *entrepreneurial manager*. An oxymoron? Not if you buy into the fact that a *professional* manager can adopt an entrepreneurial style. It may take a while, however, for the corporate culture to accept and endorse this and, more importantly, for the belief systems to change. The reason for this is simply that it violates the comfort zone. Behavior which historically has been rewarded is behavior which most managers will gravitate toward unless some crisis dictates otherwise. However, change is inevitable. We are in the midst of a huge catharsis—socially and in business. Our old belief systems are being challenged. Managers are evaluated on the basis of performance. They are being held accountable for results. This change is seen as "good" by the entrepreneurial manager.

Professional Characteristics

Let's examine more carefully the professional and personal characteristics of this entrepreneurial manager:

First and foremost, entrepreneurial managers are apolitical. Politics will not be tolerated because they are seen as time-wasters, counterproductive, and more importantly, destructive. Although some might argue that politics are inevitable, it is the unwillingness to recognize or support action which *is* political which is critical to the entrepreneurial manager's ability to create an environment which is conducive to maximum results.

Entrepreneurial managers are team builders and team players. Rank or title is not important. No one is better than anyone else. Entrepreneurial managers are non-secretive. They share everything and believe all members of the organization should be fully informed. They operate in a participatory, open management style and strive for alignment within the organization.

Entrepreneurial managers place just as much emphasis on human resources as on capital resources. They recognize the need for talent throughout the organization and are not afraid to hire someone better than themselves. They encourage their people to challenge them; they abhor "yes-men" and "yes-women." They invest in their people and in their development. They effectively utilize talent.

Entrepreneurial managers are good listeners. They create an environment which fosters and encourages idea-generation. There is no such thing as a bad idea.

Entrepreneurial managers are solution-oriented. They train their people to come to them with solutions, not problems. They look for ways to make things work rather than for reasons why they won't.

Entrepreneurial managers encourage mistakes. They guard against and discourage perfectionism. If people are not making mistakes, they are probably not getting as much done as they could or are not taking enough risks. Or worse, mistakes *are* being made—they're just covered up or blamed on someone else.

Entrepreneurial managers delegate authority, not just responsibility. Even if they think they would do something differently, they guard against the tendency to direct. This has two benefits. First, the person doing the work will be more "vested" in making it work. Second, the best way for someone to learn is to make mistakes. And, when a mistake is made, entrepreneurial managers don't say "I told you so," they help them fix it.

Entrepreneurial managers are risk takers, willing to try new things and new ways of doing things.

Entrepreneurial managers have a long-term orientation and are willing to sacrifice short-term results for long-term gains.

Entrepreneurial managers are intuitive, have a compelling vision, and set a clear direction for the company. They are inspirational leaders and motivators whom others naturally want to follow.

Entrepreneurial managers have a positive outlook, and are not easily discouraged. They have a winning attitude. They have confidence that the plan will work—they find a way to make it happen.

Entrepreneurial managers are results-oriented, not process-oriented; they create a sense of urgency, and "manage" to get things done. They push people with aggressive timeframes so that they are themselves amazed at how much they are able to accomplish. As a result, capacity for work and frames of reference for change become self-motivators as their accomplishments are reinforced.

Entrepreneurial managers set objective and measurable goals. They provide recognition and an effective reward system for meeting or exceeding performance standards.

Entrepreneurial managers have a strong sense of personal integrity as well as business ethics. They are driven by doing the right thing; in doing so, the "right things happen." They are fair with their shareholders, their suppliers, their employees, and their customers. Profit is an objective, but not an obsession.

Personal Characteristics

Now, on the personal side:

Entrepreneurial managers are well-organized.

Entrepreneurial managers have a strong sense of purpose.

Entrepreneurial managers are typically spontaneous.

Entrepreneurial managers possess a high degree of sensitivity to people and situations.

Entrepreneurial managers believe in themselves and exude confidence in others.

Entrepreneurial managers are typically fun to be around; others soak up their time and thoughts like a sponge.

Entrepreneurial managers possess a natural curiosity about almost everything; they have a tremendous love of learning.

Entrepreneurial managers are persistent—almost tenacious—if they believe they are right.

Entrepreneurial managers are driven and almost compulsive about their work. They lead by example.

Entrepreneurial managers' enthusiasm is refreshing and contagious.

Characteristics of the entrepreneurial manager

Professional

- Apolitical
- Team-builder, team-player
- Values talent
- Good listener
- Solution-oriented
- Discourages perfectionism
- Delegates authority

- Risk-taker
- Long-term orientation
- Compelling vision
- Positivity
- Results-oriented
- Sets goals
- Integrity

Personal

- Well-organized
- Strong sense of purpose
- Spontaneous
- Sensitive
- Self-confident

- Fun
- Naturally curious
- Persistent
- Driven
- Enthusiastic

Now that we've created the paradigms of an entrepreneurial manager, what about the rest of the organization below him or her?

What if a company crisis leads to the recruitment of a "new generation" entrepreneurial manager? How does this manager cope with the resistance to change, resistance to new ideas, and an *old* belief system?

More importantly, how does an entrepreneurial manager effect a culture change within an organization? How does an organization "unlearn?"

Change

In most instances, companies are limited only by their own internal boundaries. A company's performance is more affected by its internal organization and the organization's history than it is by external factors and constraints in the marketplace. It is the ability to use an explosive crisis to create "learning value" and rise to the challenge of change which will ultimately define success.

Many managers may not be able to buy into this change. They believe they were hired for their specific skills, and in the past they have been rewarded for use of these skills.

In other words, they don't believe change is necessary.

The need to change the culture means you may need to change the people. This must be balanced against the obvious benefits of management continuity, experience, and knowledge base. It is always, however, much easier to teach new people new ways than it is to have existing people unlearn their old ways. The key is their attitude and receptivity to change.

Care also needs to be taken to make sure that what they are saying to you is the same that they are saying to others. In other words, they may suffer from the "I need a job" syndrome. Loyalty is by far the most misunderstood attribute desired by managers; it is easily confused with motivation.

Management changes must be identified and acted upon post haste, lest an atmosphere of fear and uncertainty preoccupy staff time. Nothing is more divisive in an organization than a pervasive fear over job security.

Look for a willingness to communicate frustrations and an openness to talk candidly on the part of middle-managers—traits which may not have been recognized or tolerated previously by senior management.

Often times, these more junior managers make excellent candidates to replace senior managers. In part this is because excessive layers of management may have contributed to the under-utilization of talent and cumbersome delineation of authority, as well as unnecessary overhead. Tomorrow's organizations will be much leaner, streamlined, and efficient.

Senior managers are typically more resistant to change and set in their ways. Junior managers may even be closer to the business and have more of the hands-on knowledge which is critical to the decision-making process.

Having the right people and the right structure in place are seen as basics of good management but they become even more important to the entrepreneurial manager. Again, this is one of the key differences from today's stereotyped entrepreneur who may be quite talented, but limited in effectiveness due to the inability to leverage those talents through others.

Entrepreneurial managers recognize resources at all levels, not just from senior managers. The source is not as important as the substance. They listen for ideas; they hear solutions; they put it all together. They enroll people and enlist their help—not only for the help, but also because the "helpers" will be more committed to making it work.

When entrepreneurial managers are CEOs, they also need to understand that there is no "right" or "wrong" way to do something. What's important is to pick a direction; where they lead, others will follow.

The Leadership Art

The vision for the company must clearly come from the CEO. The successful CEO has the ability to instill that vision so deeply throughout the organization, that managers, and those who report to their managers, actually believe the ideas are their own. This is the "art" of being a CEO.

Everyone in the organization should be able to articulate clearly, and with conviction, what the vision is and how they are important to that vision. Teamwork is integral to achieving company goals. Interdepartmental communication is as important, if not more important, than good intradepartmental communication. The right hand must absolutely understand what the left hand is doing.

It is quality, not quantity, of projects which is important. The average person can become overwhelmed if nothing gets done; he or she becomes frozen in inaction. The team must concentrate on two or three key priorities, and work on the most important tasks first. It is okay to relegate less important work to the back burner. As a colleague so aptly puts it, "first things first, second things never."

Entrepreneurial managers must know people's tolerance for workload. They must be prepared when they feel their people are ready for more. They must guard against giving a project to someone so that they can "get it off their desk."

They will share openly and honestly, with everyone, everything about the business. Even if people aren't financial wizards, they are flattered to receive a report on financial performance. They feel they are respected and that senior managers think they're smart enough to understand, even if they don't.

People in an organization should always be learning. If they're not, boredom will set in and they'll let the work push them, rather than pushing the work themselves.

Above all else, they must have fun. If it's "just a job," they've already quit mentally. They just haven't told you.

Not Just Good—Great!

Entrepreneurial managers must focus their organization on being *great*, not just *good*. Great isn't *what* you do, it's *how* you do it. It is a way of thinking.

Great doesn't mean you have to be the *biggest*. It means being the *best*. Great doesn't mean you're perfect. It means bouncing back from the ups and downs.

Great isn't temporary. It endures change—even change in management. Entrepreneurial managers who build great companies today are the architects of companies which will be great tomorrow.

Greg Steltenpohl is the Founder, Chairman, and Chief Executive of Odwalla, Inc., a fresh beverage company head-quartered in northern California. Since its inception in 1980, he has led Odwalla from a backyard venture to a publicly-held company run by a group of "freshness" entrepreneurs. Odwalla is a pioneer in the fields of store direct distribution systems, creative corporate culture, and "living juice" production.

Steltenpohl's business philosophy is based on the practice of holistic and sustainable principles, evidenced by Odwalla's award-winning environmental programs ranging from commitments to organic agriculture, recycling, and alternative fuels to eco-auditing. He has maintained Odwalla's focus upon the vision of community nourishment as an essential corporate practice. A graduate of Stanford University with a BS in Environmental Studies, he is co-founder of the Whole Earth Institute and has been a featured speaker at the Stanford Business School. Steltenpohl is also an active member of the Social Venture Network and Business for Social Responsibility.

4

Vision, Mission, Values, and the Environment:
A Conversation at the Stanford Graduate School of Business

Greg Steltenpohl

Entrepreneur Greg Steltenpohl was a guest speaker at Michael Ray's 1993 class, "New Paradigm in Business," at Stanford Graduate School of Business. The following is an excerpt of his meeting with students who were encouraged to ask him questions.

Q. Greg, we know about Odwalla from the outside, but what has it been like for you personally?

I'm glad that you started with that because I usually don't have the opportunity to talk at an intimate level. It's one of my ideas that one of the challenges for business people is to learn how to become "intimate" people in most of their transactions.

Odwalla was started in 1980 by myself as an idea bearer. Then I asked my best friend and girlfriend at the time if they wanted to join. An entrepreneurial situation tends to create a vortex. Anyone who happens to be around at the time either gets sucked in or spit out, one way or another! Odwalla definitely followed that type of pattern.

During the late 1970s I graduated from Stanford, studying environmental systems. After that I was basically following an interior process. I was doing a lot of studying on my own; some philosophy and also trying to learn more about musical composition and particularly about improvisation. I found it quite interesting that the initial impulses of my twenties later became externalized in the business principles that I was trying to work on. Sometimes this was unconscious, but the longer I've been at it, the more I've been able to bring to the surface some of the things that were intuitive to me in my twenties.

Somebody once said that what people really want to do usually surfaces very early in their lives. A lot of times we come up with reasons why we shouldn't do them or reasons why we should be doing something else. So one of my messages to you is to try to be conscious of the messages you're getting from yourself about what your mission really is in life and what you want to do. If you're tuned in to what you're doing, my experience is that the world keeps putting new opportunities in front of you. But most people don't recognize them because they haven't acknowledged their own goals and processes.

Our initial impulse for the business was to earn some money in order to create some educational presentations for high schools about the state of the environment. We were looking for funding for that. I decided that having a business would be a lot more expeditious than trying to get supported through grants.

So we started the business. We were esoterically oriented. We wanted to choose a product that reflected the ideas that we held very strongly about what the world needed. If the world had to have more things, then what kind of things did it really need? Food was the basic thing. And besides, we figured, if the business didn't work, we could always live off the juice! I think there was a survival motive embedded in the choice.

Q. How did you fund the company in the beginning?

Well, it became interesting right away, because it was apparent that the growth opportunities were fairly large. The capital constraints began immediately. I always say to people who are just starting out that I think the discipline of having to work through capital formation problems is some of the best possible training that you can ever get. You will be better equipped to face the challenges that come later in that process by having struggled early on to articulate what's necessary to attract even meager capital.

I think it hones your story for one thing. It also makes you keep digging for what you really want to do, because in the early stage there's little evidence of anything. You've got to have a good story. Then later all the trappings come, and you develop all the structures that are evidence to the banks and so on.

I still believe that it's an eternal challenge for a company of any size to maintain the feeling of being on the edge. We're at a seventeen to eighteen million dollar run rate per year right now. That's a small company in my mind and even at that size, structures start to get in the way of keeping on the edge of things.

Q. How is that, keeping on the edge, for you?

Personally, it's a real desire for me. I had a fondness for outdoor sports and for improvised music (usually performed in front of a group of people with very little structure in the music ahead of time). There was very little predetermination. We had to try to make something that was engaging and positive for people, and not a waste of their time. Putting yourself in that kind of spot is something that I find continually in business situations.

What's really interesting to me is finding internal states that resonate with the external situations and challenges that you find, particularly in business. The reason I got so excited about, and sort of fell in love with, being in business was that in school I was studying systems theory, environmental and natural systems theory. In particular I was attracted to the interface between human systems and natural systems. Today that is really my main focus and reason for being in business. My personal view is that we are very rapidly destroying the quality of the environment for people. I'm not too worried about the planet as a whole. I think we're something that can be shrugged off at some point if we make it too annoying. But I think we're destroying it for ourselves. So even for self-centered reasons, I think logic and reason dictate that we should be focused on sustainable solutions instead of becoming obsessed with chasing after an idea of progress that we haven't really understood.

An analogy might be that, in our culture, we are in a car, a metal box, hurtling on the highway at a hundred and fifty miles an hour to an intersection with a red light. And that intersection is full of cars. It's like two big highways crossing and coming together at a stoplight. We give no sign of slowing down. We're headed right for it.

I'm not going to go into all the evidence for that in terms of environmental problems, because you don't have to dig very hard these days to see it. But despite that, most of us are going about our work as if it's all fine.

A deeper level of that is the relationship between your own interior environment and process and how the planet is reflecting that. I believe our exterior world is a manifestation of our own interior preoccupations.

Q. But is that ecological concern actually reflected in your business?

Within Odwalla, the thing that I'm trying to wrestle with and that holds such a fascination for me is that the natural environment has certain rules and ways in which it operates. Human beings have taken mental processes and have imposed these. They now intersect this natural environment. With our company for example, we are now trying to undertake a comprehensive eco-audit. How many tons of material are we moving in and out? What does it cost in terms of BTUs, calories, degradation of water, degradation of air, degradation or enhancement of soil? What impact are we really having on the shared environment, the natural environment?

This is a very interesting concept, even to communicate within the company and have the company embrace. Our company is now about two hundred people. I'd say that half of those people have joined the company in the last two years. The idea of communicating why something like this was initiated within this organization is a real challenge.

Today the company is basically an integrated sourcing, manufacturing, distribution, and marketing company. We have about twenty different flavors of juice that are usually available at any given time, overall around fifty different flavors that rotate and change seasonally.

To give you some idea of how we are trying to explore joining the natural and human world in a more integrated way, our basic marketing plan is to make available and promote seasonal varieties of fruits and vegetables. Then as a consumer you get an opportunity to have a feature of apples and apple juice or blends in the fall of the year. During each time of year we base our whole retail shelf management around this idea—the idea of cycles and seasons and change in a product. That sounds pretty basic. But it's something that very few consumer packaged-goods companies do. Packaged goods have not been based around a lot of change.

We have adopted the idea of a "trade dress environment" in our package rather than a logo. We have a logo that we use, but it's really a minor part of the whole imagery. We try to use certain symbolic elements which have our typical resonance in them as parts of our trade dress and packaging. It's something that we have found very interesting in terms of how people respond to basic visual elements.

Q. Greg, can you tell a little about how the business got started from an experience you had being on your father's boat and having juice there?

I was going to music school in New York and when I left there I had no idea what I was going to do with my life. I had absolutely no idea. I visited my father; that's always a good idea if you don't know what you're going to do—see your father. He was living on a boat in Florida. He had a little ritual of going on shore every day and getting a bag of oranges and coming back and squeezing them. I was there for about ten days and had this really great glass of fresh-squeezed orange juice right off the tree every morning for ten days.

When I got back to California, my body was addicted to this experience from all the fresh vitamins and so on. I was looking around desperately to get some of this. I had no money to buy my own squeezer. I was hoping that I could get a bottle in the store or find somewhere that had fresh juice, but it just wasn't there. I pondered the concept that if something was that good and there was none of it around, there was an opportunity. It's pretty basic stuff. That was the first little clue.

The second clue came when we were trying to do these slide shows on the environment. I went into the bookstore to look up grants for doing these educational presentations. The business section happened to be next to the nonprofits section that had books on grants. I looked over there at the business books and saw this book on a hundred businesses you can start for a hundred bucks. I flipped through it and there was a model for a juice stand. This one had a comment that said: "This is the only suggestion in this book that has unlimited opportunity for growth—you can open these things all over."

That sort of stuck in my mind. Then one day I was lying in bed and a light bulb went off. "Wait a minute." I wasn't too interested in setting up these stands, but I could make the juice and deliver it in the morning and play music all night. That was the theory. Of course the music all night quickly turned into juicing all night.

In our first plant we managed to line the back office with egg cartons and actually play some music in there during the early years. In fact, now we make audiotapes for our route people. We call these "infotainment tapes, Odwalla-style." They're a mélange of music and information about our product. If you sublimate long enough, it starts leaking out no matter what.

Q. How did you take the next step beyond pure orange juice to mixing funky flavors like Strawberry GoManGo? What was the cognitive process there? I assume that there wasn't that much on the market in the early eighties?

There were a few small operators like ourselves who were doing different things. But being interested in natural foods, one of the common practices at that time was to make fruit blender smoothies—you know, throw a banana in a blender and that kind of thing. We've just glorified that to some degree, with our line of smoothies, blends, and so on. It's just been a natural extension and elaboration of process.

We think we've defined our niche fairly narrowly. We have said that we will not heat treat our products. Our juice is fresh. It is not pasteurized. It's not from concentrates and remixed or sweetened with concentrates. We have tried to focus and say that we are not going to be in the salsa business or the salad business for example. However, we may try some other beverages that compliment fresh juice. But that's how we've defined our mission statement in terms of product.

Q. The first thing was marketing the fresh orange juice like you had on your father's boat, but how did you come to the rest of your product mission?

I do have to qualify that first part of the story. My mom got upset when that story first got publicized, because she said that she was the one who squeezed the oranges all the years I was growing up.

The development of our mission statement was part of a more comprehensive process. I would like to talk about vision and the role of vision in enterprises. I want to make a pitch for that. Having an articulated vision is one of the most powerful things that you can do in building an organization.

Once you've done it, it becomes a relentless taskmaster. People give you endless grief about how you're not performing according to the vision. This is one of the best methods of self-discipline for entrepreneurs—discipline in a positive way. I think following a path of joy can become a natural system of discipline. Doing what you want to do and what you really love in life creates standards by which to live life. We call that the vision, mission, and values process.

Vision, mission, and values. It's kind of the upper tier before you get to the strategy and tactics and so on. It's a hierarchy with the vision as the overarching guiding principle as to why people are involved and what the enterprise is all about. That's the first thing.

Our vision statement ends with the capstone line, "Nourishing the body whole." Central to that is really the process and principle of nourishment. That is a fundamental principle to us, but it certainly is overlooked by most major food companies in the United States. So there's lots of opportunity there.

The mission statement is how, in terms of business guidelines, the vision is achieved. In that process we determined that the nutritional properties of heat-processed foods were not optimum. That was not the most efficient, energetic form of nutrition delivery in terms of nutrients per ounce. In an environmental sense, we don't think we're just delivering thirst quenching properties. We think we're delivering micronutrient food properties. That's really how we're starting to analyze our business.

Q. You're talking about the mission statement as it now stands. When you just had the orange juice, did you have a sense at all for what your personal mission statement might be?

I think that I definitely had a vision, but I didn't have my mission at that time. Finding your purpose is really finding your personal vision. That process is a gradual articulation. The real process is in keeping that vision inside of you and using it as a focusing device—always using it to reconnect with the source of your energy. It works on an organizational level, and it works on an individual level as well.

In the early days I was interested in educating people about the environment and also in the idea of transformation of the basic activities of the industrial world into a series of activities that were more harmonious with natural system processes. I had that vision before I even started the company. When we started the company, I thought, "Well, this business is a great vehicle for actually taking ideals out of the theory realm and trying to practice them."

Q. I'm a little surprised at the environmental background to the concept of Odwalla. There is no real communication to the consumer that the ethos of this firm is based around environmentalism. I'm wondering whether you have intentions to go more in that direction.

That's a good observation. We really have not done much of that kind of communication—pretty much intentionally. As I said earlier, I come before you as part of the problem, because we use plastic, we run trucks. We're out there creating problems in the daily activities of our business at the same time we're supplying nourishment to the human body. But it's not a completely positive process at this point.

From an environmental science and analytical standpoint, I do happen to believe that plastic bottles are more energy efficient than glass. But there are many different components of trying to introduce environmental thought into a business. Until we've made a map of what we do [the eco-audit], we don't really want to talk about that to people. I also believe that too many people try to say they're environmentally-oriented. Just because I have an environmental background and we've done a lot of recycling, we don't think that's enough to really start talking about it on the bottles. When we start to make some changes and know what effect we're having, we'll communicate it more.

Q. How do you deal with the problem of time and stress?

I don't believe that I'm a particularly good example of a holistic approach to life. I became so enamored with the business and all the business could do that it's been difficult to balance my personal life with that. I have a family and the reason I have to leave before the end of the class is that it's my son's birthday today. If I get carried away and turn up late for his party, that's a real bad example.

I think that in entrepreneurship there's a certain mystique and glory that gets exaggerated. I think that what the world needs now is more of a balanced approach to all of it. Just going out and having high growth companies is not the solution to anything.

Q. What can you tell us about some of the aspects of your work that give you the most satisfaction?

Creating new products is something that I'm really excited about. We have a new product coming out at the end of this month that's going to be called "C Monster." It's mainly a blend of synergistic nutrients with fresh juices and some extra Vitamin C. We researched the Vitamin C content of various fruits and put together four of the highest Vitamin C content fruits that you can find and then added some Vitamin C on top of that. So it's got two thousand percent RDI Vitamin C. I think it tastes great. People seem to like it. Kids like it.

In reviewing the nutritional literature and hard science that's been done on micronutrients, we've found that Vitamin A and Vitamin C are the two most fundamental micronutrients that can boost the immune system. I believe that anyone who's in a high-stress environment can benefit from them. I'm really excited about that.

I really like putting together a whole package—the design of the product, the product itself and trying to get the essence of the label to somehow be connected along with the name. Getting a whole little package that has this kernel of essence is what gets me excited.

I also like joining communities together with their visions. I don't know if any of you have seen an apple blend drink that we came out with just a week ago called Wild River Rapids Berry Apple. We're dedicating five percent of all our sales of that drink to trying to save this wild river in the High Sierra which is in danger of being dammed. There's over twelve hundred rivers and something like fourteen hundred dams in California. There are only four rivers left in California that are not dammed. Just the concept of a wild river which can complete its course is a fundamental thing that I think is sort of neat. Neat is sort of a trite word. I don't know what to say. It's like, "Hey! You should keep those rivers around, because there's something about them which speaks to the human spirit."

Now there's a plan for these dams that doesn't appear to make economic sense when you really get into the numbers. It's going to cost more for the rate payers in the utility district which it serves. But it would be a great project for the contractors and developers.

Anyway, we did an educational label on the back of that product which talks in some detail about the issue and gives addresses and telephone numbers for people to call and register their feelings about it one way or another. That's something that I'm really excited about, because there is a whole community of people who are trying to protect this river and we've been able to leverage our visibility to contribute to that common goal of saving a certain section of the natural environment.

Q. What was the process you went through to create C Monster?

We started really thinking about, and talking to people about, what they were buying in the wintertime. Although orange juice sales go up, we found people weren't buying a "drink." They were buying orange juice to get well or keep them well.

So when we saw that people were looking to buy the beneficial effect of Vitamin C, I thought, "Well, when you get a cold, it may be too late for orange juice to have an effect." Orange juice is great if you're drinking it right along. But it is not going to clean up a cold. You've got to take large doses of Vitamin C if you're at the point where your immune system has become weakened.

So we thought it would be great to make a legitimate Vitamin C-fortified drink. Then we started doing the research. The way we do our naming process is to creatively brainstorm and then do an internal poll and see what pops up as people continually talk about it. You have to give it a little time. We did that and people said things like,"It's got 2000 RDI of C, so we should be calling it C2000." Others said, "It should be Super-C." But, people kept coming back to "C Monster".

At the same time, my son is really into dinosaurs. He's six years old today. He's into dragons and all this monster stuff. One day he came home with a tattoo. (It was the kind you can take off, fortunately.) It was right on his chest, a tattoo of this sea monster dragon with fire coming out its mouth. And I said, "Yes! C-Monster!"

A little analysis, a little vitamin C, and keep your eyes open for the synchronicities.

Part Two

Implementing New Visions

The Corner Shoe Store:
Gangbangers to Merchants
Ron Kovach

Ten Principles of Corporate
Intrapreneuring
Jeff Sholl

Peacemaking for Profit:
The Years I Ate an Elephant
Jacqueline Haessly

Entrepreneurship Through Misadventure
David P. Jasper

With all the articles and books being written about the emerging paradigm of society and business, it is easy to become intoxicated with concept or philosophy. It is tempting to speak or write solely about ideals and altruistic objectives. But, where does all this rhetoric turn into useful activity? Where does "the rubber meet the road"?

In this part, four authors write about implementing their visions for doing business in a new way—some because of their inner drive and some because of external circumstances. All these essays are practical—based on real experiences by true entrepreneurs.

In a powerful recount of post-1992 riot-ridden South Central Los Angeles, Ron Kovach reports his own experience in converting gang members into entrepreneurs—business owners who ended up playing basketball with President Clinton during his visit to the area months after the upheaval.

Green Giant intrapreneur Jeff Sholl tells the story of growth and learning inside a large organization as he and his team rode the roller coaster of a new business launch.

Jacqueline Haessly writes about an unusual approach she has taken with her business—peace education and consulting in a for-profit structure.

David Jasper, who has started his own entrepreneur incubator in Minnesota, tells his story of turning around a business venture and learning from his own misadventures.

Ron Kovach
formed his outdoor adventure company in 1985, with his wife Linda.
Outdoor Enterprises publishes a
fishing newsletter, organizes fresh-
and salt-water expeditions, offers lectures and seminars at colleges and
trade shows, publishes Kovach's syndicated articles and best-selling books,
and sells specially-designed fishing lures and apparel.

Kovach has also served as an executive with Big 5 Sporting Goods
for twenty years and now serves as an industry expert in sports shoes. He
served as an independent consultant for Adidas America and now is an
executive with Turntec/Nevados Athletic Footware Co.

He and his wife Linda have been married since 1969 and have two
children. He holds an MA in Sociology from UC Riverside, and was an
NIMH research fellow at UCLA. He is listed in *Who's Who in the West*.

5

The Corner Shoe Store: Gangbangers to Merchants

Ron Kovach

For as long as I can remember, I've had parallel business lives. My wife Linda and I have operated our own outdoor adventure business since 1985. Yet, I have also held significant corporate positions in the sports and leisure industry. This essay is an excerpt from my corporate life.

From Suburb to Inner City

I live in a predominantly white, beach community in Orange County. Like most Southern Californians who reside behind the "Orange Curtain," my images of the inner city to the north were primarily those most often portrayed by the media: urban blight and violence—hardly a place where I might want to do business.

Since 1972 I have been an executive in the retail athletic footwear industry. I've made a career out of selling sneakers to the white suburbs of Southern California. Athletic shoes are now a ten billion dollar business in this country, with California leading in many different sales categories.

After a twenty-year career in operating retail stores in the suburbs, I was recruited to expand a small chain of shoe warehouses in L.A.'s inner city. Like the proverbial stranger in a strange land, I had to quickly familiarize myself with the retail pulse of this new marketplace.

As I soon discovered by venturing into the barrios and ghettos of this metropolis, the inner city can be a commercial melting pot, with the potential for significant enterprise. In the commodity where my expertise lies—athletic footwear—I found these neighborhoods to be an incredible "mother lode" for sneaker sales. Let me explain why this is the case.

Many residents of this part of Los Angeles find themselves living in an economically-impacted situation, frequently below the poverty level. However, many people in this inner city are not confronted with the major financial exigencies found in the suburbs. Luxury car payments, bone-crunching mortgages, and escalating college costs are not high on their priority lists. With whatever discretionary monies remain once basic food and shelter are secured, residents of the inner city will often purchase high-ticket shoes and apparel.

These items—which are usually strongly endorsed by professional athletes and pop music groups, and then extensively promoted by athletic clothing and footwear companies—become major status symbols in the barrios and ghettos. Athletic shoes in particular, remain a hot product, very much in demand by urban youth and gang members.

The L.A. Riots

During the 1992 Los Angeles riots, three of our shoe warehouse stores were looted and burned. Initially, the company executives felt a sense of outrage and resignation. On one hand, we were helpless in our efforts to save the shoe stores. An angry mob ransacked the sales floors, taking practically every pair of shoes they could loot from the shelves.

The company also felt outrage, since this was a community, in their opinion, that had been served well by the retail stores. Each outlet prides itself in providing the customer with an awesome selection of over 1,500 name brand models to choose from, and at highly competitive prices.

Without oversimplifying arguably the most tragic civil disturbance in this country's history, the riots were the explosive accumulation of frustrations of the economically disenfranchised. Perhaps what we witnessed wasn't so much a "riot," but rather a "caste" revolt. The televised scenes of the widespread looting seemed to illustrate the classic distinction between the "have" and the "have not" castes.

In the aftermath of the violence, some law enforcement experts felt that much of the rioting and looting was actually orchestrated by organized, urban gangs. The "gangbanger" to some extent is the prototypical member of this disenfranchised caste. He is typically either "un-" or "under-" employed. A common prescription that was voiced following the riots was, "give us *meaningful jobs!*" This may be the single most important ingredient in the formation of some type of game plan to re-build L.A.. The people need jobs that provide them with a clear level of self-esteem and financial empowerment, gang-member and "civilian" alike.

The Aftermath

Immediately following the riots, the shoe company decided to return to the inner city to rebuild its damaged stores. Pragmatically speaking, there was little choice but to return. The inner city is where we conducted most of our business for years. We felt a bond with the neighborhoods where the warehouse stores were located. A majority of our managers and sales people also live in those same neighborhoods. We didn't want to abandon them.

Prior to the riots, the small shoe store chain also had established philanthropic programs providing local high schools with scholarship funds. But, the company felt that after the riots, maybe something more could be done for the community. As long-time shoe merchants, we believed that the violence perpetrated against the stores was not aimed at us as a company per se. As a matter of fact, some businesses that were African-American-owned were attacked during the three days of mayhem. This was a community that was angered over a social and economic structure that had not really changed that much in twenty-seven years since the Watts riots.

The shoe merchants took out large advertisements in the *Los Angeles Times* announcing their return to the inner city as part of the re-build L.A. campaign. The ad—which did not promote any particular product— more importantly encouraged other retailers to have the courage and vision to rebuild their establishments, returning to an area of the city that had supported them well up until the riots.

The next phase for the shoe store chain was centered on aligning themselves more closely with the most disenfranchised sector of the communities where they did business. We wanted to explore the possibilities of involving hard-core gang members in some form of retail business venture.

To do this, company executives met with gang contingents from both the African-American and Latino communities—on the gangs' own turf. Imagine veteran "shoe dogs" presenting their business proposal initially to the Bloods and Crips—L.A.'s most notorious rival gangs—then later to their Latino counterparts.

We explained to the gang members that we were clearly not representing a liberal, inner city social or political cause. Rather, we were merchants whose primary objective was to make a serious proposal to launch a joint venture selling athletic footwear deep in the most economically impacted areas of Los Angeles.

In contrast to the "gangster" stereotypes seen on TV, we found these young men to be both articulate and extremely savvy to the idea of forming some sort of business partnership.

From this landmark meeting, other opportunities quickly emerged. We also wanted to involve some of the formerly active gang members in the actual design of a new athletic shoe line. This turned out to be a major windfall. The gang members functioned as paid consultants, showing the company's R&D team precisely what was "dope" (hot!) in the inner city. Rather than using a traditional focus group, we instead relied upon the street knowledge of some of the "OG's." These are the "original gangsters," the members of the gang with the highest respect and longtime standing.

As shoe people, we were quite impressed with the understanding our new consultants had with regard to both the functional and fashion elements of the product. On many occasions the OG's provided us with the precise balance of color and interpretations of patterns. Their input was extremely instrumental in helping us design this dynamic new line up of shoes. We actually launched the brand as "PURE STREET," reflecting the lifestyle of the inner city.

But there is often a serendipity effect that occurs in business, especially when creative minds meet. Although the small shoe store chain is well-represented in L.A.'s inner city, there remain a wealth of other neighborhoods situated deep in this zone that have been neglected by mainstream businesses. Fear and racial stereotypes are prevalent among many merchants when the idea of doing business in the heart of the inner city is presented to them. After the 1992 riots, the anticipated sense of danger in these neighborhoods became a major, contributing reason why many merchants still have refused to return to the inner city.

The fact remains, however, that the residents of these communities still desire certain consumer goods that may be obtainable only by driving or walking some distance to outlying areas. So, in a relatively unprecedented move, the shoe merchants turned not to commercial realtors, but instead sought the advice of the formerly active gang members to direct them to locations where there would be considerable vehicular and pedestrian traffic in the heart of this zone.

The plan would be for the shoe people to secure the properties recommended by the gang members. Organizations like Jim Brown's Amer-I-Can Program or the Delores Mission which specialize in educating and resocializing urban youth and gang members, provided us with their promising graduates to move into retail management.

Our job as shoe merchants would then be to train the ex-gangbangers in the skills needed to become accomplished footwear retailers. The company would also set up a series of miniature outdoor outlets, similar to the "tranquies" popular in the mercados of Latin America. Each outdoor street-corner operation would then be stocked with shoes purchased from the corporate warehouse.

The retail chain would thus function as a franchise agent, providing job training, product, financing, and the location for the mini-outlets. The social organizations would in turn be responsible for referring potential management and sales personnel who had gone through their life-skills programs.

In less than three weeks from the inception of the plan, the ex-active gang members and the inner-city shoe store chain opened their first joint venture. Sales were instantly realized, as residents of the neglected neighborhood found affordable name brand foot-wear available in a casual, informal retail set-up on a popular street corner.

Interestingly, we also solicited and received full cooperation from the local law enforcement people who provided the outdoor market with a modicum of security. The police wanted the new venture to work as a means to send a solid message to the community that they also supported the idea of generating new jobs in the inner city.

The formerly active gang members gravitated to their new role as inner-city proprietors with remarkable skill. Immediately they seemed to internalize a strong pride in ownership as equity partners in this new joint venture. The most rudimentary rules of proper retail stewardship were embraced by the ex-gangsters. Stock levels were routinely monitored, sales trends were reviewed daily, margins were maintained, and product turn-around was maximized. A new business had been launched in a riot-torn section of L.A. that had been pretty much ignored by most commercial enterprises!

The Future

With the success of this pilot street corner shoe store, other outlets soon followed. Each has generated considerable business in their own, small neighborhood niche. But what about the future? What are some of the basic ingredients that might help to continue this and similar commerce in the inner city? And, what are the potential pitfalls of such enterprise?

To begin with, mainstream business people will have to suspend stereotypes of the inner city. On one hand, it would be foolhardy to have a cavalier attitude about setting up a commercial venture deep within the barrios or ghettos of Los Angeles. There is undeniably a degree of danger present in many of these neighborhoods, fostered to a large part by organized street gangs. It is essential that local law enforcement also lend support to this kind of project by working with the street corner merchants. Both retailer and police must outline the kind of security, if any, that is needed for a particular street-corner operation.

Nevertheless, there is a wealth of potential buyers who reside in these economically impacted communities. Like consumers anywhere else in the country, they too want name brand products at affordable prices. Up until recently, such consumer goods had to be purchased primarily in the suburbs at mainstream discount stores. The problem is that many of these inner city residents have limited means of transportation, or less inclination to travel to some shopping mall 10-15 miles from their neighborhood. Thus, many have learned to live without those products.

The miniature shoe-store outlets might serve as a true, primordial model for doing business in this zone. By having the courage and vision to proceed into the heart of the "hoods," the shoe merchants tapped into an entire enclave of consumers who had been neglected by the conventional business sector.

An integral feature of the success of the street-corner shoe stores was the fact that the shoe store chain actively recruited indigenous members of the neighborhood to staff the outlets, with the possibility of the local people acquiring equity in the operation. Unlike many other inner-city businesses that are making money in the community by absentee owners who commute outside the "hood" to their homes each night, the mini-shoe stores have prospered primarily because the salespeople and management team *live* in the community where the street corner shop is situated.

It certainly helps to have highly visible, formerly active gang members working in the shoe stores. Many of these men had been perceived as either folk heroes or villains. They now present a new, positive role model of economic self-empowerment. By no means, however, will such ventures work only by recruiting ex-gang members, paroled felons, or the like. But certainly, if these extreme members of the "have not" caste can be transformed into successful entrepreneurs, the model should work for other less notorious, disenfranchised peoples.

The point is that the little street-corner shoe store outlets might indeed serve as a blueprint for practically any business wanting to penetrate into the heart of the inner city. Other popular consumer goods such as clothing, auto parts, hardware or records, tapes, CDs and videos may all be saleable through such casual, low-intimidation sales units.

However, as the expression says, "Good help is hard to find." The potential success of such an operation depends upon the recruitment of reliable inner-city help. This is where programs like Amer-I-Can and the Delores Mission will be of great value, in providing businesses with people who have the potential to properly staff such operations. Keep in mind, that most small merchants will not have the time nor the experience to teach ex-gangsters or similarly disenfranchised persons the basic life skills needed to function in mainstream business.

The reality is that the inner city of L.A. is also a potential powder keg unless wide-scale major socioeconomic changes occur. As the Spring 1992 turmoil illustrated, a single event can trigger pent-up anger and frustrations into a major volatile expression of these emotions.

It is too early to predict whether these miniature retail store outlets will sustain themselves in these communities. Nevertheless, some sort of small-scale model for indigenous business has been created with the formation of these street-corner stores.

Hopefully, other outlets will successfully be put into operation. These and similar models featuring other retail products might serve as "seeds" spreading throughout these neighborhoods. There is a real chance that such ventures might truly cultivate an entrepre-neurial spirit that has been dormant for so many years in this zone, because traditional business never gave it a chance to really blossom.

Several months after the gang members were launched on new careers as entrepreneurs, they were viewed by millions on national television playing basketball with a shirtsleeved President Bill Clinton during his tour of South-Central Los Angeles.

Jeff Sholl
is the vice president and general manager of the Green Giant Fresh division of Grand Metropolitan PLC. He has held positions in research management with Pillsbury where he was the recipient of a number of patents, principally in the fields of microwave technology and food chemistry. He has led the marketing functions of the Haagen-Dazs Company and Paul Ecke Ranch, Inc. Most recently, he directed the development of the Green Giant Fresh venture.

Sholl has long been a student of the new business development process and has assisted a number of companies in the evaluation of their new business development programs. He attended the University of Minnesota and completed an undergraduate degree in chemistry followed by a graduate degree in food chemistry and nutrition.

6

Ten Principles of Corporate Intrapreneuring

Jeff Sholl

Most corporations have experienced significant difficulty in the successful commercialization of internally developed new business expansions. In fact, many large corporations have given up or sharply curtailed investing in new category development, preferring instead to fund product proliferations based on existing core competencies. As a result, they resort to acquiring and integrating ongoing companies as their approach to pioneering "new" businesses.

Intrapreneuring represents a powerful alternative to traditional internal innovation processes, but only for those corporations which are willing to adopt fundamental new business practices. Along with real organic growth, intrapreneurial business development programs can be counted on to introduce new systems and processes into the corporation. Inherent in their nature, intrapreneurial activities function as "islands of cultural change" in an enlightened organization providing a venue for introducing new business practices. My own story began in 1988 with the takeover of the Pillsbury Company by Grand Metropolitan PLC [GrandMet]. GrandMet looked to the acquired Green Giant business to be a leading contributor in their drive for prominence in the food industry. Green Giant was a premier brand in the Pillsbury portfolio and GrandMet was expecting a significant contribution to growth from the company during the 1990s.

GrandMet is one of the largest international companies in the United Kingdom, and a world leader in branded foods and drinks, with annual sales in excess of $14 billion. GrandMet is a world leader in the distribution of wines and spirits, marketing a portfolio of brands including Bailey's Original Irish Cream, Smirnoff Vodka, and J&B Rare Scotch Whisky. The Food Sector manufactures and markets products under the Pillsbury, Haagen-Dazs, Totino's, Burger King, and Green Giant brands.

During the 1970s and 1980s, GrandMet developed a large international business in wine and spirits, and felt that marketing globally was a key corporate growth strategy for the recently acquired Food Sector. Green Giant, having already been established in a number of important international markets, provided GrandMet with an existing food distribution infrastructure upon which to build.

In 1989, a market research study, appropriately titled "Giant Step," was conducted in Green Giant's domestic markets to identify important potential growth opportunities for the brand. The results of the study confirmed that Green Giant was the number one consumer brand in both canned and frozen vegetables. The study also identified Green Giant as the brand of choice in fresh veg-etables as well. This result was, to some, surprising. The recognized leader in premium quality vegetables, Green Giant, had only dabbled in fresh vegetables during their eighty-year history. Green Giant had never launched a serious fresh vegetable initiative capitalizing on existing core competencies in the growing, harvesting, manufacturing, and marketing of vegetable products. However, fresh vegetables were emerging as one of the fastest growing retail food categories, generating over $17 billion in wholesale sales compared to canned and frozen sales at less than $5 billion annually.

This growth was driven by a number of important consumer trends. Aging baby boomers had started to alter their eating habits to include more healthy and nutritious foods. This resulted in vegetables moving from a side dish item to a center-of-the-plate main meal. Vegetables had become a food of choice due to their naturally low caloric content and high vitamin and mineral levels. GrandMet immediately recognized the opportunity that existed and aggressively moved the Green Giant division into this rapidly expanding marketplace.

At this time, I was employed by an agricultural firm involved in floriculture. The president of Green Giant, an acquaintance from my previous years spent at Pillsbury, had contacted me to discuss the challenges he was finding in the marketing of perishable products. I soon found myself a part of the Green Giant Company, as Vice President and General Manager of the "Fresh" business.

The Fresh team was struggling. This was surprising since the team was made up of a number of very capable and experienced professionals, all sharing a deep commitment to the program. Although many outstanding business opportunities had been identified and researched, the team clearly lacked a unifying vision.

My earliest memory of the Fresh program was a team meeting held on the day of my arrival. A large conference table was surrounded by a dozen gray-suited professionals with overheads in hand. They earnestly debated whether the Fresh development initiatives should be based on infrastructure development (i.e., building factories and distribution centers) or the creation of new products. The debate continued for some time. There was little evidence that decisions, or any form of progress, would emerge from this forum.

I found it alarming that such an esoteric debate could have polarized the team to the point of paralysis. I later discovered that this polarization was not new and that the resulting paralysis had affected the team for some time.

Within days, a number of equally energy-draining discussions had taken place in my office. I began to wonder if I was missing some key understanding of the program mission? On the other hand, perhaps these issues were simply symptomatic of a business team unable to see where it wanted to go.

The Fresh team was organized along functional lines as part of the existing New Business Group of the Green Giant Company.

Team members were divided into two groups; the first group had ongoing business responsibilities with the remainder of the team dedicated to the creation of new business opportunities. This traditional approach to new business development was not working for the Fresh team. Where and how to proceed became my first significant management challenge. Clearly, the team had to move beyond the current state of polarization and paralysis.

Traditional new business development programs are handicapped by the shortcomings of functionalized business structures and bureaucratized approval systems. Successful creation of internally developed new businesses require looking beyond traditional thinking.

Intrapreneuring has developed as a "hybrid" approach to internal new business development. Intrapreneurial ventures are formed by melding entrepreneurial management philosophy with employees and select systems of the existing corporation. Intrapreneuring has emerged as the organizational approach followed by big companies desiring to perform in an entrepreneurial fashion. An intrapreneurial venture requires individuals on the team to act in an entrepreneurial manner, encouraging them to find ways around the innate limitations of corporate cultures.

Importantly, intrapreneuring permits the corporation to select the field of innovation to be pursued to meet their business needs. Entrepreneurs are dedicated to building new brands; intrapreneurial ventures are most often dedicated to building on existing corporate brands. The real value of intrapreneuring to the corporation is to maximize new business success, thus increasing shareholder wealth through a cost efficient strengthening of existing corporate brand equities. Intrapreneuring, like all good hybrids, can bring the greatest strengths of entrepreneuring [small, lean and quick] and big company muscle [highly experienced and resourced] to the new business development process.

The primary operating difference between entrepreneurial and traditional corporate thinking is the acknowledgment that *businesses cannot plan their way to success*. Corporate training leads to the belief that a blueprint can be developed detailing the path to success for most new business programs. The fatal flaw present in all new business development efforts resides in this erroneous belief.

The nature of the corporate culture is to demand a plan, then measure progress against the plan every step of the way. Entrepreneurs inherently think differently. They are not *against* planning. In fact, entrepreneurial plans are often as detailed and as well thought out as any corporate planning calendar. The fundamental difference is that the entrepreneur keeps sight of the final destination and is willing to replan [change directions] as often as necessary, to reach the final vision. From the corporate viewpoint, not sticking to a business plan can be seen as lack of management ability, knowledge or control. In an entrepreneurial environment, sticking to a course at all costs is best described as an inability to adapt to reality or capitalize on opportunity.

During my stint as Senior Vice-President of Marketing for Haagen-Dazs, I spent a great deal of time working directly with Reuben Mattus, the company founder. Reuben enjoyed telling me how, during the early years of Haagen-Dazs, he constantly made significant changes in the company's direction, mainly due to day-to-day realities of the business. He would tell me that he had built Haagen-Dazs by making nothing but "bad decisions." Every morning when Reuben arrived at work he would be faced with a number of immediate issues. He'd say that each issue presented him with making a choice between a bad decision and a worse one. "So I always choose the bad decision!"

During the evolution of Haagen-Dazs as a company, Reuben never lost sight of his overall desire to be the marketer of the world's highest quality ice cream. However, he was the first to acknowledge that the Haagen-Dazs company he sold to Pillsbury had little in common with the business he originally set out to build during the early 1960s.

Here is a summary of how we proceeded based on what I think are ten keys to intrapreneural success.

Principle #1. Intrapreneurial team members share a common dynamic vision that is permitted to continually evolve. Fluidity of the vision is required.

By early 1990, after weeks of intense study and internal debate, the Fresh team was ready to present their vision and program proposal to the Chairman of the Food Sector. The program would be built on marketing a fresh vegetable-based main meal product line marketed under a new brand name FRESHTABLES by Green Giant. The proposal was inarguably bold and visionary. The growth potential was exciting and almost unlimited. The costs to implement—admittedly—were staggering. The interest expressed by the Chairman? NIL!!

The message was clear. Don't expect the corporate funding spigot to be turned on for an unproven "dream."

Principle #2. If you are going to organize as an intrapreneurial venture—act like one!

The team had learned an important lesson of intrapreneuring: maintain control of your program by keeping the up-front corporate investment small. Entrepreneurs seldom enjoy unlimited bank-rolls—why should the team expect one!

The Chairman returned to London and the team went into a "hurry-up offense" to develop an alternate proposal. This time the proposal would be based on proving the vision on a low cost, low risk basis. We also recognized we had created a need to provide the Chairman with reassurance that the venture was going to proceed with appropriate corporate overview.

To meet that need, several senior company officers with a direct reporting relationship to the Chairman were recruited to act as a Review Board for the venture. The members of the Board were selected based on their support of the program and ability to influence the Chairman. An important role for the Board would be in ensuring that the venture did not get buried under corporate control/reporting requirements.

Principle #3. Keep senior members of the corporation well-informed and involved in the venture's progress by developing a "Corporate Advisory Board" early on in the program.

Venture team management tends to include individuals who are very independent and, by nature, high risk takers. Venture management is often made up of a heavy percentage of what might be unkindly called "Corporate Misfits"—typically, very bright and capable individuals, who may never have been very adept at internal corporate politics. Once they become members of the venture management staff, the latent desire of these individuals to operate very independently from the corporation advances into full flower. The stage is thus set for immediate and recurring conflict between accountable corporate senior management and venture management.

To be successful, the intrapreneurial venture must not only survive and thrive in the marketplace, it must learn how to successfully manage the internal relationships with the corporation. In my experience, marketplace issues can often be less of a problem than the management of the internal relationship issues that develop between the venture and corporate management. Preventing negative relationship issues from occurring requires an active management of all key interactions between the venture and the corporation.

Principle #4. A healthy dose of the venture leaders' personal time and attention must be devoted to managing the interaction with the larger corporation.

From a standing start seven months earlier, the team had developed a line of value-added products, constructed a manufacturing facility, and created a direct store-delivery system, including the required information systems. The team had been successful in launching the Green Giant Freshtables line into a controlled store test in Minneapolis. This was a remarkable team accomplishment. The primary reason for the rapid progress was the corporation's recognition of the intrapreneurial necessity to allow the team freedom to operate outside internal approval systems.

Principle #5. The venture management team and the corporation must enter into mutual agreements that allow the venture the "required freedom to act."

The corporation must accept the reality that the venture will behave in ways that may be unfamiliar and, perhaps, uncomfortable to management. However, the willingness of the corporation to stick to the up front agreements detailing the venture's "freedom to act" is absolutely critical to its success. The corporation must also constantly work to remove internal barriers to program success, while they learn to live with the experimentation that is the nature of a venture program.

Ventures are very vulnerable during their formative years. Senior corporate management accepts certain risks with the initiation of the venture. This does not render corporate management immune to being surprised with "bad" news by the venture. However, the corporation must be prepared to accept some short-term "fumbles." Venture activities are, by nature, high risk.

Principle #6. Launching an intrapreneurial venture is not for the corporate faint of heart.

The nature of a venture is to travel in new and different directions. Corporate management may perceive these shifts in direction to be indicative of loss of program control by the venture team. However, to the venture, these changes in direction may be very important responses to changing marketplace conditions, technology advancements, or infrastructure requirements.

If the corporation is going to encourage the success of the venture, then they must develop a relationship based on mutual trust with the venture team. Trust between the parties must be substantive—not just talked about. Trust must actually exist. Once trust exists, open communication can also exist. The corporation has to recognize and accept the volatile nature of the venture. It must believe in the business plan and the competence of the venture team. The team must believe that corporate management is supporting them in good faith, through good as well as the tough times.

After ten months in test market, Green Giant Freshtables were exceeding all marketplace expectations. Feedback was very positive, with some of the highest consumer acceptance scores ever recorded for a Green Giant new product. The venture team was ecstatic and looked forward to an aggressive national roll-out of the products. Frankly, we all began to act pretty smug about our accomplishment. We didn't realize that we were about to receive a nasty dose of "corporate reality."

The Green Giant Company had been experiencing very difficult market conditions for an extended period of time, and the prospects were not good for an immediate turnaround of the division. In an environment of corporate contraction, Fresh was about to trumpet our investment message to financially shell-shocked ears. We expected the corporation to open the funding floodgates. After all, we had delivered what the company had requested—test-market proof that our business concept was sound.

As the team gathered to share expansion plans with senior corporate management, no one in Fresh had any clue that the venture was on the corporate chopping block. Early in the meeting, however, the message was clear: "The project is over! Withdraw from the market and shut down!" Instead of leaving the meeting with a blank check for the expansion program that we had expected, the project looked terminal. The venture management team had two immediate reactions to the news: first, shock that we were caught so off guard by corporate unwillingness to invest capital in our business and, second, that we would not let this answer stand!

Principle #7. The relationship between the venture and corporation requires both parties to assume an obligation to maintain open and effective communication channels.

In a sincere attempt to protect the Fresh business from the day-to-day problems affecting Green Giant, senior management had not shared their sense of where the Fresh venture was headed. Thus, we were caught totally off guard, finding ourselves well down the road to potential oblivion.

My management staff returned from the meeting and immediately started working to identify a path out of this dilemma. The management review had occurred late on a Friday afternoon. Green Giant management had agreed to give us the weekend to come up with an alternate business proposal that would significantly reduce investment. The time had come to mobilize the entire team to find a path out of our dilemma. After lengthy hours of analysis and debate, the team succeeded in creating and convincing corporate management to accept a viable new approach to the marketing of Freshtables. The business would no longer be infrastructure intensive. We would not, as originally planned, be building company-owned plants and distribution systems. Rather, the business would accept lower operating profits, trading margin to pay contract producers and distributors.

Throughout this crisis, the team had demonstrated the same commitment to the business that is seen in successful entrepreneurs.

They accepted total responsibility for the future of the venture and did not allow the corporate decision to kill their program. The venture had developed a culture where adverse decisions led to learning, not paralysis or recrimination.

Principle #8. The entire venture team must be allowed and encouraged to participate in planning business direction.

A venture team cannot afford to allow lack of trust to develop between team members. In small start-up organizations, room does not exist for lack of confidence between team players. In a small team, there are no "non-key" players. Excluding any team members in formulating strategic direction is a sure way to plant the seeds of non-commitment.

I know of no better way to form a single-minded focus on the business objectives than that achieved by involving the entire team in the strategic planning process. The internal managing of a venture presents significant opportunities for team managers to find solutions to unfamiliar problems. Most team members usually have limited experience in new business start-ups and find themselves working in high pressure situations without traditional resources at hand. None of the usual corporate "escape" routes are available. Team members soon learn that intrapreneurs, like entrepreneurs, can't just buy solutions to their problems; they must creatively solve them. They soon learn to structure decisions and business activities so, even if the current approach fails, the team still advances. Individuals discover that their personal success and career advancement is truly dependent on their functioning as a team.

Principle #9. If a team lacks a "passion" for the business and each other, it rapidly comes apart.

The largest venture management challenge is to sustain an environment where the team can continually develop internal supportive processes that keep the team dynamically alive and collectively functioning.

By fall 1992, Green Giant Fresh had successfully developed a profitable commodity business selling premium quality potatoes, onions, and asparagus. However, the future was clouded not only by the recent market entry of aggressive competitors, but also by internal venture team management issues. A "we/they" situation had developed internally. The Fresh venture had evolved into two separate business teams and a problem had emerged between members of the commodity team and members of the Freshtables team. Having experienced some real marketplace success, the commodity team had become resentful as their hard-earned profits disappeared as Freshtables expenses. Freshtables team members had become frustrated watching competition gain distribution by marketing Freshtables product "knockoffs." While we had received permission to introduce Freshtables into Northern California, further expansion had not been approved. Our continued inability to convince the corporation to provide working capital for further regional expansion was at the root of this problem. The need to move forward was obvious; the "how" was not clear. The Fresh business had evolved to the point where reorganization of the venture along with renegotiation of the venture/corporation relationship was necessary.

Establishing a new relationship with the corporation which would allow the venture additional independence from the many corporate approval and overview processes, and more "freedom to act," was necessary. The venture had to be distanced from division performance issues. Thus far, these issues restricted growth opportunities for the venture. The Fresh management team recognized that the business had developed two very independent initiatives, and that each initiative required separate infrastructure and management systems. The venture team had also learned that financial independence from the corporation would lead to operating freedom for the Fresh business. The venture enjoyed significant freedom to act, when the corporation was not asked to provide all the funding for a project. While the Fresh business was able to internally generate limited investment funding, our pockets were not deep. This lead to the classic dilemma of balancing investment in growth and generating profit. Fresh management choose to restructure the business with a focus on driving the business to profitability in as short a time as possible, with the objective of minimizing corporate investment in the business.

We proposed that the management team "share in the venture investment" with the corporation. This "shared investment" required both the corporation and venture management to assume financial risks and associated rewards for the business, providing both parties with significant incentive to succeed. The corporation placed their investment dollars at risk and the venture management team signed employment agreements that coupled their career advancement opportunities to the venture's success. Each person in management made an actual financial investment in the business.

Principle #10. Venture team members become "owners" of the business when compensation is directly linked to venture success in ways they never would if they were on a conventional compensation plan.

A month had passed and I was enjoying a few days of downhill skiing in Colorado. I had promised to check in with the Food Sector's chief financial officer to discuss the status of the proposed Fresh business plan and reorganization. The CFO informed me that the corporation had accepted the business plan and was prepared to support the proposed venture organization structure.

Upon my return to Minneapolis, I gathered venture management together and opened discussions around forming a more intrapreneurial team structure. By early 1993, the Fresh Team had successfully restructured the business. Responsibility for strategic plan overview and evaluation of progress fell to an Advisory Board. The role of the Board was to approve annual and long range plans, and any significant deviations from the plan. The Board would meet semi-annually, scheduled to coincide with the corporations long term and annual planning cycles. A document, referred to by the venture team as the "Whitebook" was also prepared. The Whitebook detailed financial expectations, growth objectives, and other important understandings agreed to by venture and corporate management. The Whitebook was intended to document all agreements reached that would effect the business plan, providing a mechanism to ensure that these agreements were interpreted similarly by both parties.

Conclusion

The Fresh team has developed a unique culture based on a real and living passion for the business and a belief in our abilities to succeed. The team continues to learn what is required to thrive at intrapreneuring in the corporation. The Fresh venture didn't just happen. Rather, the program evolved through a number of development stages, with each stage providing a new set of learnings. The team accepts the fact that intrapreneuring is a evolutionary process so no team member will be surprised as business conditions and internal requirements lead us to another stage of development.

Members of business teams within Grandmet have spent time with the Fresh team discussing the nature of the intrapreneurial process. These groups are searching for ways to capture the positive benefits of an empowered independent team. The corporation stands to benefit as these individuals create new "islands of intrapreneuring" in their businesses.

Jacqueline Haessly is the founder of Peacemaking Associates, a for-profit educational and consulting company. She is the author of several books and more than one hundred articles which have been published in more than thirty national and international publications. She is a co-author of *When the Canary Stops Singing: Women's Perspectives on Transforming Business,* which was named one of the top ten management books for 1993 by *Industry Week* magazine, and is author of *Learning to Live Together.*

Haessly has been named to more than twenty *Who's Who* international biographies, including *Business and Professional Women, Women of the Americas, Authors and Writers,* and *International Leaders* for her extensive work in the field of peace and global awareness education.

She offers consultation, lectures, workshops, and retreats to local and national business, educational, and community organizations. She is currently pursuing doctoral studies at the Union Institute in Cincinnati, Ohio.

7

Peacemaking for Profit:
The Years I Ate An Elephant

Jacqueline Haessly

The year was 1987. I had just completed the first session of a six-week mini-course for women and minorities in business. As of that evening my business, Peacemaking Associates, had existed for almost fifteen years. I was an educator, responding to increasing numbers of requests from the community to provide education programs for adults or youth on topics related to peace and non-violence. Except for balancing the checkbook and filing year-end tax returns I knew almost nothing about running a business.

Toward the end of the first class, I felt overwhelmed rather than empowered. I didn't know where or how to begin to address the complexity of business-related problems that I had brought with me to class that evening. During the question period at the close of the class, I raised my hand and timidly inquired, "What does one do if one has been in business for almost fifteen years and never knew, or did, any of this." Our instructor paused and gently responded with a question of her own. "How," she asked, "does one eat an elephant?" "Slowly," I replied. "One bite at a time." The task seemed mammoth—but not insurmountable.

My professional work as a peace educator dates back to 1964, when I began incorporating racial and social justice concerns into my religious education classes in a rural Wisconsin community. Ten years later I started my business—a consulting, teaching, training and publishing enterprise dedicated to promoting educational programs for global living. While I didn't understand it at the time, it is clear to me today that the entrepreneurial spirit has been with me since the beginning when I identified a need and recognized an opportunity in a unique field. Two friends and I responded by opening an office in a small storefront in order to meet the growing needs of a public who expressed an interest in peace education. We established a resource library and invited the public to come, see, and learn. They did. I consider myself one of the lucky ones. I work in a field I feel passionate about; I have received international recognition for my work; and I even get paid for what I do. How I came to work in this field, and why, is explored in this essay.

A Journey Toward Peacemaking

My business is rooted in the experiences of my childhood and young adult life. I was born in Milwaukee and spent the first sixteen years of my life in a low-income public housing project. I soon noticed that those who were poor, or deaf, or belonged to a different faith tradition, or who had skin of a different hue, were often ridiculed, negated, and excluded from participating in play or social activities as equals. It was there that I first witnessed racial and cultural slurs against those who seemed different, and first experienced incidents of family abuse and neighborhood violence. It was there, too, that I first became aware of issues of economic disparity and discrimination. While I didn't know how to change those patterns, or even name them then, I knew that people had a right to be treated with dignity and that those patterns had to be changed if there was to be peace in our families, our community, and our world.

Thus my concerns for peace, for family and community justice, equality, and wholeness date back to my childhood—as evidenced by the questions I raised both at home and in school. I asked lots of questions, sometimes to the consternation of teachers and other adults. "Why," I asked my third grade teacher in 1944, "did our country celebrate the discovery of America by Columbus when Indian people, who were here when Columbus arrived, had obviously discovered it first?" I was not yet nine. There were other questions on my mind—having to do with poverty, race, family disruptions, and war. When I didn't get satisfactory answers I searched further.

After graduating from high school I worked as a nurse, caring for psychiatric and geriatric patients. My commitment to justice and compassion found expression in caring for people who themselves were often victims of discrimination in the community. Still questioning, I returned to college ten years later, in 1967, to complete undergraduate studies. A college education would, I believed, help me to find answers to my questions.

In 1967, race riots broke out in Newark, Detroit, Los Angeles, and in my town, Milwaukee; anti-war riots at universities in Madison, Columbia, Berkeley and Boston made the news. I was living and working at an inner-city parish at the heart of the riot scene and had become an active participant with Father James Groppi in the open housing marches then taking place in Milwaukee. Daily, I witnessed racial discrimination and experienced the fear and hatred which surrounded me and the people I had come to love. Anti-war protesters on campus aroused another level of awareness. At the time I knew little about the Vietnam War or the issues surrounding the protest movement. However, I quickly discovered parallels between my own childhood experiences, the events then taking place in Milwaukee in 1967, and the war taking place so far away in Southeast Asia. Poverty, racism and powerlessness were themes common to all these experiences. My interest in the peace movement began there.

In 1969, I accepted a work-study position with the Wisconsin Civil Liberties Union that radically changed my life. I was assigned to investigate and report on citizen complaints of police brutality. Much of the recording and documenting of evidence took place in the patient wards of local hospitals. I felt horror at the evidence of beatings I witnessed during those investigations. I felt dismay about other practices also. The dehumanizing of the "enemy," which resulted in name-calling, labeling and beatings, was almost identical whether practiced by police officers, racial minorities, anti-war demonstrators, soldiers in Vietnam or seemingly ordinary citizens. Only the labels—"niggers," "honkies," "pigs," "gooks," "traitors"— were changed. I struggled to maintain my own humanity and to respect the dignity and humanity of others in these tense and traumatic situations.

A Search For Alternatives To Violence

The racism and violence that surrounded me during those years seemed massive and pervasive. Frightened that I myself might internalize the violent rhetoric that I heard daily, I attended a seminar on non-violence which was offered at a local university. Participants shared personal stories and heard stories of Gandhi and others who had integrated non-violence into their personal and political lives. Throughout the process we were gently encouraged to discover a new way of living with others peacefully. I did not know who Gandhi was, nor did I have any idea what pacifism was but, after attending the first meeting, I knew I had found a spiritual home. Participants at the weekly seminar quickly established close bonds, and it was there that I met Dr. Daniel Di Domizio, the man who would later become my husband.

We married within the year and together have shared in the fun, love, tears, laughter and homemaking tasks associated with the care and nurturing of a busy family. Much of what I later taught in Peacemaking for Family workshops and at cooperative play festivals has first been tried and practiced on one or more members of our family. Our five children are now all young adults, working and living on their own. It fills me with joy to know that each in their own way incorporates the principles of peacemaking and cooperation in their own activities at home and where they work.

Becoming A Peace Educator

My introduction to "peace education" as a specialized field occurred during that seminar on non-violence. I took an active role as a volunteer for a local peace education committee, giving presentations to schools and religious congregations. I enjoyed developing curriculums and teaching adults. Attracted to peace studies and undaunted by the reality that neither the University of Wisconsin-

Milwaukee, nor most other campuses in the country at that time, offered courses in peace education, I requested and received permission to design my own program. I enrolled in courses off campus when necessary in order to create an education program with a peace and global interdependence emphasis, earning my undergraduate degree in 1971 and my Master's degree in education in 1976. During those years Dan and I offered peace and non-violence courses at local colleges, religious congregations, and through a "free university."

Today peace studies is a growing field in the academic and educational communities. However, in 1974, there were still few peace education programs on college campuses and most peace and justice groups focused on single issues such as militarism, the nuclear threat, hunger, or the environment. It was an awareness of a growing need for people trained in holistic peace studies and conflict resolution that led me to start my own business.

The Business of Peacemaking

My company has, from its inception, been committed to bringing issues of justice, peace, and values for global interdependence to all segments of the metropolitan Milwaukee area through education, reflection, and non-violent action for social change. Today, we offer consultations, educational programs, in-service training, and retreats for educational, religious, and social service organizations locally, nationally, and internationally. More recently, we have provided consultations and training for business groups.

There are three components—subsidiaries if you will—of my company: Creative Playtime, which evolved from my commitment to incorporate cooperative play in peace studies programs, offers intergenerational festivals for community organizations, business meetings and employee parties where adults and children of all ages are encouraged to play together cooperatively. A variety of cooperation games are also sold. Peace Talks Publications publishes and sells original material, reprints, curriculums and books as well as audio and video tapes on peace themes. The Milwaukee Peace Education Resource Center, a non-profit organization, houses an extensive curriculum library consisting of materials on a multitude of peace, justice and global interdependence topics for pre-school through adult education. The library, one of the most comprehensive in the Midwest, is of special interest to educators, students, scholars, parents, and leaders from community organizations.

Visitors to the Center come from across the city and the globe for consultations on effective ways to develop their own education programs or to research peace curriculums or peace history, and to purchase books or cooperative games. Phone calls and letters from people seeking to establish their own programs or who want to share ideas come in daily from all parts of the United States, Canada, and occasionally from such far away places as Australia, Japan, England, Poland, Russia and South Africa. Each call or letter generates an excitement and expectancy that our work does make a difference. Funding is still limited for this work at this time; we have no paid staff but depend upon part-time volunteers to meet the continuing demand for information and services.

What—Me An Entrepreneur?

When I first started my business over twenty years ago, I did not consider myself an entrepreneur. Indeed I didn't really understand the meaning of the word. I considered myself an educator who was responding to requests for peace education programs in the community. James D. Gwartney and Richard L. Stroup, writing in their book, *Microeconomics*, define an entrepreneur as "a profit-seeking decision-maker who decides which projects to undertake and how they should be undertaken." They say an entrepreneur adds "value to existing resources." An entrepreneur is also commonly described as "one who assumes risks." There are all sorts of risks in the world, some financial, some personal, some professional. One who undertakes the business of peacemaking assumes risks in all of these areas.

In 1974 I took a risk. I made the decision to establish the Center as a business. I didn't understand that I was an entrepreneur and that a part of the definition of an entrepreneur included the concept of making a profit. "Food for people, not for profit" was a common cry of the day. Profit, for many people in peace and justice work in the 1960s and 1970s, had come to mean exploitation of people and resources. I knew I didn't want to do that! I did recognize, however, that through my work as a peace educator, I would be adding value to the lives and work of others. Although I lacked understanding of the economic dimensions of the concept, I was also aware of a growing phenomenon in the business community, the concept of socially responsible business. My enterprise, I thought, would be such a socially responsible business!

Two key factors figured in my decision to be a for-profit business rather than a nonprofit organization. First, given the political and social climate of that period in history, funding from foundation, corporate and government grants was limited and, as a result, competition among nonprofits for scarce funds at the time was extremely high. I wanted to avoid dependency on grants for our survival. Secondly, I believe strongly that if we want to create peace in the world, we need a peace economy, one which pays people to work in peace and not just war-related fields. It is increasingly clear to me that in order to achieve this goal, the business of peacemaking, like all businesses, requires sound business practices and management skills.

A Herd of Elephants

A laundry list of "mistakes" led to that herd of elephants that seemed to overrun my office and, for a while, my life. These mistakes developed due to my lack of general business knowledge and skill regarding financial and management aspects of running a business. One costly mistake involved the way we managed our records and fulfilled orders, tasks made more complex by the inefficient ways we were using our computers. Another costly mistake involved the way we charged for our services. From the beginning, we had depended upon fees from our workshops and lectures as well as the sale of our books, cooperation games, and other resource materials for our income. In the beginning, modest honorariums were occasionally provided for workshops and consulting services. When agencies and organizations did request fee information, I lacked knowledge of how to set a fair fee structure. It wasn't until much later that I realized that I had "underpriced" my services. Since I have an international reputation, I now charge fees commensurate with my credibility in this field.

Each "mistake" has, at one time or another, cost the business something: a loss of a speaking engagement, the loss of an order or subscription, and a great loss of time as we took steps to correct errors.

Since that introductory course in 1987, I have been "eating away at the elephant," one bite at a time. Today elephants have become dear friends, sharing space in all rooms of my office and our home, reminding me that no task is impossible if one seeks to manage it "one bite at a time."

Today, I can say that I have made some progress. I have moved the office and resource library to our home, joining the growing ranks of home-based businesses. From here I continue to pursue my professional work as writer, consultant, and trainer. We are maintaining responses to current requests for information, programs, and book orders. However, there are still reams of back orders not yet addressed. There are times when I think that I have managed well, only to discover that a new herd of elephants has emerged from hiding in one of the multiple boxes which holds the "to be done later" files. I no longer experience discouragement at the slow progress. I sense that I am on a journey of discovery. The business part of peacemaking is only one small part of that journey.

Impediments to the Business

There are impediments to this business. There are professional risks which often have financial implications. In today's violence-prone society some parents believe that children really need to be taught self-protection (with guns), not peacemaking skills. There are teachers who suggest that peace education ended with the "Sixties." Some school superintendents refuse to approve requests from teachers for peace education in-service programs. There are college administrators who, quick to introduce new programs in business administration, seem more cautious when considering programs in peace studies. A publisher once suggested a name change for one of my books because "peace won't sell." Some in the business world have suggested that I could market my consulting and training services to businesses, especially in the areas of conflict management or diversity (and get paid substantial sums of money), if only I would change the name of the company from

Peacemaking Associates to something less "threatening," something like JH Associates.

There are financial risks also. Currently, the business still depends upon fees from workshops and lectures as well as the sale of books, cooperation games, and other resource materials for income. Most of our client base still comes from the nonprofit sector, and often from groups which have limited budgets. While funding remains limited for peace work at this time, I believe that the momentum for peaceful alternatives is growing and that, in the near future, people and organizations who are able will be willing to pay a just fee for services that will enhance these skills.

There are personal risks as well. Family members and friends may not understand the work of a peace educator, especially if there is a divergence of political opinions among the members. This is especially true when a family has no tradition or experience with honoring and treasuring differences of opinion. Unlike teachers in some other fields where one can provide information without being evaluated on how well one integrates that information into one's personal life, peace educators need to "walk the talk." My children have, more than once, reminded me of this important truth. Their words, spoken in love or anger, teach me the importance of integrating peace values and peaceful behaviors into all dimensions of one's personal, professional and political life.

Like many of us, I did not learn the values and skills of peacemaking and non-violence in childhood. Indeed, my family of origin has a long history of dysfunction. My family of origin—and the family Dan, I and our children have created—are constant reminders of the fragile nature of relationships and the interconnectedness of the generations. I am especially aware of this interconnection as I cradle our new granddaughter. I know she is linked to people, past and present, who form a family. She is a clear reminder that honoring each other's love and holding it as a sacred gift for future generations is one of the tasks and joys of peacemakers.

If we as a society want our economy, and our world, to move from dependence on war and war-making, we all need to be serious about the business of peacemaking. We need to create peace businesses; we need to provide jobs in a peace economy; and we each need to develop the attitudes, values and skills of peacemaking in all aspects of our personal, professional and political lives. One of our courses encourages participants to move beyond an identification of the world's multiple problems and begin to actively consider those images and actions essential to the creation of a peaceful and just world order. Responsible and just businesses must be a part of that vision.

The Future

In our society, times have changed dramatically since our family moved into that low-income housing project more than fifty years ago. However, the effects of poverty, discrimination, joblessness, racism, political oppression, economic exploitation, and family and community violence still affect people in their hearts and in their homes in many of the same ways. There is an African saying that "it takes a whole village to raise a child." I believe that children are our future and that we, as business people who are also parents and grandparents, aunts and uncles, friends and neighbors, nurturers and educators of those children, have a unique *opportunity*, indeed a *responsibility*, to join together to create a "village," where each person's needs for safety, security and love are met. Only then can we help to create a world of peace and non-violence.

The business of peacemaking is like the planting of a fig tree, a commitment to the future, the future for our children who will be the leaders and decision makers of the 21st Century. When we provide our young, their parents, their teachers, business, religious, and government leaders with the values, attitudes, and skills essential to making a difference in their families, their communities, and our world we are offering them the best gift of all, a sense of hope for their own journey into the future. I'm happy that I can be a small part of that journey.

David P. Jasper
is CEO and co-founder of University Technology Center, a 170,000 square-foot incubator for small businesses which is over ninety-eight percent occupied and has a waiting list. Over ninety percent of small businesses entering the Center are successful.

During his fourteen-year career at Control Data Corporation, he designed the CYBERNET computer network system. In 1979, he left and formed Quest Management Associates, the corporate umbrella for his several unrelated ventures. Jasper is an investor and is actively involved in several businesses. He is owner/operator of an OMNIMAX theatre which he has successfully turned into a substantial cash producer.

Jasper has a Bachelor of Science degree in physics from the College of St. Thomas. He lives in Minnesota with his wife, Sharon, and they have six children and four grandchildren.

8

Entrepreneurship Through Misadventure

David P. Jasper

Like nearly everyone, I have my own code of entrepreneurial success. I say "nearly everyone" because even non-entrepreneurs know entrepreneurs and believe they know how they succeeded. You've probably heard many comments about how Ross Perot or so-and-so made it. It's because "she was lucky" (which, by the way, I believe is part of it) or "they are aggressive, hard, and merciless" (which I believe ultimately is an unsuccessful strategy).

I have an opinion based on my own experiences from multiple small business successes. Each venture was quite different but the basic strategy was consistent. Here are a "lucky thirteen" set of principles I've derived from my experience.

Principle #1: Never play zero-sum games with employees or customers. Find the win-win strategy.

First off, let me define "success" as I view it. Since we are speaking of livelihood and not spiritual life or family or social life, my first criterion is that one earns a sustainable living. I have learned that "too much" of anything is unhealthy, just as much as "not enough." Too much money will soon focus all one's energies toward preserving and managing it, to the loss of other aspects of one's life. I believe in a win-win strategy. If I have success, it means others around me will too. In other words, the reason I am earning a living is because I am contributing something positive that benefits others, and they pay for that benefit. My success means a living is earned by me, and the general population (i.e., my customers) is, in some way, a little better off. If I earn a living in a way that requires help, my employees also earn a living. If my employees are able to feel fulfilled and happy, that, too, is an additional measure of success. So, beyond earning a livelihood, success also benefits others—customers and employees—in non-monetary ways.

I find that I feel good when I can help others feel good. When I feel good, I do better and others do better. It's that simple.

Principle #2: It's not an adventure unless there is some discomfort.

From grade school on, some people seek conformity and comfort (Group 1). They want security and predictability. Others want challenge and seek to lead extraordinary lives, to be different, unconcerned with comfort or security and predictability (Group 2). They are the adventurers.

Some discriminators of these two types of people are:

The adverturers do not fare well in structured environments and may not have done homework exactly as prescribed in school. They probably have difficulty following orders.

In my case, I was never a "bad boy." I found academia to be structured for someone else. I learned from every course I took but may not have done well on tests or assignments. Decades later, I remember more from many courses than others who studied to get an "A." I never studied for grades and so I didn't get very good grades. I studied for what I wanted to know.

An adventurer does not plan vacations in detail either but, rather, seeks the thrill of the unknown. He or she may not plan beyond the first night and the number of days in a locale, because the process of discovery is enjoyable and the unexpected is a delight. The adventurers are comfortable with the unpredictable and are self-reliant. Group 1 is put off by this type of vacation.

I've noticed a common element whenever I or anyone else is telling "war stories" or our own personal adventures. There is always a measure of discomfort. I believe that discomfort is the result of being stretched outside of our known operating zone to the unknown. In a word, we are learning. Adventures are therefore learning experiences. Often we learn what not to do, but we nevertheless learn.

Principle #3: The opposite of success is not failure—it is discouragement.

When Sharon, my wife, and I were looking at an $850,000 debt and mounting losses in one of our ventures, we discussed the possibilities of losing our home to a second mortgage and having to start all over. We concluded that we still would have our health and our family, and our mutual love, and a sense that God was still with us. We thought we might move to a small rural town where expenses would be lower, and possibly make pottery and handi-crafts to sell. We were not frightened or discouraged by this pros-pect, however much we wanted to avoid it. What I learned from this "near death" experience was how to let go. Not to quit, but rather to let go. There is a big difference.

Principle #4: It is the primary task of management to remove barriers and to enable employees to remove barriers.

I believe successful entrepreneurs come from Group 2: not easily discouraged, self fulfilling, adventuresome; but it's good that not everyone is in Group 2.

Perhaps my own story will further amplify how I arrived at my own code of entrepreneurial success.

I love art. To create a painting which simultaneously balances composition, color, value, and is a faithful drawing is a constant challenge which I have never fully achieved. But when it is close to perfect, it is great art. In high school, I concluded that I was a good artist but not great enough to be what I perceived as one of a handful of great artists who made a comfortable living. Fortunately, I had an equal interest in how and why things worked. And I thought I could earn a living as an engineer and still create. I found in school that fundamentals and research attracted me most and so I majored in physics. After five and a half years, I was married and had a son and daughter and still no degree. I had wrestled with the academic system and now it was time to go to work.

While I was interviewing for a technician's job, a man (whose name escapes me) advised me that I would quickly become bored with the job he had for me, but I should try computer programming in another department where they were always seeking potential talent. That advice changed my life. I was hired and took to programming with a passion. It was 1961 and I was a natural in an environment that was too new to have structure and rules. Still, there is always some structure. I loved it so much that I often punched out after eight hours and then went back to my desk. After one pay period, I was called in and told that I was punching in late— five to fifteen minutes after 8:00 A.M., and, although I carefully punched out at exactly 5:10 eight hours later, it was still not proper. And what's more, I was seen there at 6:00 P.M. Was I planning on coming in later still? When I said I came to learn and work, and precisely eight hours just didn't seem to fit me, I was encouraged to "try not to upset the system." Soon thereafter, I left to find a more flexible company.

After a couple of more years, I was an excellent programmer at the top of my game. In fact, I had inadvertently created some "structure and rules" to simplify my own efforts. Rather, I should say *we* created. My mentor who had taught me programming in the beginning, Ken Mackenzie, and I developed some programming techniques and conventions that simplified our own work. We taught these to Larry Constantine, who further codified them in a book he called *Structured Programming*, which started a whole movement to refine programming from pure art to a teachable skill. This also meant that program code could be read by more than the original author. Some years later, someone I supervised was aghast to discover my early involvement in *Structured Programming*. I guess he thought he knew me better.

I had a supervisor in the early 1960s who often asked what he could do to help me do my job. Charlie Crichton's sole objective as my supervisor was to make it easier for me to do my job. I never forgot what that felt like as his employee.

Principle #5: It has often been said that information is power, but what makes data become information is understanding.

Consistent with management practice early in my programming career, another supervisor identified my programming performance as "managerial potential" and promoted me to supervisor. I was really disappointed and asked to be passed over since I didn't want to start shuffling papers and playing politics (my view of management). He said that I was mistaken and I should try it for six months. As a manager I could accomplish the work of many by leveraging. These two seemingly divergent views served me well, as I was promoted an average of every nine months for over ten years.

I ultimately became an executive of Control Data Corporation (CDC), primarily by communicating between the technical people and management. In other words, I contributed understanding.

Principle #6: Learning to let go may really be learning to listen.

While my company and the industry were new and unstructured, I thrived. As both became more mature and bureaucratic, I began to flounder. I tried several areas at CDC, including technology licensing, hoping to again find my 'bliss,' as Joe Campbell might put it, in another emerging unstructured area.

I finally left CDC in 1979, disillusioned with the future of the company and the industry. I had six children, $10,000 given to me as an incentive to stay, but with no strings, and a small consulting contract. I tried consulting for the Fortune 500 Companies on a principle I started advancing while still at CDC—that technology was a resource that could be managed like real estate, or any other more conventional resource. It could be bought and sold, inventoried and counted. Although many were intrigued by the notion, I found they were not ready for this as a practice.

While still at CDC, I did volunteer work at the local Science Museum while it was undergoing a massive expansion. Four of us had formed a committee to design and build the world's second

OMNITHEATER and produce an inaugural film, "Genesis." OMNIMAX films and projection systems are very impressive and expensive, offering 360-degree views for the observer. They use a fish-eye lens to project onto a domed ceiling, which inserts the viewing audience into the picture and sound so that they feel that they are experiencing the film story directly rather than vicariously. There are only about twenty of these theaters in the U.S., mostly operated by museums.

The project was very successful, so I found some paid consulting work there and, in addition, obtained rights to distribute a couple of films to the now half-dozen OMNIMAX theaters around the world. Earning a living had brought me a long, long way from my first love, art, and my second love physics, and programming.

Jack Hoeschler, an attorney and one of the committee of four mentioned above, and I intended to produce OMNIMAX films using our fledgling distribution efforts as leverage. We called on the world's first private venture OMNIMAX theater in Seattle to license the run of one of our films. Having experienced dismal attendance and even worse revenues, they could ill afford it. It appeared that they were losing $1,000 per day. As a venture separate from the hundreds of conventional movie theaters they operated in Canada, an OMNIMAX theater was a mystery to them (they lacked understanding). They heard my opinion that we had been very successful in St. Paul and saw no reason for a failure in Seattle, so they asked if I would manage it for them. I was not looking for a job. I really enjoyed my freedom to pursue what I liked and believed in. So I said I would only manage it if I owned it. I believe they recognized my understanding of that little unique piece of their business.

I negotiated for three months, hoping to close a deal before the lucrative summer season. I ran *pro formas* and knew I would need $250,000 in working capital to turn it around. I had nothing and, in fact, my family was surviving on three-fourths of what I had earned at CDC. Here, again, what I knew about OMNIMAX theaters was in the context of an emerging industry with no guidelines or precedents. Moreover, this theater was the only non-museum-related private venture ever attempted. I managed to negotiate $100,000 in working capital as part of the purchase and another $25,000 for capital improvements which I determined were necessary. I never met the man I negotiated with. We communicated by phone and letter. While it was an incredibly big deal for me, it was but one problem theater out of six hundred for him. You see, Jack and I had managed to "bump" the negotiation to the top of the organization, a technique I had learned at CDC. I wanted to keep it as easy and simple for him as possible. My strategy worked and on June 30, 1981 I signed a note through a newly formed corporation for $600,000—less than half of his net book value.

Listen to where the markets are going. Listen to what you are good at. Listen to what works. Go with the grain, not across it.

Principle #7: Hire first on the basis of attitude, because you can teach the job but not the attitude.

I hired a local manager after an exhaustive search. The plan was to move my family out to Seattle for the summer only, and teach the new manager what I thought I knew about how to run an OMNITHEATER. Then I could return to making films in the fall.

The new manager lasted six weeks. While he was almost over-qualified in experience and skills, he lacked attitude. He really thought that a turnaround was hopeless.

Principle #8: Part of being a good listener is to not lose sight of the ultimate goals.

I was so discouraged that I felt it was hopeless to find another general manager who looked as promising as the first one. The winter doldrums were approaching and we were going to be cash poor. So, I asked myself, "why add another salary?" I brought the family back home to Minneapolis. I negotiated the rent-free use of an unsold condo across the street from the theater. I was able to fly home only once or twice a month while I worked 12-hour days. Film-making was out of the question. Jack decided to go back to practicing law, urging me to get out before I ran up a debt. It was heartbreaking news. I hung up the phone and walked downstairs to the theater lobby to ponder getting out. The City of Seattle was our landlord and had a very controlling lease. My first line of contact at city hall, Howard Bogie, dropped by as I stood in the lobby and I confided in him—I gave him my grim news. He was stunned. Our attendance was up nearly 200% over prior years and the public was growing in awareness. If we weren't going to make it go, there was no hope. Couldn't he help in some way? Could the City defer rent? Now, I was stunned. The City was willing to be flexible, accommodating, supportive, and I hadn't even asked. I took him up on his offer.

Over the next three years I learned a lot. I had another unsuccessful manager who lost $240,000 in one year while I was distracted by expansion plans. We went back out to Seattle for another summer and turned it around a second time. While I was there calling all the shots, everything worked out fine; but I could not seem to negotiate a "hand off" to a manager. I have often heard that said by other entrepreneurs. In fact, few companies survive their founder. Or, if they do survive, one would hardly recognize them, as in the case of my former employer Control Data.

As I saw it, I had only two choices: 1) move out to Seattle and make a decent living running an OMNIMAX theater or 2) figure out how to run it remotely. But wait! My criteria for success is to earn a living and create benefit for others while doing it, not to completely change my life in ways I never intended.

We had family and friends in Minneapolis and we liked it there. I closed down the theater for one winter to consider options. I figured I'd lose less money while closed. I went back to the original owners and told them that, although I expected we could operate at a small profit, we would never be able to pay back the $600,000 plus back due interest I owed them and have enough left to make it worth my while. They did not want the theater back, so we tore up the note! Another win-win negotiation! I received some concessions on three other large payables and tried re-opening in the spring with no manager; just a skeleton crew on week-ends. My trusted projectionist, Dale Fletcher, who had been with the theater from the beginning, counted the money and made deposits. We were cash-flowing so we packed up the family for a third and final summer in Seattle.

Principle #9: Chaos is the result of internal conflicts and contention. A good system has well-defined boundaries which lead to growth and success.

We trained college students to supervise operations on a day-to-day basis. I suppose many fast food operations are the same: a highly structured environment where employees can come, be trained, and train their successors. I don't like structure for myself, but I do recognize its value and the value of Group 1 people (those who want predictability).

While still in Seattle that summer, I discovered a theft ring among my employees. I did not know how widespread it was, but I eventually determined that 14 employees were involved and about five were not. It had cost me thousands of dollars, but it forced me to devise a virtually foolproof system of checks and balances for cash handling. Averting future problems would be critical if I was to be an absentee owner/manager.

Being 2,000 miles away, I needed to develop some skills previously unknown to me in management. Internal strife was a problem. I found that I needed to define job boundaries precisely, with no gaps or overlaps. This removes much of the stimulus for competition, divisions, and blaming. I discovered that, if I focused on measurable objectives and not the process, I could defuse nearly all grievances. Energy would be focused where it was most productive. I reinforced those objectives by putting everyone except the projectionists on an incentive pay program. To this day, whether you are a cashier or in group sales, 20-30% of your income is by incentive pay. There are daily objectives for operating staff, weekly objectives for operations managers, monthly objectives for group sales, and annual objectives for advertising and marketing.

Principle #10: Focus on the ultimate goal and avoid embroidery of it or of the path to it.

Advertising and marketing are handled by a part-time consultant, Elliot Harris, who is one of the best in the country; but I could not support him full-time. I do, however, provide him with a full-time office, phones, copy machine, fax, etc., so he can work full-time on our premises. In exchange, I have someone over the age of twenty-five to solve problems and keep people following guidelines and policies. All major decisions are made by me; but there are few of those, now that we have a highly successful, smooth-running operation in its twelfth year. I am sure that employees are sick of hearing "will it put more people in the seats" for every request they make. But I am finding that, at some distance, I can much more easily focus on my goals for the business. My wife and I approve all bills and she performs the checks and balances to manage cash and all banking from Minneapolis. We generally visit Seattle once a year for a few days now. Moreover, it pays amply for our sustenance and we have enough left over for other business ventures.

Principle #11: A person can have more than one bliss, which can change with time.

The same instant that the OMNIDOME got successful (which also meant routine), I began to look for something in Minneapolis to do that had new challenges and was local. I did not want to spend several years commuting to another city to start a second theater. I was not a theater operator, remember, I was a physicist/computer techie/technology manager/film maker slightly off target. But I still had bliss. I knew because, if I asked myself what I would rather be doing, the answer was not forthcoming.

I did some consulting for a friend, Pat Gorman, on small business incubators—you know, a building with support services for start-up companies. Using data from twenty or so attempts, and with spreadsheet analysis, I thought I understood what the key elements of success were.

One day, a local incubator was being foreclosed and it was only a little more than two years underway (like the OMNITHEATER in Seattle). We bought it with City of Minneapolis revenue bonds and a relatively tiny amount of our cash, but with personal commitments on $5 million in bonds. There were three partners and I was managing partner. You remember, I needed something local and this industry was unstructured, immature, and an all-new challenge. This time I knew I did not want to do this for any length of time, but I now had some experience letting go. We invested about $3 million in the remodeling of the former high school, defined our service offering, and had it nearly leased up when I was able to reduce my effort to about three days per month.

Principle #12: Each employee can meet or miss the objectives for their part; no one else can. When

they know they have sole control (equates to ownership) of their area, they soon are working as hard as the owner of the enterprise.

This time we had a much more senior crew to manage the business on a day-to-day basis. We are still not able to hire perfection. I tell Barry Bosold, the general manager,

> All employees are defective (as are all humans including me and you, unless you are not human). It's the manager's task to get the work done, amplifying the employees' strengths and reducing dependence on their weaknesses. You can change none of either their strengths or weaknesses. Only they can (i.e., we must get the job done with dull and broken tools).

I still make the strategic decisions; I still keep my eye on the goal. We have a 170,000-square-foot building that is filled with 120 start-up companies, a waiting list, and a satellite building with plans for expansion. The job definitions, goals, and approach are radically different from the theater, but the same principles apply. Everyone knows the objectives for the whole and for their part.

Employees were all hired based on their attitude and basic skills. I still believe you can teach most anything but attitude. Or at least we don't have the time in business to change a bad attitude. I know. I've tried many times.

Principle #13: Understand the systems you are linked to.

I am now involved in two ventures which are based on patents. One is a simple consumer device that is really clever. The other is a highly technological device for industry. Additionally I have started to develop a product on my own, which takes me back to my physics and computer programming. I am also working on a new OMNIMAX film, which could be my own artistic outlet. But now it is all different, because I can no longer measure success the same way. I have met my maximum point of livelihood and now work exclusively to make a contribution.

In 1977, more than ten years after leaving college, I returned to sign up for whatever it took to complete my degree. I was told that, by their calculations, I already more than qualified to graduate. So I graduated with my choice of a BS in physics or math with no additional work. I chose physics.

I realized that, while I was struggling with the educational system, it was not struggling with me. I simply did not understand the system I was working in. If I had but one principle to lean on, this last one would probably be it, for no effort—no matter how hard one works or how good the intentions—will ever be effective if the effort is outside the system. I perceive systems as encompassing the human relations level; the obvious but often overlooked physical systems, the systems of government, the system of finance you must work with, and the systems of a given market with its competition and customer expectations.

With a solid understanding, all efforts have the potential to be effective—the unexpected becomes rare—tension is reduced and you will become a successful entrepreneur.

Summary

To summarize, there are 13 principles that I have extracted from my experiences as an entrepreneur. In the order I related them, and not of equal weight, they are:

1. Never play zero-sum games with employees or customers. Find the win-win strategy.
2. It's not an adventure unless there is some discomfort.
3. The opposite of success is not failure—it is discouragement.
4. It is the primary task of management to remove barriers and to enable employees to remove barriers.
5. It has often been said that information is power, but what makes data become information is understanding.
6. Learning to let go may really be learning to listen.
7. Hire first on the basis of attitude, because you can teach the job but not the attitude.
8. Part of being a good listener is to not lose sight of the ultimate goals.

9. Chaos is the result of internal conflicts and contention. A good system has well-defined boundaries which lead to growth and success.

10. Focus on the ultimate goal and avoid embroidery of it, or of the path to it.

11. A person can have more than one bliss, which can change with time.

12. Each employee can meet or miss the objectives for their part; no one else can.When they know they have sole control (equates to ownership) of their area, they soon are working as hard as the owner of the enterprise.

13. Understand the systems you are linked to.

Part Three

Personal Responsibility

Personal Response-Ability:
Choosing to Respond for Success
Richard Bliss Brooke

Crisis to Transformation:
Transition as Opportunity
Sharon Gadberry

Executing the Entrepreneurial Adventure
John H. Stearns

Creating New Futures in Turbulent Times
Cheryl Alexander

Marjorie's Maxims for Social Entrepreneurship
Marjorie Kelly

Reengineering Entrepreneurs:
Creating Emotionally Healthy Organizations
Chris Manning

Somehow, all these ideas and examples, all this idealism and all these formulas for success, boil down to one key factor: people taking personal responsibility for doing what's right.

As much as we want to avoid it, individual responsibility for our actions—those we carry out and those we allow others to do—is absolutely essential for any of these ideals to reach reality. We must be accountable for our condition and for the impact we have on one another.

In this section, six authors collaborate on this personal trait—this need for true character in business. Network marketing guru Richard Brooke shares some of his own path to success in addition to his perspective on "living where the buck stops."

Outplacement service provider Sharon Gadberry advises corporate refugees to take advantage of the crises in corporate America and find opportunities for transformation in the transitions.

With a wealth of experience, John Stearns examines the need for responsible execution or implementation as a key factor in successful entrepreneurship.

Executive search firm owner Cheryl Alexander calls for new attitudes by those corporate veterans who may find the sleeping entrepreneur within themselves.

Business Ethics magazine co-founder Marjorie Kelly shares her own learning—how to be responsible for her business' success—striking a balance between visionary ideals and pragmatic implementation.

Finally, entrepreneur and consultant Chris Manning shares his own personal insights for an emotionally healthy workplace and challenges many outmoded attitudes that are no longer effective in business.

Richard Bliss Brooke
is President and CEO of Oxyfresh
USA, a personal-care products marketing company with over 13,000
distributors world wide. He has been featured on the cover of *Success*
magazine and is a primary spokesman for the network marketing industry.

He has also been a collaborator in the founding of the World Institute
for Life Planning Group, instituting a leadership program for his distributors
based on what he calls "do the right thing leadership."

While his father was educated at Stanford University and his mother
was a graduate of Mills College, Brooke did not obtain a degree. He left
home at seventeen and, by the age of thirty, had made his first million
dollars and had developed a 30,000-distributor network. He moved to
Oxyfresh in 1986 and has since accumulated a controlling interest in the
company.

9

Personal Response-Ability: Choosing to Respond for Success

Richard Bliss Brooke

At the age of four I stole a pair of sunglasses from Red's Market. When Mom asked where I got them I told the truth. Of course, I had to take them back to Red and apologize—I was humiliated. *And, I decided telling the truth was painful and not a smart thing to do.*

In the fifth grade a girl I liked sat with me at the movie. We held hands. The next day she "dumped me." *I decided I wasn't good enough for the women I liked.*

In the sixth grade we moved to the city. The cool guys (those the girls liked) wore powder blue Levi cords. I was still wearing Kmart jeans—the ones with the double knees. I asked my mom to buy me the cool stuff. I think she said no or not now. *I decided I didn't need her or anyone else. I'd buy my own cool stuff, and I'd always be cool.*

Just like millions of other kids my age. I experienced life in such a way that I formed a personality to cope with life as I perceived it. As a result of a few everyday circumstances, my beliefs and my personality were created. It was hardly a winning personality—low self-esteem, driven to be accepted, and a compulsive liar.

I was raised in an upper-middle-class family. My father, a star

123

athlete, graduated from Stanford. My mother is a graduate of Mills, a private women's college. Their marriage was volatile and by the time I was seventeen they had divorced. It wasn't pretty.

Graduating high school by the skin of my teeth, I started my career pumping gas at Pearson's Arco. I also *lived* at the Arco station in my pickup camper with Chinook, my faithful, obnoxious dog. Eventually, my ambition led me (after I failed to lock the front door of the gas station two nights in a row) to Foster Farms, the largest single poultry-processing plant in the world. This was a union job paying $3.05 an hour with benefits, seniority, vacation and best of all—retirement. I jumped at the opportunity. My job was to cut the chickens into parts as they flew past me on the production line...billions of chickens. That's what I did for 450 to 530 minutes a day. Production people exist in minutes.

Although I was a hard worker, ambitious and intelligent, there were aspects of my personality that held me back. I disliked most other people as well as myself. I refused to let anyone whom I didn't consider extremely competent tell me what to do. This included my bank when they told me I couldn't write any more checks. I made $1,000 per month and was addicted to spending $1,500. Those idiots kept screwing up my checking account.

I loved the chicken plant—still love the people with whom I worked. At the time, I fully expected to spend the next forty years at the chicken plant, building seniority (power), vacation time (independence), and clicking off the years to retirement (freedom). I really thought I was cutting it and I fully expected to be there today. That was 1977. I was twenty-two.

The Rest of the Story

(Please excuse the forthcoming arrogance. I believe it is necessary to make the point.)

I made my first million before the age of thirty. Today at age 38, I am the president, CEO, and majority owner of a $13 million privately held international marketing firm. Our company, I expect, will be a billion dollar enterprise by the year 2000 and multibillion beyond that.

Our company has thousands of health care professionals from dentists to veterinarians that make our products available to their patients, clients, friends, co-workers and relatives. Oxyfresh is a network marketing company—one of the hottest distribution concepts of the 1990s What was once considered nothing but chain letters and pyramid schemes is now a fifty billion dollar industry in which twelve million people participate. Network marketing is leading edge technology for distribution and a dynamic environment for personal development, leadership training, and financial freedom.

I have visited every state in the union, most many times, and have fulfilled dreams of vacationing from the Virgin Islands to Bangkok, Thailand. I have better health now than at age twenty-two. Most importantly, I have a network of friends nationwide that would allow me to drive from Seattle to Boston to Miami to L.A. without ever buying a meal or staying in a hotel.

In March of 1992, *Success* magazine featured me on their cover. They called me a "millionaire maker" and did a feature article on how people with whom I work and train build "overnight empires of their own." Pretty hypey stuff!

I hope by now you're asking "What the hell happened?"

Well, a lot obviously—fortunately I got swept up in the emergence of network marketing as it came of age. The people involved in the particular company I joined had a special vision for people and a passion for teaching and leading people to pursue it. Their vision was that any person, regardless of background or education, could achieve anything in life they chose to accomplish. If finances were required for the vision, they had a powerful opportunity for people to achieve financial freedom in a very short period of time. They never suggested what someone should want, they just encouraged people to dream again—child-like dreaming, for any possibilities—and then they taught us how to achieve those dreams.

I learned that no matter who you are, where you come from, how you got that way, and no matter what life throws at you full speed, you can respond, you can change, and you can live the life of your dreams. To do so requires that *we* become responsible—100% unconditionally responsible for doing whatever we must do to succeed.

I learned that I am responsible for whether I stay who I

became at age ten, or I grow up and create some personality that supports my success as an adult. I learned that what the majority of society and I believe is the truth about life may not be a truth that supports our dreams. Whatever the truth may be for us, we can change it. Obviously these lessons apply to all aspects of our lives.

In this book we are addressing business, careers, and professions. Therefore, the balance of this chapter will focus on how the general lessons I learned apply more specifically to this subject.

For example, most of us were raised with a belief about financial success that looks something like:

1. Do your homework
2. Get good grades
3. Get a college education
4. Get a good job
5. With a really good company
6. With lots of benefits
7. Keep your nose clean
8. Work real hard
9. Save your money
10. Retire to either fishing or knitting

These were the the "rules for success" we were taught.

People have believed that if they would just land on those ten steps financial success would be assured. For many it was. Unfortunately, for at least this past decade the rules have been eroding; the game has been rapidly changing right in front of our eyes and most of us didn't see it.

The ten steps to financial freedom is now a bankrupt paradigm. It is now the exception rather than the rule. It has gone the way of vinyl records, low-paid athletes and "AIDS is nothing for *me* to be concerned with." What works today is personal responsibility.

The buck stops here.

If it's to be, it's up to me.

Play the hand you are dealt and play it to win.

Do it now. And most importantly, DO IT *ANYWAY*.

Whatever circumstances life throws at you, you have got to handle them. You are the source—the cause of whatever effects are surrounding you. Our world has changed more in terms of how and what we do in just the last ten years than in the last one hundred years combined.

Change has hit critical mass. The world as we see it today—bank on it—will be nearly unrecognizable by the year 2000.

This requires a whole new set of rules. The context is that the rules themselves can no longer be relied upon. They may be good for today and today only. Tomorrow *we* must be *responsible* to see what we don't see now; to seek to know what we don't know we don't know; to be completely response-*able* to meet new challenges. Those of us who are still marveling at the idea of the job market and financial freedom courses changing, have actually missed it.

Here is the new deal:

One: Job security is a historical concept. Expect now to move around a lot. Be unemployed and change professions several times over a forty-year career. Respect and admire the company that acts on technological advances and new ideas to eliminate jobs even if it's yours. Companies will either be acting on new ideas and technologies or they will be out of business. *You're either eating the bear or the bear is eating you.*

Two: Education is an asset. Applicable skills and leadership are what employers will pay most for. *Leadership is now a profession,* and the best top management jobs will be filled not with managers but with leaders.

Three: Anyone can accomplish anything they choose to—no exceptions—no excuses. During the last ten years while most people struggled just to stay ahead, Bill Gates, a 37-year-old college dropout went and made himself eight *billion* dollars. He quit college, borrowed $1,000, and turned it into eight billion dollars (excepting the billion or so it fluctuates whenever the market burps). To put that achievement in perspective, if *you* earned $1,000 a day you would have a *million* dollars in less than three years. It would take 300 years to earn just one billion dollars. That's 2,400 years at $1,000 a day for Bill who is *not* eight hundred times smarter than you and I.

Four: We are either on track to achieve our goals or we have already achieved them. The idea that some people achieve their goals and others don't is bull. We have been confused in thinking that goals are things we want. *Goals are expectations*—not necessarily what we want, but actually what we expect—what we believe we will achieve. The human mind is teleological in nature. Like an auto pilot it steers a course for the picture we hold in our mind's eye as our prevailing expectation.

We are all goal achievers, and we always have been. What's missing is that we've unconsciously set our expectations based on our past experiences, fears, and beliefs—all of which are usually opposed to, or fall short of, what we want. We have believed that we are victims of our beliefs, our experiences, and our fears such that once we have these ideas firmly rooted in our heads, we are stuck with them.

As humans, we are incredibly closed-minded and arrogant. We actually believe that what *we think* the truth is true, and what someone else believes is *just their opinion*. This arrogance and foolishness sticks us with our beliefs—blinding us to any other possibilities, possibilities that may propel us toward success. For example, let's say that you could earn $1,000 cash for each "F" that you read in the sentence below—but you have to find them *all*. If you want the money, read the sentence below and count the "Fs."

> Finished files are the result of years of scientific
> study combined with the experience of many years
> of experts.

Now grab a pen or pencil and write your answer in the margin. I will assume (your being educated, well-read, etc.) that you believe your answer is correct. In other words, you believe it is the truth. It may be, but only if you counted seven of them. Go figure.

There are a zillion examples of you and I seeing *today* what we didn't see yesterday.

A truth is that there are many possible truths about a given subject. We can and must choose the one that motivates us to accomplish our dreams.

Decide what it is that you want in life. Look objectively at the beliefs, experiences, and fears you have around it. Discover where they limit you and then go to work changing them. By the way, if you missed some "Fs" it's because you were blinded by your expectation that "Fs" are only present when you hear yourself pronounce "F" versus the "V" as in "of."

Five: The universe is run by a set of laws. These laws are like invisible boomerangs—use them to win and winning is inevitable. Violate them and prepare to get whacked in the back of the head.

1. What you contribute to others and the world comes back to you ten-fold in sometimes the most mysterious ways.

2. Treat others as *they* want you to treat them. Everybody is different. You will want to honor other people's values versus your own.

3. The harder you work *on your expectations*, the luckier you get, or life's battles don't always go to the strongest or fastest, but to the first who *thinks he or she will*.

4. Your brightest days of accomplishment will follow your darkest days of despair. Push through just one more step, past one more setback. Bliss awaits you.

5. Love yourself and the world will love you.

6. Be thankful—the universe has a deep appreciation for those who are thankful and despises those who are not.

7. Your body is a delicate living organism. Don't poison it..

8. The earth and all the rest of its inhabitants are delicate living organisms. Don't poison them.

Six: Self-motivation is the key to success. It's totally possible and sustainable. Self- or internal-motivation is a somewhat nebulous term. It describes such energies as:

Enthusiasm
Confidence
Persistence
Physical Energy
And, believe it or not, Skill and Creativity.

Ask yourself this question: If you could create and sustain enough of the above facets of motivation, could you propel yourself along a progressive course of achieving your goals?

If your answer is like most, it's a powerful "yes," creating a clarity that self motivation *is* a key to success. The good news is that creating an abundance of self-motivation is very do-able for all of us. We can all start right now and continue to build a roaring fire of accomplishment within ourselves. Self-motivation is created automatically, naturally, and free-flowingly to the degree that our realities contrast with our expectations.

Contrary to the popular myth, motivation doesn't necessarily have anything to do with desire.

For example, if you have a deep-rooted expectation for how much money you should earn (expectation), you will be motivated to earn it (reality). Once the income starts to approximate the expectation the motivation decreases progressively, and once the income equals the expectation motivation is only unleashed in quantities sufficient to maintain the income.

Motivation and reality work just like a thermostat or an auto pilot. The heat/cooling or thrust is directed to accomplish the pre-set objective. The mind, however, does not care what you want and it doesn't even care what you expect. It just serves by motivating you to stay on track to achieve the expectation.

There are three ways to illustrate the effects of self-motivation. One where the expectation exceeds (in the direction of what you want) reality; one where it equals reality, and one where your expectations are below reality.

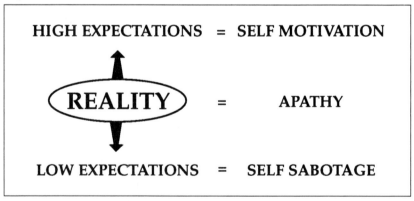

The effects are either self-motivation, apathy, or self-sabotage (which is a form of self-motivation.)

The key to creating and maintaining self-motivation that

supports our dreams and desires is to consciously create an expectation that matches it. This process is proven, it's powerful, and it's magical.

Seven: A life purpose that serves. Each of us has a special gift, be it a natural talent, quality, or passion. This gift can create the context for discovering a purpose for our life rather than something to achieve. Our purpose can be the theme song for who we are and what we do, a theme by which we could resonate through life being totally fulfilled.

When a life purpose is focused on serving others our lives take on a quantum leap in meaning. I know that we will rise above failure, mediocrity and personal success to the degree that we dedicate our lives to a contribution theme that's much grander than us. This purpose creates a context within which much of our humanity seems to just get handled.

My life purpose is to inspire others to play life full on— sometimes referred to as "Mach II with your hair on fire!"

There are no secrets to success. This chapter and those that surround it are the type of resources everyone will want to absorb in their quest for success. Some of these ideas have been around for centuries, others certainly for decades. They are not secrets, but rather truths that give each of us access to a life of fewer regrets, a life of accelerating the momentum of experiencing full on what's most important to us.

Sharon Gadberry is the founder and CEO of Transitions Management Group, a San Francisco outplacement service business. Her clients include Bank of America, Nestle Corporation, Firemen's Fund Insurance and Levi Strauss. The firm has counseled over 15,000 people since she began the company in 1982.

Gadberry is very active in civic affairs, serving as commissioner for San Francisco's Human Rights Commission and as a director of The City Club. She is an active volunteer for the Global Fund for Women and the Women's Campaign Fund and, through her company, she hosts Student Career Days for college-age children of her corporate clients. She has a doctorate in psychology and has worked as a clinical psychologist, a university professor, and as a business consultant before she started Transitions Management Group.

10

Crisis to Transformation: Transition as Opportunity

Sharon Gadberry

The ominous headlines loom from newspaper pages almost daily: "Conglomerate X Lays Off 100,000 Workers." "Y Industry Predicted to Suffer Sharp Cutbacks." "Middle Managers Squeezed Out in Corporate Restructuring."

Outplacement firms such as ours, hired by companies to help their laid-off employees navigate the difficult career transition, are sometimes considered "crisis companies." We constantly deal with clients for whom life is not going smoothly. The companies—the clients who pay us—are caught in an economic squeeze that forces them to let some of their most talented employees go. The displaced employees—the clients we work with—are suddenly facing economic jeopardy, not to mention a strong threat to self-esteem. The future appears uncertain. Anxiety, guilt, resentment, and fear knife through the atmosphere like sharks in a pool.

What makes it all not just bearable, but exciting and stimulating, is the knowledge that we and our clients have an opportunity to participate directly in both individual and organizational transformation—societal transformation, in fact. The very concept of "outplacement" reflects the changing role of business in society.

In the 1970s, the idea that companies should pay to provide a service to ex-employees would have been laughable. Today, companies are much more cognizant of their partnerships with all their stakeholders: employees, customers, the community, suppliers, and shareholders. Companies that provide assistance to their laid-off employees are motivated by more than the fear of lawsuits. They realize that when large numbers of employees lose their jobs, the community suffers, and the company is part of the community. They know that their corporate image depends partly on how they handle layoffs, and that this corporate image affects the behavior of vendors, investors, customers, and remaining employees. In other words, they are systems thinkers—at least in this respect.

Crisis

To a true systems thinker, a corporate downsizing is not a "crisis" in the negative sense. The problem side of crisis is inseparable from the opportunity side. "Down" can be "up" when viewed from a different perspective. When companies, job candidates, and outplacement firms focus on opportunity, positive transformation begins to happen.

Sometimes the crisis itself can open up opportunities that would never have been possible before. As I work with displaced employees and corporate clients, I learn from them and their experiences just as much as they learn from us about how to deal with transition. Our company (Transitions Management Group, or TMG) and we as individuals have dealt with crises too; what applies for them applies for us as well.

Worst-Case Scenario

Often, when people are laid off, they are so anxious that all they want to do is find a new job, just like their old job, as quickly as possible. They feel so stunned and frightened by the sudden loss that they become fixated on old behavior and attitudes. Like drivers whose rear wheels get stuck in the mud, they just keep pressing down on the accelerator, burying themselves even deeper. They are ready for change, they need change, but change doesn't happen until a shift occurs in the way they view their careers, lives, goals, and strategies.

One of our job seekers could not stop talking about what a tyrant his old boss had been. Even when we pointed out that this was unhealthy for him, he communicated his blame-the-boss attitude in body language and in damning the boss with false praise. Somehow his job interviews always seemed to focus on why he had left his old job and he kept coming in second and third as a candidate. When he finally thought he had been hired, it turned out that the hiring manager had not possessed the requisite authority and the job fell through. Our client plunged into deep despair. He threw up his hands and said, "I just don't care any more."

At this point his personal transition began: he stopped being caught up in the past. The worst had already happened. But he continued to go to interviews and was surprised to discover that the subject of why he had left his old job never came up. His transformation produced a dramatic result. Almost immediately, he began receiving job offers, and accepted a position which closely resembled his ideal job description.

For most displaced workers, just losing the original job is enough to constitute a "worst case" scenario. Yet in every crisis lie the seeds of transformational opportunity. When "the worst" happens, many employees realize that it's time to explore other options that take their whole lives into account—their families, their personal goals, their lifestyles, their values, their dreams. Lifting their noses from the grindstone gives them a chance to look around and see how work fits into the total picture. They may realize that they haven't seen their kids much in the last ten years, or that they had forgotten what they started out to achieve in their lives. They are now able to focus on what might really fulfill them.

A job seeker we'll call "Bill" was puzzled and angry when he lost his old position in a corporate cutback. However, he had been very dissatisfied with that job. For ten of the twenty-five years Bill had spent with the firm, he had been stuck in an operations middle-management function, crunching numbers and keeping paper flowing. As the result of a psychological assessment, he realized that his real interest was in corporate culture and that he had some great ideas about how people could work better together—ideas he had never had an opportunity to implement. He re-targeted his job search, became a consultant to the CEO of another firm, and was hired three months later as a strategic planner. He is delighted with his new job, which is several levels up from his old one.

Entrepreneurs

When we ask our clients to describe their "fantasy goals," we discover that about half of them have dreamed of starting their own businesses. Some begin turning the fantasy into reality. They prepare business plans, brochures, and portfolios. They research the industry and the competition. They focus on their own strengths and skills. Although some of them may later opt for employment rather than self-employment, the process boosts their confidence and provides fuel for interviews.

The family system, we believe, is part of the personal system and should never be considered separately from the career; each affects the other. One of our clients was surprised to discover, in a session with us and his wife, that she and the children had never been happy in the San Francisco Bay Area and wanted to move back to Chicago. He had been basing his job search on false assumptions about what was best for the family. Had he been "successful" in locating a California job, his personal life would have deteriorated. When he began focusing on the Chicago area, with more clarity about what he wanted, he found a suitable position in one month.

To turn a crisis into a positive transition, it is essential to stay open to new ideas, especially if they seem risky and out of your normal realm. I have learned to listen to people when they tell me I should be doing things differently. I may still argue, but I try to get to the bottom of the matter, reasoning that these people are likely to see things I don't see.

A crisis may force my hand. Several years ago, when my partner announced that he wanted to leave the firm and move on, I almost panicked. First I tried to persuade him to stay, and then I focused on finding someone to buy him out. I was convinced that, even if I could manage the business alone (which was doubtful), I couldn't afford to. When I failed to find a new partner with enough knowledge about the business and enough money to invest, my anxiety grew. Then I showed the books to a friend, a financial expert, who said, "You can afford to run this company yourself if you increase your business and arrange a leveraged buyout." I had to listen because I saw no other choice. The LBO could be arranged, but how was I going to increase the business?

At his suggestion, we changed our compensation system so that everyone in the company received a percentage of the firm's total business. With everyone motivated to bring accounts in *and* work in cooperation with each other, the business did increase. And I had a company full of "partners."

Later, when a business downturn began affecting us as well as our clients, I felt very threatened. I knew we needed to change the way we were doing business, but I didn't know how to do so without compromising the quality of our services. Our corporate clients wanted us to start working with 100 people at a time, and again I resisted change, thinking, "We can't do that; we're used to working one-to-one, and we're too small to handle large groups of people." Then I realized that the reason we were small is that I had been thinking small. When I acknowledged that we could be twice as big, in terms of income and clients, we began moving in that direction. We found a new way of delivering service: through career centers where we offered consulting, transition workshops, and "survivor programs" to a thousand people at once. By listening, staying open to fresh ideas, taking risks, doing what I hadn't done before, and looking at myself and my professional role in new ways, I had been able to turn transition into an opportunity for positive transformation. So have millions of other people who have looked crisis in the face.

Networking

There is one particular employment skill—and habit—that is essential in a world characterized by constant flux: networking. Many people believe that networking means asking friends if they know about any jobs. In fact, networking is like sailing a boat across a lake: you work with the prevailing wind, and sometimes you seem to be heading in the opposite direction from where you want to go.

You talk to people who do *not* have a position for you, or know of one, but who possess information that can lead you to new contacts. You are prepared to discuss your targeted industry and explain your skills and desires to anyone you meet. You ask for introductions and look for jobs that don't exist yet. You maintain your networks even when things are going smoothly. People in your networks are your partners in change.

Ninety percent of our clients find their new positions through networking. In this process, Bill, the aspiring strategic planner, reconnected somewhat reluctantly with a person from his old company. He had felt resentful because this man had bypassed him on the way up the corporate ladder; but he discovered that the man was a generous source of useful leads, one of which ultimately resulted in Bill's getting a new job.

The network has begun to replace other structures, such as the pyramid, as an effective model for both individuals and businesses. Personal and professional networks have been of immeasurable help in keeping our business both solvent and vital. I operate on the assumption that work life, civic life, and personal life are all part of the same web of connection. I consider many of my clients personal friends and I often invite job seekers to accompany me to professional meetings, where they can augment their own networks.

Opportunities

When organizations lay off large numbers of people, they find themselves with leaner structures, trying to stay competitive with limited resources. For many of them, this constitutes a crisis that forces them into new ways of thinking. Senior management may actually become desperate enough to consider some of the innovations that they have been reading about—or that their Human Resources people have been advocating—for years.

For example, knowing that they will probably have to restructure more than once, they become receptive to flexible employment schedules. They begin to rely more on contingent workers: part-timers and consultants, who are more mobile and who prefer not to be tied to one job forty hours a week. These workers do not require costly separation packages when the company experiences a downturn, and they can come back when business picks up.

Downsizing leaves organizations with flatter structures, which is better for rapid decision-making and provides an opportunity for reinvention. Sometimes, however, it also results in a dearth of management talent. When a company realizes it cannot afford to hire expensive executives full time, old objections, such as "Hiring managers from the outside on a part-time basis just wouldn't work," "They don't know the industry," "They wouldn't be loyal," etc., melt away. Today, twenty five percent of executive employment-seekers at the $150,000+ level are choosing part-time or consulting positions. The idea that neither they nor their employers need be stuck with each other forever can be liberating for *both*.

One Example

Corporate restructurings and mass layoffs can be particularly painful for companies that have carefully built a culture of team-work and mutual trust. One such company was Itel Rail Corporation, which was absorbed by General Electric. Unwilling to destroy this culture, Itel management informed employees immediately of the impending merger and GE's intention to eliminate positions, then asked for their input as to what types of assistance to provide. The company helped employees write personal profiles, which were compiled into a professionally produced "talent bank" book highlighting the achievements and employability of those who were leaving. Itel mailed the book to recruiters and employers, and nearly 100 of them responded with requests for résumés. By the time the merger was finalized, employees were prepared and no one felt insulted or betrayed.

Itel, which had taken a large risk with its proactive early communication program, was rewarded when nearly all employees stayed until an agreed-upon departure date. As a result of their open support of their employees, senior managers gained a reputation for being forward-thinking, which helped when their own jobs disappeared. For Itel, as for many other companies confronted with the need to downsize, necessity had become the mother of innovation.

Most companies that go through downsizing later find themselves in a position to hire again. This time, their flatter structures and competitive challenges require them to seek employees who are entrepreneurial, creative, and self-motivated. They need to know how to work in teams and to gather information through networks rather than through hierarchies. What better candidates could they find than people who have weathered the career transition process?

These people are more likely than others to have assessed their needs, values, skills, and strengths. They have a strong sense of what it takes to create their own opportunities. They have had to cast off authoritarian styles and reliance on hierarchy and entitlement. In many cases, they have had to ask those who used to report to them for job leads. They have learned to work in partnership with each other and have become experienced, flexible networkers.

Some of them, after researching industries and talking with representatives of many organizations, have become experts in evaluating business needs. They have learned what types of jobs are necessary to accomplish particular business goals, and they know how to apply their skills in practical ways. After enough interviewers have asked them, "If you were going to solve the problems of this business, how would you do it?," they become more creative thinkers. For example, in his new strategic planning job, Bill introduced so many innovations that the company changed from a rather stuffy, by-the-book organization to a flexible firm that was more responsive to both its employees and its customers.

Walking the Talk

Since our clients—corporate and individual—are people who are dealing with change, we at Transition Management Group need to look at how well we deal with change ourselves. We try to be role models; how can we expect clients to take our advice if we don't follow it ourselves?

For example, because we consider networking and community involvement so important, we practice these on a daily basis. We attend professional events and participate actively on corporate and nonprofit boards. We urge our job-seeking clients to volunteer their time, which is a good way to open up your options and your life in general. Likewise, every consultant in TMG is committed to community service on an individual level, and we offer pro-bono seminars to out-of-work job seekers. I firmly believe that the "abundance principle" works: if you give even when you think you don't have enough to give, you will always have enough. When our company was in a financial slump, that's when I decided that from then on we would donate ten percent of our profits to charities and other causes. We have never regretted the move. Casting one's bread upon the waters by giving to the community is satisfying and rewarding, often in unexpected ways.

We also strive to model the type of organization we are helping our corporate clients to build: flexible, collaborative, diverse, democratic, and oriented toward individual as well as organizational development. Each of us handles an area of specialty and also becomes involved in any other aspect of the business that appeals to us. We continually ask ourselves, and each other, "What would we like to do if we weren't doing this?"

All clients and job candidates receive the attention of our entire team. At weekly meetings, both the consultants and office staffers review the progress of every candidate and every client account. All of us report on our accomplishments and ask for what we need from each other.

The candidates, who use our offices to prepare résumés, attend workshops, contact prospective employers, and videotape practice interviews, become part of our corporate "family." They can walk into any of our offices—consultants or staff—to seek help or advice. They quickly learn, however, that our staff is there to work *with* them, not *for* them. We are all equal team members.

Staying Entrepreneurial

We advise our clients—individual and corporate—to stay flexible—to broaden their thinking and keep an eye out for new trends that may affect their working lives. Most of them are successful at this, and it keeps them entrepreneurial. In a dynamic industry such as ours, we need to remain entrepreneurial too. The priorities of our corporate clients are changing so quickly and dramatically that it is difficult to predict what they will require from us and when. They may even go out of business, which means we have to seek new clients. We need to be ready to handle a huge account, yet not depend on it. Like other companies, we have developed a flexible workforce of independent contractors who can be called upon for specific services.

Some time ago, we realized that we needed to expand beyond the local area in order to serve our corporate clients better. Many of them, such as Bank of America, Qantas, and Porsche, were undergoing restructuring throughout their worldwide operations. We could have sold our company to a large national or international organization as some other small, local outplacement firms were doing. Or we could have acquired or launched branch offices in distant cities. We decided instead to create our own international corporation—and we did it in an unusual way.

The corporation, Outplacement International, is owned by its members, about thirty outplacement firms in various parts of the world. There is no "boss," no hierarchy. We conduct projects in teams. For example, when our firm lands a national contract, our sister companies subcontract from us in their local areas. Likewise, if one of these companies secures a contract, we will subcontract from them. The organization shares databases, including international talent and opportunity banks, and conducts joint training programs. We meet as a group six times a year, taking turns hosting the meeting in our offices, and we talk to each other's corporate clients. Our voice mail network keeps us up on each other's latest discoveries, problem-solving methods, and innovations.

The Transformation Web

Downsizing, reinvention, and restructuring are likely to become "normal" as organizations respond to a rapidly changing global environment. Both businesses and individuals are transforming themselves in the process of career transition. Those who have survived downsizings and layoffs, who have analyzed their strengths and developed networking skills, are better prepared for whatever turns their lives will take. They know that they are responsible for taking care of themselves, because employers cannot promise them a secure future. With a deeper sense of their own needs and capabilities, they can integrate their life goals with their work goals in a way that is satisfying to them and their families.

Since individuals, families, and businesses are interdependent and changing, society as a whole is undergoing profound transformation. As I observe these changes and participate in many of them, I marvel at the richness of the dynamic human web.

John H. Stearns
is President of JHS Enterprises, Inc.,
consultants in the area of strategic
planning, product development,
program management, and management development. He specializes in
management services to high-technology start-up and emerging companies
as well as in project work for major corporations.

For over twenty years, Stearns has led entrepreneurial efforts in
personal computers and network systems, air traffic control, newspaper
automation systems, advanced display systems, credit and identification
cards, smart cards, and financial payment systems businesses.

Currently he is consulting for Visa International in the area of credit
card security technology, card personalization, and card manufacturing,
for CampusCard Systems to develop multi-technology identification card
programs, for CollectorCard Corporation of America to market prepaid
collectible sports cards, and for universities to develop universal card
solutions for the higher education market.

11

Executing the Entrepreneurial Adventure

John H. Stearns

With over two decades of experience in senior management, I now help high-tech start-up companies and corporate project teams develop effective strategies. While my appreciation for the entrepreneurial adventure will be readily apparent, I see a real need for more effective implementation of the visions and plans of entrepreneurs if they expect to be successful.

The advice I share in this essay has been gleaned from my own experience and the experience of my clients. Sometimes the advice will seem to contradict pressing short-term requirements. You will feel the need to react rather than to plan. Wishing we had been more rigorous in our planning brings little satisfaction, but is great experience on how to do it right the next time. I will try, in this essay, to help you do it right the first time so that you may never have to do it over again.

The need to get it right has been made more pressing by the rush of talented people into independent ventures, replacing their confidence in large corporations with confidence in themselves. Historically, the 1970s and 1980s were characterized by a loss of confidence in large bureaucratic corporations. In the early 1970s, consumers lost confidence in American-made goods and started buying Japanese products in ever-increasing quantities, finding them a better value. Then, in 1987, the financial community lost confidence in the management and growth potential of these corporations and reduced their market value by over twenty percent. Since then, most of these same corporations have demonstrated little confidence in themselves and are pursuing downsizing, reengineering, reinvention, process innovation, and other massive changes. Faced with diminishing success, large corporations are trying to become more entrepreneurial and the number of start-up companies continues to increase. In Minnesota, for instance, 5,539 new corporations were formed in 1970. By 1992 this number had jumped to 13,096. The literature is also replete with case histories of American corporations attempting to become more competitive through the acquisition and implementation of new ideas. In a business climate focused on starting up or starting over, what steps are critical in traveling the road to success in an entrepreneurial adventure?

Good Ideas vs. Execution

Obviously, before the planning and execution phase can take place, the entrepreneur must settle on an idea or concept for the business. Hopeful entrepreneurs are often stalled looking for just the "right" idea. Sometimes they are looking for the self-empowering idea, an idea so big that it guarantees success. In my consulting work with would-be entrepreneurs, I often hear them say things like, "I'm still looking for the right idea" or "I just can't come up with the right idea" or "I wish I had thought of that."

How did our predecessors come up with their "right ideas?" Are we talking about individual brilliance, or divine guidance? How would we know the right idea if it came along? Luckily, a good idea is easier to recognize than it sounds. Since there are so many successful ventures, there must be an alternative to waiting around for a great idea to magically come to us. Here it is: Optimum execution is much more critical to success than uncovering the "perfect" idea. Said another way, many small ideas have been turned into large enterprises by the proper execution of a plan that leaves room for extraordinary success.

A good example of this is the Regis Corporation. They started with the rather unremarkable idea of providing hairstyling and turned it into a network of 1,311 salons located in the United States, Canada, Mexico, and the United Kingdom. Their 1993 revenue was $341 million, with a net income of $3.9 million. This is good execution. Ben & Jerry's Homemade Inc., with revenues of $97 million, is another excellent example of a rather ordinary idea made extraordinary by good execution. Such successes could be repeated more often than most of us think. As Thomas H. Davenport states in his book *Process Innovation: Reengineering Work through Information Technology,* "companies can succeed with very different strategies as long as they are well executed."

That is not to say that you don't need a good, workable idea. To quote W. Edwards Deming, the late internationally known authority on quality and management process, "there is no substitute for knowledge." You must know the business you intend to be in. As a start-up entrepreneur and CEO, you will be expected to tell others why they should invest in your company, why you think your idea will work, and what the market is for your product. You must be prepared to see your idea through to completion, to execute the plan and make the idea work.

The steps to the successful execution of your idea are:
1. Setting expectations
2. Committing to the venture
3. Developing the business plan
4. Selecting the team
5. Measuring progress against the plan
6. Protecting against the downside
7. Taking remedial action quickly

Let's examine each of these steps and many of the common misconceptions about them to see how the execution reinforces the seeming "correctness" of the idea.

1. Setting Expectations

Here's where I differ with the philosophy of many of the "success gurus" who claim that your success "is only limited by your dreams." Success is relative to your initial expectations. If these expectations are not in line with the opportunity's real potential, even excellent execution can fail. You must be modest in your expectations and insure that the idea is capable of supporting your minimal financial requirements in both the short and long term. For instance, opening a small retail establishment and expecting to clear $100,000 a year is unrealistic, and would soon seem a failure. Another entrepreneur, however, expecting to clear $20,000 while gaining experience and opportunities for growth from the venture, would judge the same operation an unqualified success if, at the end of the year, the books showed a $25,000 return.

Setting conservative expectations is important—not only when you select the initial operating parameters of revenue and net income, but throughout the life of the venture. You need to be honest—not only with yourself but with those who will be accompanying you on this adventure. The entrepreneur's family must agree to and be willing to live within these modest goals. Family support is a valuable asset when the times get tough and energy and commitment are the only things keeping you going.

The company's financial partners must be given attainable expectations. The bank will be concerned about your line of credit if you are off the financial plan you submitted. And there is nothing more devastating to the entrepreneurial venture than the cancellation of a bank line of credit. The bank expects and will insist on having nothing at risk in the enterprise. Their expectations are that you will meet your plan. If goals are realistic, the shareholder community will also welcome the continued flow of good news, as each financial period produces the gift of over-achievement. With realistic goals, each surprise will be a good news bulletin. All that is made possible by setting the proper expectations and then performing or over-performing to these expectations. This is not "sandbagging," it's good philosophy.

Likewise, your employees will react to the challenges you give them with enormous energy if making or surpassing your goals highlights their contribution to the success of the venture. It makes them feel like winners. I believe that one of the failings of American corporations has been driving people through "stretch goals," confident that this tactic would produce maximum performance. Business is one of the few places where winning can be defined by the entrepreneur CEO and where exceeding the plan can be much more important than the absolute level of the achievement. If we read in The *Wall Street Journal* that analysts expect us to grow at 15% per year, and we take that as our plan, and if we achieve a 14% growth rate for the year, we can still feel like losers even if our performance by absolute standards was extraordinary.

Another downside of unrealistic expectations is that long-term goals don't get set and pursued. Tactics become reactionary and do not contribute to the company's vision. If the entrepreneur becomes totally focused on unrealistic short-term expectations, decisions affecting the survivability of the venture are likely to be poor.

2. Committing to the Venture

Even before you develop the business plan that will prove beyond a shadow of doubt that this is a good and reasonable idea, you must examine the level of commitment you are prepared to make to this venture. This commitment must be personal, financial, emotional, and total.

Personal responsibility: The successful entrepreneur's pride and feeling of accomplishment are tied to the success of the venture. You must take every shortcoming, setback, missed schedule, and customer disappointment personally. There can be no excuses and you must feel responsible for it all. The whole enterprise needs to be a personal expression of your goals, beliefs, and integrity. Admittedly, this can be a problem later in the life of the corporation when success demands a significant increase in personnel. This personal commitment must be shared by other executives and employees. But if the personal commitment is not there, the venture is not likely to be successful.

Financial commitment: The entrepreneur should have something at risk in the venture. Once in a while, it is possible for an entrepreneur to get started without raising any outside capital. When capital must be raised, either through equity or debt, however, the entrepreneur should be prepared to share the financial risk with those people who have put their trust in the venture. This sharing of financial risk can take the form of a direct equity investment, of securing the loan through a mortgage of assets, or even of the investment of time at compensation rates greatly below the market ("sweat equity").

Emotional commitment: There will be times when entrepreneurs are called upon to make sacrifices that would seem unreasonable in other contexts. You must be prepared to work hours that seem impossible, and to love doing it, because that's what it takes to make the venture successful. Luck is a most precious commodity, but hard to plan and schedule. Fortunately, if entrepreneurs have commitment, their need for luck is reduced. Commitment means giving yourself no acceptable alternatives to making this venture successful, and then doing what it takes to make it become so.

3. Developing the Business Plan

I find that, all too often, entrepreneurs view the business plan simply as a document required by the bank or by the investor community to raise capital. Nothing could be further from the truth. The business plan contains the design for the venture, and will be as important to its success as blueprints to the architect.

The business plan is an orderly, disciplined way to express the premise around which the venture will operate. By itself, a business plan is neither a good thing nor a bad thing, but it is fundamental to success. If the market is undefined, the customer need unknown, the vision unclear, the products or services ill-defined, the support requirements obscure, the financial requirements and payback unrealistic, or the team inadequate for the challenge, then it's best to know it up front and forget the whole venture.

The business plan is a test of your organizational skills as an entrepreneur. It is also a test of the soundness of the vision and a reaffirmation of your ability to achieve the financial goals around which the venture is to be organized. The financial goals section of the business plan shows the expected results of the operation, the score card by which it will be judged. An adequate gross margin is the result of the selling of the product or service for a sufficient price and the delivery of excellence against this sale in a cost-efficient manner. Hence the price and the cost are the business of the entrepreneur and must be addressed in the business plan.

The business plan should also indicate those areas where unknowns exist or where circumstances are outside the control of the entrepreneur. The plan should help you minimize the effects of these unknowns, but sometimes variables do exist that we can't control. These should be included in the plan, not as potential excuses but as areas of concern to which the entrepreneur will give special attention.

The business plan is also the vehicle used to secure financing. Several words of caution are appropriate at this point. First, there are three times you can raise money: at the start of the venture; when the business plan indicated you would seek intermediate financing; and when the venture has met its commitments and you don't need the money anymore. Raise as much as you can in the initial round of financing and make sure you have identified the need for intermediate capital in the business plan or it will be very difficult to raise. You cannot raise too much capital and there are times when the market will not be receptive to any offering. The second caution involves starting the enterprise before the total capital has been raised. It is tempting but very dangerous to proceed before this most important step is completed. If you decide to proceed, you must re-plan your expenditures to match your resources. The entrepreneur must take these factors into account when determining the time to raise capital and the amount of capital required to meet the expectations set forth in the business plan.

4. Selecting the Team

The careful selection of associates can be the entrepreneur's biggest challenge. The start-up phase is characterized by rapid accomplishment with minimum expenditure of capital. To get through it successfully, associates need the same commitment as the entrepreneur CEO. Every venture needs its special mix of talents, but some needs are common to them all.

A strong scorekeeper is required, someone with the total confidence of the CEO. This means that the entrepreneur must follow this person's judgment in all financial matters. The CFO/scorekeeper position need not initially be a full-time one, but the importance of this function cannot be overstated. This person becomes your partner in the development and execution of the business plan.

The marketing, product development, support and service functions are also critical to your business, but before taking on people to work in those areas, step back and examine what you are trying to accomplish. This venture will be successful if enough customers are willing to pay an adequate amount for the product or service offered. Customers do not want to pay for your overhead if they can help it. Hence, the entrepreneur must take steps to minimize unnecessary costs. Remember that the customer wants the product or service, not the company. For instance, only start-up high-tech engineering services companies require a world-class technical group, but every enterprise needs world-class products. If the product can be brought to market without permanent staff, so much the better. There is plenty of time to hire staff when the incoming monthly gross margin is sufficient to pay their salaries. Organizing and staffing around those functions that supply value to the customer should be the heart of the staffing matter.

5. Measuring the Progress Against the Plan

Measuring against the plan is a good habit for all phases of development, corporate and personal. Whatever the goal, progress is measured against the plan of achievement toward that goal. Setting goals is a way of being held accountable. Ignoring your goals, or dynamically changing them to fit the situation is, in effect, changing the plan without the conscious effort you took to develop it in the first place. If the plan is to be reviewed on a monthly basis, you need interim milestones in every critical plan line so progress can be quantitatively measured every month. If you get behind on the critical path, action must be taken, expenditure rates must be reviewed, resources must be reassessed. Getting behind in a start-up venture delays the arrival of margin-producing revenue and extends the duration of unabsorbed costs. This is a double-edged sword, since the customer will be unwilling to pay for your additional costs. Never will the need for accurate measurement of progress be more critical than when the entrepreneur is trying to bring a product or service to market on a fixed budget.

Another reason to be fanatical about the measurement of

progress on a detailed task-by-task basis is the tendency to let the most pressing needs of the moment take your focus off the plan as a whole. The danger is in thinking that you'll have time to get to other matters later. Not so! Time is the entrepreneur's least renewable resource. A rigorous monthly review of the expected progress against the plan throughout the life of the venture is the best tool known to keep a company on track.

What does one do when the unexpected occurs and the schedule must slip to accommodate this new event? Most important, never deny the problem. This is the new reality that you must deal with through the life of the venture, and tough decisions must be made. The least acceptable thing to do is to operate with an invalid plan and try to work your way out of the situation. This is why commitment is so important; the entrepreneur must sit down, go through the remaining tasks and re-plan the effort and the sacrifices required to minimize the effects of the new, unexpected variable. Often the effect can be minimized through redeployment of resources, the possible subcontracting of tasks, the addition of alternative marketing strategies, or through increasing the number of parallel paths that define the effort.

I can't say it strongly enough: measuring progress against the plan is the only sure way to determine if adequate progress is being made.

6. Protecting Against the Downside

Once you have a plan and can measure progress against it, you will need to ask "what if…" as a continuing effort to protect against ill fortune. Much of this step will have already been accomplished if you were careful to set reasonable expectations. Every entrepreneur is an optimist, but experience teaches us that, if you can look ahead and anticipate negative challenges—competitors' actions, for example, you can minimize their effect on the plan.

We are not suggesting that entrepreneurs expend great quantities of effort looking over their shoulders. The leader of any organization needs to avoid the rocks in the stream rather than to deny their existence or try to blast through them as if they did not exist. This step, the least formal of the seven steps, is often undertaken privately by entrepreneurs to keep others from worrying. I encourage a more open approach in order to consider the relevant concerns of others on the team. Worrying leads to inaction. Getting people's concerns out on the table and discussing them openly can put these concerns to rest and empower the team to move forward unencumbered.

A final note on step six: use conservative accounting and develop legitimate reserves. The entrepreneur's job is to develop options. When the money is gone there are no options. Conservative accounting forces us to err on the side of good news rather than stretching the truth.

7. Taking Remedial Action Quickly

The entrepreneur who follows the previous six steps will have a strong team committed to the plan, executing well, and measuring their progress on a regular basis. This often leads to a sense of family among the team. But things change and action must be taken. This is as true of personnel issues as it is of responding to faltering marketing plans or unsatisfactory product development programs.

A feeling of family, with the entrepreneur as the leader, is a very powerful motivating force. No one likes to let the family down. But sometimes the fit isn't right, or the pressures of a start-up venture are too great, or undetected personality traits endanger the team's effectiveness. When this happens, the venture is at risk, and swift action is in order. This is always difficult, and with willing hands in short supply it is easy to put off the inevitable. Even with advice from the board or other trusted associates, entrepreneurs have been known to stay with an associate long after he or she has ceased to be a contributor. Keeping this person on the team benefits no one, not even the individual who has been identified as the "problem." The entrepreneur CEO must act swiftly but with compassion. New ventures are high-risk businesses with higher probability for failure than for success. Replacing people who don't fit allows them to get on with their careers and be successful somewhere else.

A similar situation exists when the distribution channel, for example, does not meet the plan's expectations. Trying harder is good, but it is rarely sufficient. Other channels should be investigated and the company's internal structure and operating assumptions should be examined and prompt action taken.

This includes the possible need to cut the company back dramatically to save the venture. We would all like to believe that this never happens, but the reality is that entrepreneurs often find themselves in this situation. Logic must rule the day, and the cut must be based on the determination of what part of the venture is most likely to survive. This is not so much cutting back as it is selecting the part of the company that can make it as an independent entity. While the bigger dream may be put on hold, as long as the venture is still breathing there is hope it can to be built up again. Acting quickly will provide the entrepreneur with the maximum number of options in a bad situation.

SWEET SUCCESS

If, as an entrepreneur CEO, you set your expectations correctly with a committed team in the development of the business plan, measuring your progress step-by-step, avoiding dangers, and taking swift action when required, you may find it possible to take a vacation someday. While on vacation you may hear someone say of your success, "What a great idea—I wish I had thought of it!" And you will smile, knowing it wasn't the idea but rather its execution that they admire.

Cheryl Alexander
is CEO and founder of Alexander Companies, an executive search and consulting firm. For two de-cades she has recruited leaders to accomplish organizational objectives and create healthy, productive workplaces.

Alexander's facility with multiple languages and extensive work and travel experience help Alexander Companies serve as partner in the implementation of globalization and diversification strategies of client organizations, which include Fortune 500 companies, emerging growth firms, and entrepreneurial ventures.

She appears in the public television series, "Inventing the Future," is listed in several *Who's Who* volumes, and serves on the boards of a variety of small businesses, non-profit and professional associations. She serves on the U.S. Secretary of Energy Advisory Board and on the Task Force on Strategic Energy Research and Development.

12

Creating New Futures in Turbulent Times

Cheryl Alexander

As the founder and CEO of an executive search firm, I know how tough today's job market can be. The competition is fierce and the requirements for related experience, strong interpersonal skills, and demonstrated innovative thinking make being selected difficult for even the very top candidates in a search. Over the past decade, the average size of U.S. companies has shrunk by twenty percent. High performers are working twelve to fourteen-hour days, often doing the work of two or three people. One-company careers have largely ceased to exist. Most new positions are with small ventures, formed by people with good ideas looking for leadership and a bit of magic to bring them success.

What it means to work for a successful company is rapidly changing. Take, for example, the recent break-up of a very successful TQM consulting firm. The partner assuming control is going to reduce the permanent headcount from twenty-eight associates to two. The consulting will be outsourced, most likely to the former associates who will become autonomous workers. Next, they will eliminate the bricks and mortar and replace rented office space with people telecommuting through the use of PC's and modems.

Or take the experience of one of my clients who became CEO of a troubled medical device company two years ago. The product line was outdated, manufacturing costs were too high, and cash flow was limited. He struck a deal with two highly skilled engineers to develop a new product line. The engineers agreed to work for expenses only, provided they had the right to manufacture the product for the first two years and receive a royalty on each unit produced. Within six months a new product was designed with updated technology that, even with the additional royalties, is less expensive to manufacture. The engineers have launched a new business and within a short period of time are making significant profits. The company has a new product line and a strategic partner who shares the risks and the rewards.

A final example: In a recent conversation with a product development manager at a major medical products company, I learned how lean her department had become. To continue to develop products, acquire patents, and conduct scientific research, she now relies on individuals and small companies in different parts of the world. She no longer manages the laboratory but rather the objectives, relationships, and results of a variety of strategic partners. These relationships continue to evolve as parties tackle patent applications, royalties, and ownership of the technologies.

In short, the need for talent, skills, and ideas has not diminished. But the cost of hiring and firing, the expense of benefits, and the demand for continually updated technology are causing organizations to rethink and restructure the way they do business. Large companies are becoming smaller, and small businesses are forming alliances, entering new markets and creating new jobs. Automation and the access to instant information are great levelers. To quote Casey Stengel, "The future sure ain't what it used to be."

Three major trends account for such changes:
1. The ever-increasing access to information and electronic networks and the corresponding shrinkage of the workforce, requiring more knowledge, analytical capability, and problem-solving skills.
2. The restructuring of business into smaller, more flexible, fluid enterprises, leading individuals and organizations

to focus on their core competencies and to extend their capabilities through a network of individuals and partners.

3. The globalization and diversification of the workforce, markets, and relationships, requiring new cross-cultural awareness and interpersonal skills.

Of all of the above trends, the one that remains least understood is the fact that our economy has become truly global, where ownership of, investment in, and alliances between companies fluidly cross international borders.

Globalization and the Diversification of the Workforce

Increasingly, organizations and individuals based in different regions of the world are engaging in joint research, development, manufacturing, and distribution. Businesses are taking their work to whatever part of the world will offer the greatest strategic advantage and the best return on their investment. Businesses trying to place their goods have discovered that markets that are saturated, overly regulated, or difficult to enter in one country show great potential and ease of access elsewhere. This is no longer a simple case of one country exploiting another, but a potential win/win situation that can meet all parties' needs.

Within the United States, one cannot escape the diversity among customers and employees. The composition of the workforce continues to change rapidly. Women, people of color, and foreign nationals are making significant contributions and offering new perspectives. Multi-disciplinary business teams include a mix of people of different genders, ethnic backgrounds, age groups, and nationalities. While they may encounter initial challenges in communication and in learning to work together, given a bit of time and good leadership, diverse teams are proving to be lively, innovative and challenging to the status quo.

As unsettling as such changes often are on a macro level, they also create challenges and opportunities at a micro level.

Implications for
Surviving in Larger Organizations

To survive and flourish in the face of all these rapid changes, managers in all kinds and sizes of organizations will need to demonstrate a new agility, a new willingness to take risks. They will need, that is, to adopt an entrepreneurial attitude.

An entrepreneurial attitude implies looking at the big picture, finding your competitive edge, forming a plan, taking risks, assuming responsibility, and operating with minimal resources in a hands-on manner to accomplish objectives. Each person is critical to the success of the whole. Small teams representing the marketing, sales, product development, manufacturing and financial perspectives are responsible for moving the company and products forward. Structure and process are of less importance than frequent communication, rapid decision-making, a sense of urgency, and a bias for action. In-house research is often replaced with information or expertise acquired from the vast resources available externally.

What does this mean for your performance as an owner or manager? Buy expertise wherever possible, yet develop contracts that offer opportunities for knowledge transfer. Keep fixed overhead as low as possible. Look for opportunities to develop mutual benefit or synergy between enterprises. Create relationships that will allow you to function as partners with vendors, consultants, marketing organizations, technologists, manufacturers. Maintain the flexibility to change direction or to transfer resources in response to specific customers or competitive challenges. Expect change, chaos, and uncertainty when making decisions. Flexibility and speed are required to capture opportunities.

As organizations continue to downsize in favor of automation and flexible resources, attention to internal culture-building becomes increasingly important. People are working harder and longer, taking more responsibility for the whole, and offering more creative input. As more is demanded, their other needs have to be met. Fairness, honesty, appreciation, open communication, flexibility, attention to individual needs, and skill development will build loyalty and team spirit. Communication of values, strategies, competitive pressures, and significant directional changes will allow each participant to respond to the challenges and participate in the solutions. Full communication of both good *and* bad news relieves fear of the unknown.

To remain competitive, accept the global paradigm. Learn a foreign language. Learn about and experience different cultures at work, in your community, and through travel. Develop skills and confidence in dealing with a wide range of people. Be willing to modify your point of view, to consider and accept other perspectives and beliefs. This is not to say that you shouldn't be true to your values, but that you should recognize not only the existence, but the usefulness, of multiple points of view, priorities, and approaches to problem solving.

One of the greatest points of challenge for executives or team leaders occurs when they delegate responsibilities and accountability and it becomes clear that other team members have markedly different approaches and methods than they had. It's important that leaders not let their fears about such differences cause them to end a project, to turn good people away, or to stifle creativity. Critical to the success of the team is the ability to recognize the individual talents of each team member. A strong leader will find ways to encourage the flow of ideas and communication, thus allowing all members to develop their full potential. Team leadership of multifunctional, diverse team members requires a delicate touch, much encouragement, and clear communication. With objectives, tasks, accountabilities, and expectations clearly defined and agreed to in significant detail, there will be fewer unpleasant surprises for everyone. Delegation and follow-through that include attention to individualized coaching as needed will work wonders at removing fears and avoiding set-backs.

Take charge of your career. Realize that single-company careers are becoming rare. Labor experts predict that we will each have five to ten careers in our worklife. That implies continuous new skill and knowledge-building, assuming different responsibilities in more than one industry.

To accomplish this, it is essential that you identify and develop your core competencies. Know what you do best and build on it. Identify your areas of expertise and develop new depth and breadth. Learn from other people. Attend seminars. Develop a larger view of your industry and the external world through reading and participation in professional organizations. Continue with formal coursework when appropriate to keep up-to-date and to challenge your own assumptions. Keep your mind agile.

One of the quickest ways to get a broader perspective on how business works is to volunteer to work on multidisciplinary, cross-functional teams. Listen to people in your business with other perspectives. Help bring people of multiple backgrounds and levels, both internal and external, into the team. Think big: more of the world and its expertise is available to you than ever before. For instance, contact authors of books you've admired or seminars you've attended. Industry experts are just people making a living; if they're not available for your project or for consulting, ask them for other recommendations.

As your organization gets flatter, it's important for you to remain flexible, and comfortable moving between different roles as individual contributor, team member, and team leader. Remember that in the new business structures it is not a demotion to operate without a staff or a significant budget. As vertical moves become rarer, do not hesitate to take lateral moves to build skills and expertise.

Take care of yourself. Find ways to keep your mind flexible, your attitude positive, and your body healthy. You will need the energy and the perspective. Workaholics have a much more difficult time maintaining networks. Over and over again, studies have shown that creative people tend to get their best ideas when doing something other than working. They need time for building relationships, for staying challenged and stress-free enough to let the creative parts of their brains kick in.

Recently I was talking with a commodity trader whose job requires rapid response, and quick thinking while processing information coming at her from all sides. With so much stimuli in her daily work it was sometimes difficult for her to think through problems and issues in a quiet, deeper manner. She began taking evening university courses, some related to her work and some simply for the stimulation of it, and has continued to do so for more than ten years. She has developed stronger analytical and problem solving skills, broader interests, and increased work opportunities. Analysis and synthesis of large amounts of data, continual learning, and development of your thinking skills, are required in today's business world.

Realize that old structures have to change. Learn to "think outside the box." Corporations are calling for a fundamental re-thinking and redesign of work processes. Offer suggestions, observe information flow and process. Take risks. There can be more "security" and opportunity in making a large contribution than in keeping your head down. Look for new business opportunities, new resources.

Build and maintain your network. I am amazed at the number of people going through outplacement who are learning to network for the first time. They often find it exhilarating and swear they will continue building and contributing to these networks for the rest of their work lives. Remember, however, that networks only work if there is two-way information flow. You must give as much as you receive—another reason for continuous learning.

Respond to headhunters or other recruiting calls. You can't afford to miss hearing about an opportunity. If the position is not for you, refer a colleague.

Polish your communication skills. We most often think of these as speaking and writing and forget that listening is the other half of communication. Learn to hear not only what people say, but what is being implied and what isn't being said. Learn from other people's base of knowledge and perspective, and respond in kind. The successful executive is no longer the person with all the information and resources but the one who can best facilitate communication and shared activity with other people.

Lastly, watch the health and politics of your company. Whole-sale changes are occurring in business structures that often result in entire groups of people being laid off. Divisions are closed, busi-nesses relocated, companies sold, executive teams replaced with minimal notice. Remember that it is still much easier to change jobs while employed.

Security and personal marketability no longer come auto-matically from spending one's entire career in a large corporation. Too many factors not related to performance can result in job-loss. If and when that occurs, a career history that shows evidence of entrepreneurial experience, the ability to work with a wide range of people, and a willingness to take risks becomes an asset. Several two-career households are discovering that there is more family security and greater flexibility when one partner remains in a corporation and the other joins a small company or becomes independently employed.

Implications for Starting Anew

The old wisdom held that entrepreneurs were born, not made. But increasingly new businesses are being created by people who never dreamed they'd go off on their own. Often they don't have a choice. Highly qualified people are being forced out of companies during restructuring and downsizing. Industries decline. Product lines are dropped. Companies decide to outsource manufacturing, data processing, or accounting. With little forewarning, you are out. This is a great time to consider the option of becoming independent and starting a business, especially if you have a severance package that eases the transition.

The majority of people I see who have decided to become entrepreneurial decide to find a small company to run, invest in, or buy. Although the prices and valuations never seem right, the products are often past their peak, and the infrastructure may be all wrong, an existing company presents an entrepreneur with a revenue stream and seemingly solvable problems. If you take this direction, look for industries or for weaknesses in a specific company that match your major strengths. Don't underestimate the unknowns, the steep learning curve in a new industry, or the issues to solve that do not play directly to your strengths.

If you don't have financial backers or a two- or three-year window to find a business to buy, consider starting your own small business or consulting practice. Identify your most marketable skills. What would companies or individuals be likely to buy from you? What problems motivate you? What services or products would *you* buy if they were available? How could you help people who trust and respect you solve a problem, work more effectively, or eliminate risk or overhead? What work could you better do as a consultant for your current or past employer?

Consider forming a consortium with colleagues who have different but complementary skills. Brainstorm and explore working together. Watch for motivation, follow-through, initiation of activities and ideas, chemistry, and balance. Do not feel committed to work together simply because you initiated discussion.

Begin to form a plan, a description of what you have to offer. Be able to succinctly describe your passions, your experience, and your accomplishments. Then focus on working out a plan to meet a need.

I've seen a number of these new, flexible, synergistic relationships or business formations that have been highly successful. For instance, a software designer made the decision with his family to move from California to North Carolina. He approached the management of his company with a well thought-out plan for working out of his new residence in North Carolina. The company had never considered this an option, but over a two-month period of negotiation the parties were able to select manageable projects and now a fruitful relationship is being maintained by telephone and electronic communication.

In another case, a director of marketing with expertise in telecommunications wanted a change without relocating. He teamed up with a colleague and formed a new consulting business focusing on the telecommunications market. Their first contract was with a customer of their past employer. For four years they have been fully engaged with a few large clients and are now faced with managing their growth.

I also worked with a CEO who sold his company. Instead of entering the job market, he targeted five companies with good reputations but flat revenues. He developed business strategies that could launch the companies into new market or product areas and began approaching their CEOs with his plans. He offered to launch their new business, working for them in six-month contractual increments at a compensation level similar to other VPs in the company but with a significant bonus opportunity tied to the success of his venture. He would require office space and expenses but would work from his own geographic base, traveling as necessary. The second company he approached bought his plan.

Yet another approach was taken by an experienced entrepreneur who has been launching businesses by acquiring rights to technology that has been proven in R&D but needed to be turned into manufacturable products. Since his strength was manufacturability, he was relying on other partners to supply raw materials and to market and sell the finished products.

Like many entrepreneurs, we at Alexander Companies are finding ourselves redefining our core competencies and establishing stronger linkages with key customers. In the last few years, our clients have been as interested in our understanding of the larger business context as they are in the specific search assignments for which we've contracted. This is especially true of how alternative staffing options, organizational planning, multicultural recruitment, and team building might help them improve their own operations. Under the new consulting and search arrangements that have resulted, they gain access to our wider expertise, we gain more direct involvement in their overall success. We've discovered as well that being willing to take part of our compensation in stock, warrants, or on a deferred basis, can help develop a stronger partnership and a vested interest in the success of a client.

What even reluctant entrepreneurs should find encouraging in these examples is that businesses or independent operations can be launched based on core competencies. It is not necessary to be all things to all people, as long as you can find good partners to fill the other parts of the equation.

Implications for Small Businesses Seeking to Hire Superior Talent

Tapping into the flexible and autonomous workforce is a real boon to small business. To buy expertise on an as-needed basis from experienced professionals allows you to access exceptional talent on a less than full time basis. Likewise, alliances with large and small companies allow you to extend your reach without incurring fixed overhead expenses.

Because of the pace of change in business and technology, companies aren't able to give new hires much time for learning an industry or a new technology, or for building new external relationships. In small and mid-sized companies, senior people are seldom hired solely on the basis of their general management skills. Specific knowledge, contacts, and expertise in areas critical to the success of the company will usually pay higher dividends. Organizations are typically looking for leading edge technology, processes, and knowledge that can be immediately usable. These may include specific market niche experience, industry or market contacts, and relationships to be leveraged.

Stability and loyalty were once considered important attributes. This has changed in the face of ownership changes, mergers, and divestitures or shifts in direction or leadership objectives. Further, it becomes increasingly difficult to assess the impact of one individual upon the outcome of a company and the key decisions. Both successes and failures should be expected of risk takers.

Recently I was speaking with a VP of HR in a fast-growth company who said, "Look at my own background: ten years in my first company, four in my second, two in my third, and five months in this job. I think the time periods for professionals with individual companies will continue to shorten. Infrequent are the long-term careers in one environment. As individuals we are developing portable skills, a variety of experiences that can be brought to bear on new situations, and evidence of flexibility and innovation." Careers are being built of specific assignments and projects completed in a variety of environments. What one wants to look for in hiring are patterns of experience and core competencies.

Leaders of small businesses need to remember that with each new hire, you are building your corporate culture. For most of our twenty years of executive search, finding the right fit generally meant finding someone very much like the current management team. Today, however, we and our clients are more likely to look for fresh insights, complementary backgrounds, and diversity in gender, ethnic heritage, and work environments that foster the development of varied management styles or perspectives. Likewise, the hiring of foreign nationals or individuals with international work experience often adds insight, connections, and responsiveness that result in more rapid access to new markets and alliances.

As an employer, establishing a healthy and flexible work culture will give you access to a highly qualified talent pool. Layoffs in larger corporations have increased pressure on workers, while diminishing opportunities for advancement. The 1993 National

Study of the Changing Workforce finds that workers are more willing to give up money and career advancement for more free time. Thirty-four percent were willing to make "a lot" of sacrifices to devote more time to their families; sixty percent of workers under twenty-five with children were willing to do so. We have found a tremendous pool of talented, skilled men and women with school-age children eager to work less than full time as independent or part time workers. Job sharing, though not broadly institutionalized can give an employer two highly motivated, skilled individuals, each with less pressure and more creative time for applying their minds and energies to challenging problems. Another source of talent are people over fifty years old who offer expertise and perspective that may not be needed full time.

Creation of a healthy work environment that values people as its major resource, is staffed by quality people who build trust and a sense of mission, and offers shared rewards or equity, will attract talented, loyal, and hard-working people. Attention to hiring leaders of high integrity who themselves live balanced lives will determine the quality of people you draw into your organization. Look for leaders who have vision, excellent communication skills, demonstrate flexibility, are honest, enthusiastic, able to build and sustain relationships, and have a history of successful implementation individually and through others.

In June 1993, the *Minneapolis Star Tribune* reported that there were 41.1 million homeworkers constituting thirty-three percent of the country's adult work force, according to a nationwide survey of 2,500 people by Link Resources. That total includes 7.6 million telecommuters; 12.2 million self-employed small-business people, consultants, or contract workers, and 9.2 million employees working at home on a personal computer.

Implications for Society

It may be useful to recall that prior to the turn of the century, only ten percent of the population worked for large organizations. Yet in this century, we came to believe that security and opportunity existed only in large organizations. Taking more responsibility for structuring our work lives, for providing financial stability, and for defining ourselves and our personal worth can be terrifying, but also potentially liberating and empowering. Viewing the talent, education,and experience of the people in the market who will be joining or creating new business ventures, we can anticipate a regeneration and revitalization of business and a new understanding of its role vis-à-vis our families and our communities.

As autonomous workers and entrepreneurs, we will also need government policies that take into account the changing structures and independence that is evolving. Affordable health care is a must. We need incentives for investing in small high-risk businesses and technologies. We need to provide for our own continuous education. We need to plan for irregularities in cash flow and business cycles. We need to save more, borrow less, and invest in programs for retirement.

In the past, our workplace has consumed the majority of our energy and creative power, and too often defined our value in economic terms. We have frequently created imbalanced lifestyles that have caused us to defer other priorities and responsibilities. Organizations reflect the values of the individuals who run them. We need to clarify our own priorities and values, define our own mission and purpose, recognize the myriad of options available, and create our own work environments. We need to reconcile our beliefs and cultural heritage with the larger, diverse world we now experience. We are responsible for our own realm of influence, being involved, and conducting ourselves ethically.

As we take back responsibility for our own work lives, we create our future in accordance with our dreams.

Marjorie Kelly
is the founding editor and publisher of *Business Ethics* magazine,
the only national magazine of so-
cially responsible business. She launched *Business Ethics* in 1987.

Kelly has worked in the publishing industry nearly twenty years,
including her work as writer and editor at a variety of publications, from
daily newspaper to feminist arts quarterly. She holds a Master's in
magazine journalism from the University of Missouri, where she won the
Penney-Missouri Award for most promising young magazine journalist.

She is an active member of the Social Venture Network, Business for
Social Responsibility, and the Social Investment Forum. She also serves on
the Advisory Board of the National Conference on Ethics in America.

Her essay has been adapted from an editorial she wrote in *Business
Ethics* entitled "Dangerous Vision: Social Mission Can't Substitute for
Business Basics" and is reprinted with permission.

13

Marjorie's Maxims for Social Entrepreneurship

Marjorie Kelly

"I used to think that only ideologies could save the world. But now the most important thing seems to be running things well."
—*Rolling Stone* founder Jann Wenner, quoted in *Rolling Stone Magazine:The Uncensored History,* by Robert Draper.

How does it happen that what looks so easy can end up being so incredibly complicated? How is it that something so basic can be so invisible? What I'm talking about is management, and how invisible and complicated the skills of management are—particularly to aspiring entrepreneurs, intent as they are on things more exalted than sick-leave policy or 1099 forms.

Take my friend Richard, for example. He's developed a pretty amazing new product—multi-dimensional graphing and plotting software that promises to revolutionize statistical analysis—and he wants to start selling it from his garage. "But I'm not going into business," he tells me. When I protest that he is indeed going into business, and is likely to run into more pitfalls than he can imagine, he brushes away my warnings with the wave of a hand. "How much can there be to it?" he says. "You hire somebody to

answer the phones, you put the software in an envelope and mail it."
I shake my head and wonder: Would he be so cavalier if it was a
career as a saxophonist he was undertaking? "How much can there
be to it? You put the horn in your mouth and blow."

It's an attitude that is dismayingly common among entrepreneurs. I met another fellow at a conference recently who, with a
partner, is planning to start a new business magazine. Knowing that
he was an editor, I inquired about his partner's background. "He's
an editor too," I was told. "But who will do the business side?" I
asked. "Oh, we'll hire people to do that. How many ways can there
be to skin a cat in circulation?"

Interestingly enough, that same day I found myself in a long
conversation with David Thorne, publisher of *New Age Journal,*
discussing circulation—lists, offers, pricing, gross response, pay-up,
renewal rates—all the various cats, you might say, and how they can
be skinned. And I couldn't help noticing that, in an hour's time,
neither of us mentioned a single editorial idea—though that was the
only thing my entrepreneur friend thought worth his attention. I
hadn't said it earlier, but I hoped, at that moment, to find him and
say: If you think you can "just hire someone" to run the business
part of your company and then ignore it, you're making a huge
mistake. It's not that editorial quality doesn't matter—it matters
tremendously. But business matters just as much.

It's an easy mistake to make: wanting to focus on the things we
love and ignore the rest, hoping that, magically, the rest will take
care of itself. In the good old days of being an employee, most things
did take care of themselves. All the pesky details of management—
meeting payroll, filling out tax forms, fixing equipment, emptying
trash—somehow just got done, and we only noticed when they
didn't. I had no idea how well my former boss ran his company until
I started my own. I'd always been very aware of his shortcomings as
a manager, but I barely noticed his strengths. Because strengths in
management, almost by definition, are invisible.

Management is the art of what doesn't happen: the checks
that don't bounce, the orders that aren't shipped late, the lawsuits
that are never filed.

Such things are rarely foremost in the mind of the new

entrepreneur—particularly one with a social bent. Management is what boring bureaucrats do, we tell ourselves; we have a mission, we're funky—we don't need all that Man in the Gray Flannel Suit stuff.

Yet management is like life: It's what happens to entrepreneurs when we're busy making other plans. We set out to develop a wonderful product, to have an impact—and we find ourselves spending less time on changing the world than on getting the mail out at 3:00, and remembering to print our letterhead on recycled paper with that little recycling logo on the bottom of every sheet.

Of course, trying to tell all this to a new business owner is like telling a newlywed about the perils of long-term relationships ("Not in *my* marriage…"). But at the risk of being a Cassandra—issuing warnings that go unheeded—I'd like to share a few of the lessons I've learned over the years about the perils of social entrepreneurship. "How much can there be to it?" More things than you've ever dreamt, Horatio.

And so, in true management-how-to style, I'd like to offer here a few of Marjorie's Maxims:

1. Social mission is not a substitute for business basics.

When I started this company, my goal was to make a difference. I believed that if I put out a great magazine and created the right esprit de corps, the rest would take care of itself. We were riding a wave of historic change; nothing could stop us. I still believe we're riding that wave—but I now realize it helps to have a good engine on our craft. And that engine is revenue.

My business partner, Miriam Kniaz, and I use the phrase "being devoted to revenue." It's been like a conversion experience. Because it's clear to us that every day we face more tasks than we can possibly complete, so we must constantly ask ourselves: Is this task revenue-generating? And we must ask as an organization: Are we simply spending money or are we investing in growth? Because spending $500 to generate subscriptions is very different than spending $500 on shelves for the library.

So revenue is one of the clear basics—but there are others. Like working conditions or employee relations. We ignore these at our peril, too. Jerry Gorde, founder of Vatex, said once that he had focused so much on lofty issues like company mission and employee ownership that he'd neglected things like job descriptions. "Forget taking ownership of the company," he said. "Take ownership of your *job*."

Nothing can substitute long for business basics.

2. Return on investment *is* a social responsibility.

Our mission says it quite nicely. When we started the magazine, our mission had two parts: to promote ethical business practices, and to serve those professionals trying to live and work in responsible ways. A few years down the road, we added a third part: to create a financially healthy company. It's pretty hard to make a difference if you don't make any money.

We use the phrase "financially healthy company," because it encompasses a lot: good wages (for employees), revenue growth (for the company), and return on investment (for investors). Employees we face every day, so their needs are obvious. And, as entrepreneurs, we own most of the company, so its needs are pretty clear to us. But when someone I hardly know, and will rarely see, hands me a personal check for $75,000, it gets my attention. It becomes pretty clear, pretty fast, that "return on investment" is not an abstract concept. It's my personal obligation to a handful of people who have taken a risk on me, when they could have done any number of other things with their money. And return on investment, by the way, is also an obligation I have to myself.

3. The democratic workplace is not a leaderless workplace.

You can't pretend that everyone is equal. This point was made best by Jim Autry, author of *Love & Profit*, who put it this way: As a manager, you may not feel your power, but your subordinates do. Jim, at the time, was president of a $600 million division of Meredith Corporation, but when a call came in from his CEO, he jumped to take it. The power difference was always there.

This has been a hard lesson for me, coming as I do from a background in collectives and cooperatives, where there is a fierce distrust of hierarchy. And, for a time, I tried to run a completely egalitarian office. But "power sharing" didn't work, I discovered, for, instead of creating welcome opportunity, it sometimes left a confusing vacuum. When I finally stepped into that vacuum and claimed my role as a leader, there was a palpable sense of relief among the staff—because now someone was in charge, now we could get somewhere.

The same lesson hit me again from a different angle. Like many entrepreneurs, I had the fantasy that we were all in this together—like a group of friends pitching in on a project. That worked with some employees, particularly those who came with experience in the industry and a high level of skill. But I was surprised to find that some employees considered this atmosphere irritating. Without close supervision, comprehensive training, and a clear definition of responsibilities, they felt cast adrift. They couldn't do good work. And they resented it. Claiming my power, it turned out, really meant claiming my responsibility.

4. Anarchy can be more oppressive than bureaucracy.

My old boss, Bill, would laugh if he heard this, but I've come to think of procedures as my friends.

Before I started *Business Ethics*, I worked for an entrepreneurial company that was quite young—I was the third full-time employee—and I hated how, over the years, the procedures multiplied. Where once we had written direct mail plans on the back of menus, now there were endless forms to fill out. I put a bumper sticker on my car that said, "Break the Rules." And when I left to start my own company, Bill gave me a going-away present: a binder labeled, "Kelly Inc. Policies and Procedures." It was totally empty. We laughed about it, but I vowed that my company would never, never have so many rules.

The six years since, I humbly admit, have been spent filling up that binder—and these days I welcome new procedures with glee. For example, last week I bought an alphabetized accordion file for unpaid bills. I'm like a kid in a candy store with it. I take great joy in filing invoices tidily, and pulling them out knowing that all the Federal Express bills will be in one place.

Instead of seeing procedures as oppressive, I now see them as an oasis: a welcome space where things run well, and I can make one decision instead of ten. When I envision the perfect workplace now, it is a hybrid of the best parts of both bureaucracy and anarchy: a humming, well-oiled, efficient organization, but with an atmosphere that is comfortably human.

It can be done, I know. We can create organizations with all the panache, passion, and fun of social entrepreneurship, and all the efficiency and financial acumen of traditional business. But we can't have the former without the latter.

Summary

At our office we have a lot of wonderful traditions, like office toys (cars that race down walls, wind-up walking monsters). We have a Big Blue Eraser we ceremoniously award to anyone who has made the latest Really Big Mistake, and we've been known to show up at staff meetings in yellow plastic Dick Tracy hats. We try to walk our talk however we can: letting staff bring kids to work, using recycled paper, seeing every job as promotable. I'm proud of these traditions, and they say a lot about who we are—but I've discovered over the years that they're really the icing on the cake. To do these things without having the business basics in place is like hanging elegant curtains in a room where the wind is whistling through holes in the walls.

I thought, when I started this company, that we were rewriting the rule book on business: throwing everything out, starting fresh. Since then I've put back most of the things I threw out. I've realized that social entrepreneurs aren't so much writing a new book as adding a chapter to the old one. We've made some improvements, I feel sure of that. But the old book, you know—it has a lot of good stuff.

Chris Manning,
MBA, PHD, is the founder and managing principal of Manning Advisors and the Denver office of Houlihan Valuation Advisors, a national business valuation firm. Manning Advisors is a reengineering and financial consulting firm specializing in the integration of corporate culture transformation, computer and telecommunications technology, and increasing the profitability of businesses.

While on a leave of absence as Professor of Finance and Real Estate in the Department of Finance and Computer Information Systems at Loyola Marymount University in Los Angeles, he is building his consulting practice in downtown Denver. In addition to his work as a facilitator and lecturer at executive workshops, he is widely published in both academic and professional journals, including the *Harvard Business Review.*

Manning's previous business experience includes being an entrepreneur, a corporate banking officer for a major national bank, an investor in businesses, and a U.S. Army officer during the Vietnam war. His entrepreneurship and management accomplishments have been detailed in Marquis *Who's Who in Finance and Industry* over the past twelve years.

14

Reengineering Entrepreneurs: Creating Emotionally Healthy Organizations

Chris Manning

Technological and knowledge resources are so great today that managers can no longer afford to think of leading employees, establishing alliances (partnerships, joint ventures, etc.), and exploiting suppliers as they have in the past. Old management paradigms, full of dysfunctional precedents, interfere with developing the needed teamwork and general health among people key to the success of today's enterprises.

Economic pressures caused by rapid change will more frequently force managers to think and act like entrepreneurs. The best of the new breed of entrepreneurial managers will be "plugged into" the appropriate information systems, be aware of technological advances, respond quickly to market conditions, take prudent risks, and shape their corporate cultures to reap the benefits of more productive relationships with employees, customers, partners, and joint ventures. Those companies blessed with this type of leadership will be most able to harness this rapidly growing availability of advanced technological and information resources.

To ensure their own success, the first task required of managers will be to choose a management paradigm that will work to accomplish both their personal goals and the goals of their enterprise. When choosing among competing management models, traditions, and paradigms, managers will need to think as entrepreneurs because so much that is passed off as sound management practice is destructive to human creativity, productivity, organizational morale, and team spirit.

The best management paradigm I have come across is Peter Senge's "Learning Organization Model." The dramatic increases in worker productivity recently achieved in companies through "Reengineering" and "Total Quality Management" have relied heavily upon concepts that are a part of Senge's paradigm. In his article entitled "The Leader's New Work: Building Learning Organizations" (*Sloan Management Review,* Fall 1990), Senge recommends that managers build truly cooperative organizations that support the continuing growth, learning, and adaptability of individuals within their organization. He says this alone will ensure the long-term competitive advantage one company will have over another in the future.

From the entrepreneurial manager's perspective, this means that the ultimate product that their enterprise must produce to insure success is the psychological, emotional, and spiritual health of their own organization's culture and its people. Only through enlisting the energy and efforts of the members of an organization can managers create an environment that empowers creativity and unleashes the productivity needed to compete.

Senge points out that people's natural impulse, to learn and be productive has been destroyed by our prevailing system of management. He contends that our receptivity to this destruction of our natural productivity began for all of us as toddlers—"a prize for the best Halloween costume, grades in school, gold stars, and up through the university. On the job, people, teams, divisions are ranked—reward for the one at the top, punishment at the bottom. MBO, quotas, incentive pay, business plans, put together separately, division by division, cause further loss" through their singular appeal to people's fears rather than harnessing the natural support from people's sincere caring about each other in a holistic team effort.

Senge elaborates that "the impulse to learn, at its heart, is an impulse to be generative, to expand our capability." This is why leading corporations are focusing on "generative" learning (which is about creating) as well as adaptive learning (which is about coping).

Under the learning organization paradigm, the entrepreneurial manager's primary role shifts from setting direction, making key decisions, and energizing "the troops" to one of building a shared vision, fostering more systematic patterns of thinking, and challenging prevailing mental models. Such leadership in a learning organization starts with managers infusing their corporate cultures with what Senge calls "creative tension."

This creative tension comes from people seeing clearly where they want to be (their "vision")—and at the same time telling the truth about where they are (their "current reality"). He writes, "Individuals, groups, and organizations who learn how to work with creative tension learn how to use the energy it generates to move reality more reliably toward their visions."

From my own experiences as an entrepreneur and university professor, I have found that the key to unleashing the vast creative and productive resources of our relationships is to focus upon the physical, mental, emotional, and spiritual health of the people we work with every day. While much attention has recently been placed upon reducing physical stress to improve productivity, too little attention has been placed upon creating and maintaining the emotional and spiritual health of the firms and networks we work within.

The quality and efficiency of our own thinking (and thus our own productivity) is dependent upon our emotional well-being as well as our physical well-being. It therefore stands to reason that we need to also focus our attention on how to develop healthy relationships and communication habits among the people who are key to our economic success. Otherwise productivity will be stifled. If we, as managers, wish to win the competition in the marketplace for talented employees and other partnerships important for our success, we will come to realize that our society's growing quality-of-life concerns include workplaces as well.

In starting up the Denver office of a national financial services firm in late 1993, I was impressed with the eagerness of talented people to work for a learning organization patterned after Senge's model. Fifteen years ago I had difficulty attracting successful entrepreneurs or good employees from firms such as Xerox to join my enterprises. This is not the case today. Central to this success appears to be my willingness to depart from old management paradigms through experimenting to discover what "works" for talented, experienced people. I find such people increasingly motivated as much by personal fulfillment as by money and prestige.

Unencumbered by the ossified remains of an entrenched organizational culture, where political concerns typically inhibit growth of team spirit and emotional health among workers, I found that knowledge workers can be motivated in the direction of a healthy and supportive work culture. My biggest challenge was overcoming collective disbelief that the opportunity exists to work in an empowering environment dedicated to their emotional health and to unleashing natural productivity. To accomplish this required the courage to implement what I believed was intuitively obvious to anyone who trusted their own feelings about how they would want to be treated to be more productive. At its foundation, my entrepreneurial management approach is little more than combining sound analytical procedures of our minds with intuitive knowledge of our hearts.

I selected Denver as the location to open my own firm—the twelfth office for an expanding national financial services organization—because the city offers knowledge workers a better quality of life in addition to current economic competitive advantages. This made attracting key people much easier. Sharing my vision and collaboratively planning for building this technologically-advanced financial services office has been central to aligning our goals and unleashing everyone's emotional health and productivity.

Productivity and an Organization's Emotional Health

We can begin our understanding of how to harness practical knowledge of our human nature—to further the productivity of those around us—by noticing that our thinking ability and efficiency is heavily dependent upon emotional calm and joy within ourselves. Haven't we all noticed that we don't think as well when we are upset, hungry, tired, or feeling threatened? Experience has taught me that our emotional side is the real foundation of our best creative thoughts, our physical energy, our ability to efficiently communicate clearly with others, as well as most other aspects of mental productivity.

Unfortunately, few of us have had healthy enough emotional histories to believe that what makes us joyful and at peace with the world is also that which will make us and our relationships vastly more productive. Nevertheless, courage and management experimentation will confirm to all of us that the root of our best business judgment is our magnificently efficient intuition. Thus, an important entrepreneurial management skill in the future will be to train our intuition (i.e., business judgment). Through experimentation and observation, we can uncover what does work and what does not work in a particular work environment.

As intimidating as computer analytical software and availability of data have become, we need to remember that the computer programmers who write the best software must first program themselves. This is a creative act. Can we afford to delude ourselves with thinking that the technology of computerized information systems will ever replace our need to care about each other and think creatively to arrive at sound business judgments? On the contrary, the more computerized and other technological resources we have at our finger tips, the greater the need for workers to think intuitively in order to successfully organize and weight relevant information to produce productivity and profits. Many highly successful people already depend heavily upon their intuitive faculty to appropriately "weight" the myriad of factual considerations impacting upon their decisions, but rarely is this skill sufficiently acknowledged.

But is our intuitive ability up to the task of organizing and making efficient use of all the data and stimuli that bombard each of us every day as we attempt to fulfill our responsibilities and find satisfaction in our accomplishments? My own experience tells me that we are all up to this challenge, managers and professionals alike. However, we must take care of our emotional health so that we have access to clearer feelings. The emotional health I refer to here is physical as well as psychological, and thus requires a certain degree of physical health for peak performance. Managers will realize that it is our own emotional health, as well as that of those we work with, which is the very foundation for accessing our own vast resources of intuition, and learning better how to use them.

One obvious key to emotional health is trust. Developing trust within our relationships is an essential part of good communication and productivity. Yet, before we can either earn the trust of others or learn how to assist them in becoming more trustworthy, we must learn to trust ourselves, our abilities, and our own thoughts.

Because what is often put forth in business as a standard for motivating others is so terribly unhealthy, managers today can benefit greatly from having the courage to experiment with more honest communication with workers, associates, and, most importantly, themselves. Many managers apparently don't yet appreciate that talented knowledge workers are intuitively aware of other people's true motivations or lack of concern for their welfare. The days of lying to people through omission of relevant factual information and manipulating others contrary to their better interest are numbered. As worker's emotional health further improves, this type of behavior will become increasingly transparent. Emotionally unhealthy acts by managers, whether perpetuated by an unhealthy organizational culture, or of their own creation, will cost organizations thousands of dollars in lost productivity and worker turnover.

We need to better appreciate our own human nature, its innate healthy ability to know the hearts and motivations of others, and its unbelievable capacity for practical creativity and productive energy. With most business leadership today still "muscle bound" by the past outmoded ways of organizing and motivating workers, an entrepreneurial manager can reap tremendous economic gain, as well as job satisfaction, by proactively creating emotional health within their work environments.

It is commonly accepted that most managers need to reduce unproductive stress in their lives while coping with new technology and rapidly changing markets. Doesn't it stand to reason that the successful learning organizations in the future will become more reliant upon the emotional health of their workers? How else can learning be encouraged and accelerated in competitive organizations except by acknowledging the central role that our caring about each other plays in our willingness to learn better ways of accomplishing our workloads? Furthermore, how else can the competitive company of the future foster a positive learning environment for its workers if managers don't act as entrepreneurs to break past dysfunctional management paradigms? Managers will need to take more and more "seeming risks" to uncover what enhances the emotional well-being of their workers.

I say "seeming risk" here because the feedback to managers from such experimentation with honesty and forthrightness is so swift that errors can quickly be corrected. Their own improved emotional health, as a result of adopting a healthy management paradigm, will greatly assist in empowering managers to intuitively make sense of such experimentation. Few products or services in the marketplace provide such wonderful, immediate feedback as our sincere attempts to empower our workers and other stakeholders.

If you trust your feelings, intuition, and your own creative ability to react to what a situation needs, you will have the opportunity to make immediate corrections in better serving "your customers"—the people you work with who desire the same emotional health that you do. Because the demand to work in a healthy business culture is so unsatisfied, the cost-to-benefit analysis is heavily tipped in favor of entrepreneurial managers who are courageous enough to experiment and uncover what works.

These principles have been demonstrated to me to be true when hiring employees, subcontracting work out, and enlisting partner and joint venture alliances. I have found them no less true when working with suppliers, customers, and everyone else that I deal with.

I am amazed at how short my meetings and phone conversations need to be when I trust both myself and others (who are trustworthy because they also have learned that health and productivity stem from trusting themselves). Many knowledge workers seem to be hungry for alliances that feel good to them when they can see their economic objectives being met.

Management Tools to Promote Emotional Health

An important management tool for emotional health that has worked well for me is a variation on the common theme: We must learn to be more *tolerant* of those we work with. To me, the word "tolerant" here undermines emotional health. For none of us want to be tolerated. We all want to be *appreciated!* Most of us, as well as the people we work with, have untapped talents and energy. When these are appreciated by others, we find ourselves empowered to increase our output manyfold—both in quality and quantity in the short run, as well as in new skills and better judgment in the longer run. Do we remember to listen carefully with our hearts and minds for these same things in others? Just our effort to do so will, in itself, create a healthier work environment. Sincere openness to what is good and valuable in other people costs us nothing and improves our own emotional health by consciously disciplining ourselves to listen better.

Another important tool of emotional health is the central need we all have to "focus" clearly on our present needs, objectives, and problems without muddying our thinking with details of little relevance to a particular issue. Only when we believe our most immediate physical, emotional, and psychological needs and goals will eventually get met through our efforts, can we get on with the serious business of empowered, undistracted productivity.

The most pressing issue for businesses often has to do with making sufficient money, or cutting costs, to insure financial health and viability. Usually there are many more choices of alternative courses of action to solve financial problems than "normal" managers are able to uncover, and ultimately chose between. Because of this, a sharper focus of the intuitive and caring energy of the workers involved almost always yields good creative solutions. These immensely valuable solution possibilities are born from the sheer desire and faith of workers who won't settle for a painful, inferior course of action.

Whenever I sense effort getting off track, or merely time being wasted, I refocus attention (mine as well as others) on our most immediate and pressing concerns. This is where emotional health and intuition are so valuable. Often the most important challenge facing us is the accurate identification of our highest priority and most immediate concern. No computer software or other technology is of much help to us here. It is merely a matter of turning inward and asking the most important questions such as: What is going on here? What is our true current situation? What do I want to see happen? How can this person help me get to where I want to go? How can I help the individual get to where he/she want to go, both economically and emotionally? Do I know where these people are attempting to go? If communication feels muddy, have I asked them specifically what they are attempting to accomplish?

A key question I ask that assists greatly in tapping into the vastly greater productivity of others is: "What do you want?" or some variation of asking "What would you like to see happen here?" While many people may ask this question of others for similar reasons, few listen with their hearts and intuitions. It is by listening with our hearts and intuitions to how other people answer this simple question that we are communicating the most fundamental truths of the economic, social, and spiritual realities we all live in. At the root of our emotional health is the truth that we all wish to care, be cared about, and want to believe we have the power to change things. With this simple question, we are able to support the emotional health of those we work with by simultaneously telling them (1) we care about them enough to ask, (2) we care and trust ourselves enough to think this information is useful, and (3) there is hope that energy can be expended to get them, as well as ourselves, to where we want to go.

To receive profound truthful answers from others to this question of "What do you want?," we need to first make a habit of asking ourselves the same question and noticing that we naturally desire others around us to also have what it is that they are seeking. While this is true of emotionally healthy people, we need to prudently keep in mind that this is not true for people who are still emotionally suffering, consciously or subconsciously.

Unfortunately, due to the dearth of emotional health prevalent in many organizations today, we rarely will hear a profound reply to this question that has the power to unleash that person's productivity. This is why it is so important to learn the art of listening to your own feelings and intuition. These will tell you when you are listening to what another cares deeply about. The entrepreneurial managers of the future will risk experimentation to learn the skills of business judgment and listening to people's hearts. They will also have the courage to act upon this knowledge of how productivity and profits lie just beyond the empowerment of their workers and other alliances.

Many people have different wants and goals than we do, or have a different level of emotional and psychological health. The entrepreneurial manager will more and more need to play the role of "talent scout" to find those with the needed abilities, motivations, and health to make their own endeavor succeed. To efficiently accomplish the task of screening the myriad of opportunities we encounter each day, the entrepreneurial manager needs a refined intuitive sense about people and complex situations. This skill will become ever more essential for managers in learning organizations in order to reliably know who or what might work, to creatively experiment, and to learn from the results.

Contrast the picture of emotionally healthy workers in a healthy organization to the "political" reality that too often undermines worker productivity today. Fearful managers who seek mainly to please superiors upset their workers to the point that many of them are waiting for their first opportunity to quit. Such workers feel little motivation to deliver anything more than minimal output as they "serve out their sentence." The entrepreneurial manager with a nose for profits will increasingly realize the high financial cost of such waste.

To heal an existing unhealthy corporate culture is difficult. Many large organizations will never be able to heal themselves, nor even wish to. They will merely be put out of business by entrepreneurial managers in newer organizations interested in the emotional health of their workers. This must follow when we pause to reflect that the market for worker talent will go to those managers who truly take care of the overall health of their employees. The days are coming to an end when higher pay, a good retirement plan, health insurance, day-care, an employee gym, and other perks will mask the emotional unhealthiness of an employer. Don't we all know of people working for less money just to interact with other people in a healthy organizational environment? The increasing efficiency of the knowledge worker marketplace will only accelerate what seems to be inevitable.

The financial cost to newer organizations to provide a healthy emotional worker environment is virtually nothing compared to the increased profits immediately available. While emotional and psychological health might seem to be a scarce resource, it is not. Health, and people's willingness to enjoy it, are abundant everywhere once freed from destructive peer pressure. The abundance of worker demand for a healthy work environment is only exceeded by the fears and ignorance of entrenched managers who have too few role models illustrating how to unleash their workers' productivity. Business leaders are at a crossroads where available technology, other resources, and worker desire for a better quality of life, will force them into entrepreneurship in order to compete with the ever healthier organization cultures of their competitors. While there is no shortage of workers seeking healthy satisfying employment, there is a shortage of entrepreneurial managers with the courage to creatively involve associates as a team to accomplish the evolving goals of the enterprise.

Healthy Partnerships and Other Associations

The lines defining an association as a customer, partner, supplier, joint venture partner, sub-contractor, or other singular label appear to be blurring over time. More and more, creative entrepreneurs are discovering ways to assemble multiple roles into new hybrid relationships to further their economic goals and become more competitive.

Our need to creatively explore additional possibilities for joint productive endeavor among our association networks will inevitably increase. Our need to creatively focus the shared attention in our relationships upon what each party is attempting to achieve, against the backdrop of past experience, aptitudes, and level of commitment, must also increase. Competitive advantage within the marketplace will more and more accrue to entrepreneurial individuals who can empower a true sense of team spirit and shared goals while creatively exploring productive combinations of effort.

Central to enabling such productive effort will be each of our abilities to trust ourselves to grow and learn, trust in others, and trust the intuitive feelings we call judgment to guide us through details too complex to be sorted out by our conscious thinking processes. Too many of the old management paradigms have already proven themselves to be unhealthy and highly dysfunctional.

In summary, we all need to develop and trust our deeper intuitive capabilities to find more profound solutions to the central obstacles that block our next steps. This will require entrepreneurial managers who can focus the attention of their teams upon what that next step should be and which alternative is preferable. Just as it is easier to break each stick individually in a large bundle, so it is also easier to separate and focus on each individual obstacle sequentially while keeping hearts and minds focused on the overall direction.

Part Four

New Thinking for New Times

The Non-financial Driver in Entrepreneurship
Paul Hwoschinsky

Revisioning Economics®:
(A Systems Approach)
William B. Sechrest

A Time For Collaboration
Nicholas P. LiVolsi

The Evolutionary Times: A Fable
Bill Veltrop

This last section contains four essays dealing with our think-ing—the patterns, assumptions and habits of the modern business mindset—and how a new set of assumptions is being called for in these transformational times. To sustain, entrepreneurs in this new era must be of a different breed than their predecessors, thinking and acting more holistically, and recognizing their sacred responsi-bility to the larger whole—their customers, employees, stockhold-ers, neighbors, vendors and all the non-human resources on which they impact.

In the first essay, veteran venture capitalist Paul Hwoschinsky challenges our thinking and expands our options by suggesting that financial resources are really non-financially-driven.

Dallas attorney Bill Sechrest presents a powerful case for changing our thinking about one of our most "sacred cows"—the economy—the most powerful social system in the world today.

Former marketing and communications executive and World Trust founder Nicholas LiVolsi envisions the new entrepreneur as a facilitator of collaborative opportunities and relationships within a new business/community paradigm.

In the last essay, Bill Veltrop weaves a tale—the fable of Arthur—that sets forth a vision of what can be. Arthur envisions himself as a newspaper owner who anticipates the headlines and classified sections of the future.

Paul Hwoschinsky

is a private investor, entrepreneur, corporate director, and author. He was a general partner in Callanish Fund, a venture capital partner-ship founded in 1973 with Robert N. Noyce, one of the co-founders of Intel Corporation. In this work, they spawned several high-tech companies working on the cutting edge of emerging technologies.

He has been a general partner in a real property investment partnership as well as an investor for his own account. He has served as budget director and later as assistant-to-the-general-manager of Fairchild Semiconductor and has founded several small firms as an entrepreneur.

Hwoschinsky serves on the board of ProTechnics International of Texas and has authored a book, *True Wealth*, published by Ten Speed Press. He is now writing his second book. He and his wife, Carol, have been married since 1955 and have two grown children. He holds an MBA from Harvard.

15

The Non-financial Driver in Entrepreneurship

Paul Hwoschinsky

Our world is in accelerating and fundamental change—requiring new solutions. The entrepreneur of the next century will develop a keen sense of these changes and react with appropriate interventions. This will come from increased inner-self and outer-world awareness. This, in turn, will generate fresh solutions from inventive new perspectives.

Global Competition

Change is always unsettling. When it is rapid, it can be frightening. We see this today. Competition has become global. An auto worker in Michigan is at contest with those in Japan, Germany, and/or Korea. Depending on the subsidy, a U.S. farmer is in competition with another overseas. Foreign and domestic policy starts to blend. Trading blocks are forming. The European Community and the U.S./Canada/Mexico relationship are cases in point. Within each of these communities there will be major dislocations as nations struggle to accommodate the removal of tariffs. With advancing technology, the world is getting smaller. Access to information is instantaneous. TV coverage brings war, famine, and Olympic games into our homes as they happen. All of these movements are just the start of an eventual free world market that could change the imbalance between the "haves" and the "have-nots."

Change includes many positive potentials. Whatever else it may represent, change energizes, creates alertness, and can be a springboard for individual, corporate, or national growth. It often forces one to re-examine his/her purpose, vision, and life course. It can "jump start" our lives.

Here are just a few of the areas where change will impact us:

Resources

There will be change in the way the world sees and treats natural resources and the various life-forms that live upon our planet. We are just now starting to see and experience limits to growth. The pollution levels in the old Soviet Union and its satellites are alarming cases in point. People are dying from pollution there and some of their landscapes look like death.

Power and National Security

Even now, there is a shift in the way we apply raw military power. Military might alone is starting to give way to both international peer pressures and to a nation's relative world economic position. The genesis of this new power, in turn, will be found in education, creativity, leadership, and group shared vision. This will require new accommodations in conflict resolution interventions, and international consensus. We shall all come to understand that the only real security rests in our ability to be able to take both financial and non-financial risks, to focus on the importance of education—as a base for both an able workforce as well as an intelligent voting base—and in our individual, corporate, and national practice of financial and non-financial sustainability.

Economics

In the arena of economics, the practices of one nation impact all others. No longer are there separate markets. Domestic and international marketing become a single art. Stock market fluctuations, interest rate changes, or economic policies in one nation can impact others. Twenty-four-hour world-wide trading exists in many markets today.

The Coming Transition

As the world gets smaller and breaks up into a larger group of freer nations, relationships and relationship-building take on new global importance. This transition will produce stress as well as a sense of well-being. It will also produce profits.

There will be a new "bottom line." The non-financial aspects of life such as relationships, health, life quality, and environmental imbalances will receive greater attention. The entrepreneur of the 21st Century will see that the financial and non-financial aspects of life and living need to be joined in order to optimize goals and raise the quality of living. A new level of awareness will spawn new solutions.

There are some things that are changeless within this envelope of change. Relationships and our need for one another are human needs and do not change. Loving and being loved do not change. The need for trust remains the same. What does change is our awareness of the importance of these values and how we may choose to incorporate them within our life practice.

Solutions

Einstein taught that no complex problem can be solved from within the same state of consciousness that created the problem. Entrepreneurs of the future will need to view rapid change issues and the contexts they create from a new perch—from a place that integrates the non-financial with the financial—from a place that joins the inner with the outer—the domestic with the foreign. They will not only think globally and externally, but will also pull solutions from their intuitive inner selves—places that we shall come to experience as equally global. Instead of creating separation, diversity will be viewed as an asset that produces both financial and intangible gain. Finally, the non-financial will drive the financial. This one insight will be the source of many new options.

As Einstein suggested, we will see problems from a new perspective outside of our issues and create whole new solutions. New thought forms will develop and will create energy fields that will build their own mass and lead us in new directions.

The Emergence of a New Life Practice

What does all this mean? How does one implement this perspective? The Buddhists use the word "practice" as a way of articulating how to express and merge intangible inner qualities within a tangible outer world. Here are some of the ways the new entrepreneurs will bring solutions into their life practices.

The Inner/Outer Awareness

The new entrepreneurs will begin by linking who they are with what it is they do each day. This is done by initially becoming aware of a "personal resonance" with a life quality—a deep and intangible attribute that characterizes an important part of one's life. It is a distinguishing property that holds important value. Once a quality is identified, one can start to relate to what one does and bring a sense of rightness to one's life. By so doing, one is consciously linking that inner quality with an outward activity.

For example, if you were to identify "creativity" as a quality, you soon realize that you can apply this quality as a scientist, engineer, poet, accountant, or street cleaner. The form of the work task does not matter. It is the importance of bringing a core part of yourself (the quality) to bear upon whatever it is you do each day that makes the difference. This "conscious doing" or way of acting brings what began as an awareness of a life quality into everyday life where it can be experienced and get amplified results. This linkage is a source of empowerment and confidence. We all know how vital that can be as we deal with the outer world.

I recall the report of the young Japanese woman news photographer. She had been on the coveted educational fast track in school. She was headed for a career in science. Suddenly, she realized that this was not "her." She gave it all up to become a photographer as a way to express her insights about people. She created award winning images. While she was later killed as a wartime photographer, she followed her life force and achieved meaning from it. Her work is known for its deep visual insight into people and the events that shaped their lives.

My wife and I have a son who struggled at many things until he decided to risk being who he already was—a musician. He now

Qualities

Appreciation — Admiration

Beauty — Brotherhood — Bliss

Compassion — Communion — Connection — Creativity

Detachment

Energy — Enthusiasm — Eternity — Excellence — Entrepreneurial

Freedom — Faith — Friendship

Generosity — Goodwill — Goodness — Gratitude

Harmony — Humor — Humanitarianism

Infinity — Inclusiveness

Joy

Love — Light — Liberation

Order

Patience — Positiveness — Power

Reality — Renewal

Quiet

Service — Serenity — Silence — Simplicity — Synthesis

Trust — Tranquillity — Truth

Understanding

Vitality

Will — Wisdom — Wholeness —Wonder

DEFINITION: A quality is the superior characteristic or property of something. As used within this context, a life quality represents a deep attribute that characterizes an important part of one's life. It is a distinguishing property of life. A quality will correspond to something intangible that is of great value in a life. It will distinguish the whole of something.

Adapted from an uncopyrighted list of qualities developed by the Psychosynthesis Institute of San Franicsco in the 1970s.

has his own sound studio in San Francisco. The struggle is still there. The risks are high. However, he is finding an inner fulfillment and experiencing a real connection between who he is and what he does every day. Not only will the odds for success be better than otherwise, but there is a real sense of rightness about this part of his life.

The Non-financial Balance Sheet

In doing the research for my book *True Wealth*, one of my discoveries was that financial assets and liabilities are, for the most part, non-financially driven. This illustrates Einstein's teaching about looking at issues in new ways in order to achieve workable solutions. When one experiences this, whole new opportunities emerge.

A senior executive, recently fired, came to see me. He was despondent and talked about fear and few financial resources. I spoke of non-financial assets and new options. Clearly we were having two very different conversations, seeing the world from totally different states. I saw the situation as an opportunity, although there was danger present. He saw the situation as a disaster. I could see his options. He couldn't.

Knowing that non-financial resources would generate financial opportunities, I asked him to draw up a non-financial balance sheet as a way to develop new options. He was puzzled. Slowly we worked our way along. He "owned" such non-financial assets as a Ph.D. in physics from a fine university, a deep knowledge of his specialty, and he was well-known in his field. While he thought he had health, I suggested that his overweight condition and total lack of exercise had a liability component to it. When I asked him about friends, he said he had none—another liability. Since he had come to me, I suggested that I be counted as one friend and proceeded to draw a picture of my business network. One name led to another.

To make a longer story short, with non-financial introductions, he started his own consulting company and started to work overseas as well as in the U.S. Within six months, his annual income was in six figures.

In effect, this executive used his non-financial assets (i.e., his experience, friends, contacts, education, and personality) to generate financial assets. Those who have solid relationship skills often end up in successful marketing roles and are able to earn substantial incomes both for themselves and their companies. They intuit the importance of building relationships as the platform for selling. This same capability can also be directed to making a marriage work—another non-financial asset and resource.

This principle can also be applied to non-profit organizations. Vincent Lane, chairman of the Chicago Housing Authority, had a keen insight that may well transform the inner city. After visiting a kibbutz, he experienced how the Israelis addressed the harsh realities of living in danger. He related these conditions to those within his inner city environment: gang wars, difficult living conditions, hopelessness. He saw how differently both groups handled their crises. The kibbutz held shared visions of self-contained economic and community sustainability, while the inner-city public housing developments in America fed on despair, separateness, and dependency upon public sector handouts.

His insight? Apply the kibbutz community ideals—shared vision, universal equality, and group process (a wholly non-financial piece)—to create cottage industries that could offer economic sustainability free of public sector support. He is hoping to start with two test sites within Chicago. Given success there, these could easily become models that could transform other inner cities without large infusions of taxpayers' money. The non-financial will have become the source input for both a financial (and non-financial) turn-around.

This works for companies, too. Their non-financial balance sheet assets (like a healthy corporate culture, sound behavioral practices, good market relationships) are essential—perhaps even pivotal—to their financial well being. Conversely, their potential non-financial liabilities (greed, arrogance, overconfidence, failure to positively make use of employee diversity) are often at the core of their failures.

Individually, the non-financial can also drive the financial. Winston Churchill used his enormous non-financial leadership capabilities to build a career. Bill Cosby and Bob Hope built successful businesses around their non-financial ability to bring laughter and joy to people. World-class athletes have often translated their non-financial sporting skills into financial resources.

The Entrepreneur of the Future

We have all been somewhat aware of our non-financial abundance. *The great difference is that the entrepreneurs of the future will do this purposefully and consciously.* They will focus upon relationships, education, health issues, and personal skills to build financial resources or add further to their non-financial assets. They will, in effect, create a totally new awareness of themselves and their world from which to solve complex issues. They will approach problems in new ways. They will have worked from within a new state of awareness quite removed from the outer circumstances to better address these issues.

They will not only increase their awareness of their inner resources, but they will nurture them. They will see relationship-building, health, friendships, and their connections between who they are and what it is they do each day as a way to bring a sense of congruence into their lives, their families, and their companies. They will do this in parallel with all the financial housekeeping they already do. Now, the two will be joined.

Globally, non-financial activities have enormous financial impacts, too. Non-financial technologies such as semiconductors, bio-technology, and lasers have hatched whole new industries and jobs, increased the tax base, and created millionaires along the way. Conversely, such non-financial liabilities as high debt, whether government, corporate, or individual, will eventually have a serious financial impact on interest rates, currency valuations, and inflation—to name just a few. High debt can also adversely spawn non-financial impacts on our individual, corporate and national health, educational fitness (and thus our ability to compete in business), and the quality of the environment (witness the old Soviet Union)—to mention but three.

Here in the USA we often fail to address our deteriorating environment. We deny that acid rain is harmful, to the dismay of our Canadian neighbors. We deny that the ozone layer is being damaged because changes in our habits may hurt certain business interests. At the same time, the Japanese see this non-financial deterioration of the physical environment as a job-creating opportunity and rush to create and acquire whole new technologies and businesses to address these problems. They see such activities as emerging opportunities.

We tend to separate the financial from the non-financial when, in fact, they are joined. The extent of our awareness of this financial/non-financial linkage will shape how we address such issues. The new entrepreneur will see the linkage between the two and act on these insights.

The concept of non-financial risk-taking will emerge. Avoiding risks in relationships, for example, can have large financial impacts, as anyone who has gone through a divorce can attest. Smoking or drug use can have a non-financial impact in illness or death. Conversely, taking risks to improve a marriage or other relationship can have powerful positive impacts. Herein lies a paradox: Avoiding a risk is often the greater risk.

Community and Competition

The new entrepreneur will become competitively aware that we naturally act "separately together" despite all the boundaries we create. He/she will come to understand that seeming independence is really "cooperative inter-dependence". Former competitors are having to cooperate as a way to be fully competitive. This seeming inconsistency is best explained by noting that an awareness of a new type of working community is forming. Instead of acting alone, we are now seeing companies acting together as a way to optimize their diversity and capabilities. We saw this first on a larger scale in post World War II Japan. Competitors saw more power in working financially and non-financially together as a way to rebuild their devastated economy. We see it here and now with Apple, Motorola, and IBM joining to create new computer components. We also see this in massive cross licensing agreements and the creation of large trading blocks like that of the European Community.

We are not optimized alone. Yet, we have a need to be separate. The new entrepreneur will create ways to act separately in tune with others.

Money

For most of us, money is thought of as "the" resource of choice. Many of us, therefore, postpone attention to family, health, and the development of our own non-business selves, until we collect "enough" of it. Thus, we separate money from the rest of our lives instead of using it as a resource to nurture our whole selves.

Money will come to be seen merely as one resource among many rather than an end point or as a single gauge for success. It will be "a part of" rather than "apart from" the rest of our lives.

Vision Holding

Action follows thought. Conscious individual and shared visions will determine outcomes. As an adjunct to all of the above, the entrepreneur of the future will hold a clear foresight—a vision.

Some have been doing this all the while—such as in sports. A golfer sees the ball go into the hole before he hits it. Entrepreneurs often envision a whole company before they form it. Inventors see their creation working as a first step in the invention process.

When this precognition is shared by others, group goals (a grounded form of vision) are achieved with greater ease and assurance, as if by magic.

We have all seen this phenomenon when we were in high school and met fellow students who "knew" they wanted to become a doctor, lawyer, engineer, poet, or artist! I had no such vision myself and I envied those who did, for they went directly about their task. We also saw the reverse of this in friends who followed what their mother or father did because that path seemed easier or because that was their parents' wish. All too often, their lives became hollow and they lost all contact with who they really were.

Holding a vision is an essential step in following one's passion.

Summary

These insights may not insure outright success, but they certainly will enhance the odds toward working with rapid change in any field. With the emergence of free nations from the former Communist block and with the development of Asia, South America, and Africa, the next several decades may prove to be the most economically prosperous period in world history. The new entrepreneur will grasp—and optimize—this opportunity by making it his/her practice to implement these and other insights, tools, and ways of being.

The Chinese define crisis as a dangerous opportunity. Change inherently offers uncertainty and thus holds the potential for danger. From a place of introspection, by joining the financial with the non-financial, by linking who a person is with what he/she does, by holding and sharing a vision, the 21st Century entrepreneurs will see opportunity within the envelope of danger created by change. This will bring passion into their lives and help them to be more fully alive.

Can we ask for more?

Bill Sechrest
is an attorney currently practicing
with Winstead, Sechrest & Minick,
a Texas-based law firm he founded.
With offices in Dallas, Houston,
Austin, and Washington, DC, the firm employs about five hundred people
with annual revenues of approximately $50 million. Until recently, Sechrest
served as managing partner of the firm which has one of the largest real
estate practices in Texas.

He is also a member of the Board of Directors of the World Business
Academy, Esalen, and the Dallas Institute of Humanities. Receiving his
undergraduate degree in Economics at Stanford University, Bill has
authored one book, *The Creation of Joe Bankhead* and is currently working
on a second book, *The Future History of Economics*, of which this article
is one chapter.

16

Revisioning Economics®
(A Systems Approach)

William B. Sechrest

In the late 1970s, our law firm was growing rapidly, in large part due to an increasing real estate practice. The heyday of rapid property appreciation and tax shelter deals of the early 1980s added to our workload as we expanded our practice. When the real estate crash occurred in the late 1980s, our practice expanded to serve savings and loans as well as banks, who subsequently fell upon their own difficult times.

Our clients included such institutions as MBank and First Interstate—over 100 banks and savings and loans, many of which failed. Watching all this chaos, seemingly created by outside forces beyond the control of our clients, caused me to look beyond the immediate cause-effect rationale and examine what underlying assumptions were driving this craziness.

This personal inquiry launched me into a project of enormous magnitude—my own examination of the thinking behind our economic system. The following is a summary of what I have learned thus far, based upon a book I am writing on this subject.

****

The global economy is not a pretty sight. Our planet earth is evidencing severe environmental imbalance, suffering from the strains of constant development. Meanwhile, over one billion people are existing below poverty level and a majority of countries are undeveloped. The currencies of many countries cannot communicate, having lost their credibility. For those interested in the global economy, it is a challenge to find solutions to these imbalances. Certainly, many attempts have been made. But the gaps between the "haves" and the "have nots," the "developed" and the "undeveloped" countries, and the "hard" and "soft" currencies continue to widen.

Why is this so? The answer resides in a fundamental deficiency existing in our old economic models. Based upon a belief system that emphasizes detachment, separation, and lack, results from these models can only produce more of the same. A "revisioning" of economics and measurements applicable to economics is necessary if our global economy and its sub-economics are to survive, much less thrive and prosper. Similarly, if the new entrepreneurs are to survive and prosper, they must understand this fundamental deficiency in the classic economic model and confirm for themselves that separation, detachment, and lack are an outgrowth of the model itself. A new economic model is needed.

The World of Classical Sciences

The basis of our old economic models is a belief system that emanates from the work of Galileo and Newton and their method of measurement. With the development of optics (primarily the telescope) and the development of timepieces (primarily the pendulum clock), there was an ability to measure the mechanics of the universe. Scientists like Galileo and Newton assumed the role of observers observing the unfolding of a mechanical universe. These scientists and their successors considered themselves separated from the universe. They recorded their findings of what appeared to be a detached, objective reality as new technology produced exceedingly refined methods of measurements. The conclusion of classical science was that the universe exhibited a clockwork mechanism that unfolded in deterministic ways, unaffected by man and woman whose only roles were to observe it and attempt to predict its deterministic outcome. The result has been a scientific revolution that not only substituted the sun for the earth as the center of our solar system, but also removed woman and man from the center of the universe, leaving them with feelings of alienation and a continuing need to compete for survival.

Classical Economics

The classical economic model arose during a time when classical science thrived. Adam Smith imparted his "invisible hand" to the classical equation, showing that, because of enlightened self-interest, the supply and demand of goods and services would always express itself at a perfect *equilibrium* price. In a universe where everything was in balance and unfolding in a classical, clockwork style, it was only natural to speak of supply and demand unfolding in a similar matter. "The market is always right" became the slogan. The classical economist believed in a market that functioned in perfect equilibrium, a mindset that still prevails today.

The Study of Lack

Of course, if you were existing in a deterministic universe where everything proceeded in a clockwork fashion in perfect equilibrium, and your role was simply to observe this clockwork functioning as a separate, detached observer, you would soon be forced to assume that only a limited amount of resources existed in this universe. This is exactly what classical economics presumed as evidenced by the following definition of economics:

> Economics is "the study of how people and society
> choose to employ **scarce resources**."
> —*Paul Samuelson and William D. Wordhaus,*
> *Economics, 12th edition. (Emphasis added.)*

Scarcity and lack are the underlying assumptions upon which classical economic theory is based. The classical supply-and-demand curve is therefore based upon the initial condition that, given only a certain amount of resources, buyers and sellers will ultimately arrive at an efficient allocation of these resources through enlightened self-interest and an equilibrium pricing mechanism. Given this assumption, is it any wonder that competition for those resources would result in a "survival of the fittest" mentality and the ever-widening gaps mentioned?

A Transition

When one considers the ever-widening gap between the "haves" and the "have nots" and the current environmental concerns, it is difficult to remain optimistic, particularly if the classical economic model continues to be accepted as describing economic reality. Fortunately, modern science now shows that the classical economic model's underlying assumptions of scarcity and lack are suspect. There are other models that may be more accurate. In other words, something has happened to the clockwork model of classical science upon which classical economics has been based. While classical science proceeded with its reductionistic approach (and still does so today), the fields of quantum mechanics and thermodynamics were born. What has been discovered is that the mechanics of the classical model cannot explain the actions occurring in these quantum and thermodynamic worlds. Hence, a new model of reality that accommodates these differences is necessary.

Lessons from Quantum Mechanics

Spawned from the continual quest of classical science to more precisely measure the primary substance of the universe, the molecule, the atom, the proton, the neutron, the electron, the photon, and the quark were discovered. The behaviors of these subatomic particles were found to be erratic and uncertain. Furthermore, in a four-dimensional world of space and time, light was found to bend and time and space were found to collapse at light speed (186,242 miles per second). Even more curious, light itself was found, under certain conditions, to be particle-like in nature and, under other conditions, wave-like in nature. It was a weird world—quantum weirdness—bearing many startling discoveries, the most radical of which was the principle of complementarity discovered by Niels Bohr, the dean of quantum mechanics.

What Bohr's principle of complementarity did was place the observer in something other than a detached, observing mode. What Bohr discovered was that how the universe appeared to any particular observer was a function of the method of measurement the observer adopted. There may indeed be a separate, detached universe but, if indeed it is, the observer could only obtain knowledge of that part of the universe as reflected by his or her measuring devices. Stated in another way, different methods of measurement provided different ways of understanding the universe. Utilizing one set of measuring devices, light would exhibit particle-like characteristics while, at the same time, utilizing a second set of measuring devices, light would exhibit wave-like characteristics.

All of a sudden, with Bohr's principle of complementarity, science inserted man and woman into a participating role. However, for Bohr, this participatory involvement stopped at the boundaries of measurement. To be sure, one set of measurements may produce one result, and another set of measurements may produce another result. Nevertheless, the disparities lay in the methods of measurement, not in the objective reality of the universe. Bohr only opened the door to our participation in the universe half way. This door was pushed wide open approximately fifty years later through developments in another field of science, the world of thermodynamics.

Learnings from Thermodynamics

Space does not permit a detailed analysis of the thermo-dynamic model, other than to say that the basic underlying assumption upon which the first and second laws of thermodynamics were based was that all thermodynamic systems were isolated systems. However, with the development of exceedingly precise measuring tools, it has been found that few, if any, isolated systems exist. In fact, the only isolated system that may exist is the universe itself and that is problematic.

Nobel Prize winner, Ilya Prigogine (1976), discovered that most thermodynamic systems are open systems influenced by outside sources. Each system only has a tendency toward an equilibrium state as long as the initial conditions upon which that system is based do not change. When the initial conditions upon which a system is based do change, the system will change.

Utilizing the work of Prigogine and others, new fields of science in the form of systems theory and chaos theory have developed. What these new models show is that each system has a sensitive dependence on initial conditions. What this means for the universe, for the planet earth, and for all natural and man-made systems residing therein is that, as initial conditions of any system change, the universe, the earth, and all natural and man-made systems within it will change. Hence, whereas Niels Bohr through his principle of complementarity placed the observer in a participating role when dealing with measurement, Prigogine showed that the observer can also cause changes to the initial conditions of any system, thereby causing changes in the system and all systems to which it relates.

How does all this affect the new entrepreneur? How does this figure into a new economic model? The answers lie in how we measure. Economic and monetary systems involve measurement. We, as participants, are involved, not only in the act of "measurement," but also in the actions being measured.

A Function of Measurement

Measuring devices have advanced dramatically since the discovery of the telescope and the pendulum clock. Today we are debating the value of the superconducting super collider and we have telescopes and microscopes that explore the infinite abundance of space and the infinite combinations of subatomic particles. Could it be that the universe appears to be only that which we are capable of measuring?

Certainly, it is understandable that Galileo, Newton, and a string of classical scientists would think of the universe as detached and separate, containing limited resources, if what they believed they were doing was measuring the universe, much like you measure a piece of cloth. (Clearly, the cloth will only produce a certain number of suits.) But as classical science advanced, so did the technology that it produced. And with this technological advance has come exceedingly sophisticated methods of measurement.

I submit that what these new measuring devices are now showing is a universe that is interconnected with all systems of life that has the capability of producing unlimited resources. Entrepreneurs who can accept this premise will have a much easier time of planning their abundant future!

Crossing Over Is Difficult

Now, of course, for those of us schooled in classical thought and its cause-effect equations, crossing over to this new perspective of the universe is difficult. Einstein found this transition too difficult. His response was: "God does not play dice."

Bohr also found the transition difficult, admitting to the subjective, participating nature of the act of measurement, but not of the universe.

Yet it appears that many scientists are willing to proceed beyond Einstein and Bohr. Prigogine's ever-expanding work with dissipative systems indicates that the universe and each system within it are open, interconnected elements of a reality that changes as each system changes. Hence, when man/woman as a collective system of human life negatively impacts the environmental system known as planet earth, planet earth adjusts with changing weather patterns that cause life to adjust. The result is a model of the universe that pictures both the universe and all life within it as an interconnected web of systems, each having a sensitive dependence on initial conditions.

As we approach the 21st Century, classical science has made the quantum leap of accepting both quantum mechanics and systems theory as "real." Classical economics, on the other hand, continues to be mired in its old model of separation, detachment, and lack. What science now tells us is that the old economic model is no longer valid for all situations. A new model, one based on systems theory, is needed. Entrepreneurs who want to work with this new model will need to understand what systems are and how they operate.

What Is A System

In its simplest form, a system is a regularly interacting or interconnected group of items forming a unified whole. Clearly, this interacting or interconnected characteristic is representative of the universe. With its constituent groups of quarks, atoms, molecules, double helix, cells, organisms, planets, animals, man and woman, man-made products, man-made systems, and stars, it is not difficult to conceive of the universe as an interconnected group of diverse, but interacting, systems. And, clearly, this interacting or interconnected characteristic is also representative of any economy when the economy is considered as a whole with its constituent group of producers, suppliers, consumers, laborers, service providers, etc. Certainly, ever-expanding technology in the form of aerospace, television, computers, and the like emphasizes this interconnectedness daily.

Every system has an interconnecting link with every other system. As one system changes, all other systems respond to that change and, as all other systems respond to that change, the initial system which initiated the change responds to the subsequent changes. Simply stated, a system has a sensitive dependence on initial conditions such that, when the initial conditions of one system change, all systems will adjust to that change and in doing so, will force the initial system to further adjust.

The Free Market

If you envision a free market where buyers and sellers gather with their products and services, it soon becomes apparent that each individual who buys or sells affects the market. The market establishes prices based upon these activities. However, in a market where buyers buy, sellers sell, and market prices are established, a complementary action is also occurring. As the market "feeds back" its prices to the market participants, each market participant adjusts his or her buying or selling actions. Therefore, if prices of services continue to rise, the buyers of those services may ultimately not buy. Conversely, if prices for products continue to fall, the sellers of those products may take those products off the market. There is a complementary action (feedback) between the market and its participants. The market and its participants constitute a system!

What I just described assumes a "free market" in which buyers and sellers can buy and sell in the marketplace free of any intervening rules and regulations. To be sure, the greater the intervening force, the less "free" will be the market. Nevertheless, unless buying and selling are strictly prohibited or minutely controlled, the complementary/feedback action of the market and its participants will always exist. And any intervening changes in rules and regulations will simply cause the market participants to adjust their actions in buying and selling accordingly, assuming these changes do not affect the initial conditions upon which the market relies.

Under these circumstances, the classical economic model appears to work. In fact, if prices established by the interweaving of supply and demand are depicted on a graph showing time/price differentials, the result will be an appearance of a stable pricing structure. Similarly, graphs depicting money supply and interest rates will also reflect an appearance of a stable monetary system. Indeed, based upon an analysis of these graphs, it would be easy to conclude that money supply and interest rate mechanics control economic stability.

But this conclusion appears true *only if the initial conditions upon which the free market is based remain stable.* If, to the contrary:

- the rules and regulations governing the market are constantly changing (e.g., incessant monetary or tax policy changes)
- the market experiences dramatic, climatic changes (e.g., hurricanes, typhoons, earthquakes, global cooling or heating) or
- the market experiences severe, structural changes (e.g., the removal of gold as support for the U.S. dollar, the fall of Communism, the development of new technologies such as the computer and laser technology, the move from separate nationalistic economies to a global economy),

then the market may appear very chaotic, yielding surprising and unpredictable results. Systems theory tells us why this is so with one simple phrase: **a sensitive dependence on initial conditions.** A combination of any two or more of these changes will only compound the apparent chaos.

The Past Twenty Years

Initial conditions have not changed many times in history to such an extent as to cause these chaotic conditions in the marketplace. However, during the past twenty years there have been at least three occurrences that equate to changes in initial conditions, each appearing in the early 1970s. Each has great significance.

The first occurrence (occurring from 1971-1973) involved withdrawing gold as support for the United States dollar. Before this action, the entire monetary system of the free world had become dependent on the U.S. dollar being valued based upon $35 per ounce of gold. When gold was withdrawn as the initial condition upon which the international monetary system was based, each currency became dependent on the full faith and credit of its issuer.

The second occurrence involved the advent of the money market fund. The first money market fund appeared in 1971. At that time, banks and savings and loans were limited in the amount of interest they could pay on deposits; money market funds were subject to no limitations. The combination of a withdrawing of gold as support for the U.S. dollar and the advent of the money market fund changed the initial conditions upon which the United States banking and savings and loan system relied.

The third occurrence involved the development of the computer, specifically the personal computer. The computer has changed the initial conditions upon which our social system has been structured.

Time Delays

The results of the preceding three occurrences have been the excesses of the 1980s and the economic turmoil of the 1990s. How could these changes, which occurred in the early 1970s, still be expressing themselves today? The answer lies in time delays.

Anyone who has taken a shower has undoubtedly experienced time delays. It takes a period of time from the moment of the turning of the hot or cold water valves before the water flows at the desired temperature. For the person in the shower, it can be a fitful experience of too hot—then too cold—then too hot—and so on. Adjustments to the hot and cold valves take time to express themselves. Similarly, changes in the initial conditions upon which a system relies take their time in expressing themselves within the system. Because of time delays, the changes that occurred in the early 1970s continue to express themselves today.

A New Economic Model

Somehow, economics must superimpose a systems model over the old classical model. This new model must recognize not only the sensitive dependence on initial conditions, but also a number of other elements including the interconnectedness and linkage of all systems. Through the use of exceedingly sophisticated measuring devices, there must be a recognition of what initial conditions are and how changing initial conditions can cause not only system adjustments that lead to greater productivity and abundance, but also system adjustments that lead to chaos. There must also be an understanding of the creative process that initiates change and the historical bias that fears change. Fortunately, at the same time as new technology in the form of computers and ever advancing laser technology has caused changes in initial conditions, it has also produced new methods of measurement that can explore and understand the impact of change. The only element missing is a new economic model that understands systems and their interconnectedness.

Conclusion

Presenting a new systems model is beyond the scope of this paper. Ultimately, a new economic model based upon systems theory will be developed. (I should soon have a book published on this topic that will present a possible model.) Ultimately, each of us will have to adjust our mindset about economics. There is no reason for one billion people to live in poverty or for our natural environment to be polluted in a never ending quest to "grow out" of our economic problems. We simply need to revision our global economy as a global economic system having a sensitive dependence on initial conditions. And, we need to gain a better understanding of what these initial conditions are. Once these two steps are taken, we will be on the road to establishing a new economic model based on unity, interconnectedness and abundance, rather than on separation, detachment, and lack. Out of the new economic model will come solutions that will continually narrow, rather than widen, the existing economic gaps between the "haves" and the "have nots." Out of the new economic model will come a new definition of economics: one that involves "the study of the abundance of available resources and their efficient, environmentally responsible allocation."

® *William B. Sechrest*

Nicholas P. LiVolsi
is founder and co-director of the
World Trust, a non-profit organization facilitating a process for ex-
panding consciousness and evolving common vision around social,
economic, and environmental issues. Prior to forming the World Trust in
1987, LiVolsi spent ten years with American Express in several marketing
and managerial positions, and was president of NPL Associates, a
marketing/communications company.

This essay was written in collaboration with Jane Bell and Ronnie
Butler, also co-directors of the World Trust. Bell served as executive director
of the San Francisco Fashion Institute, has an extensive background in sales
and marketing, and is co-founder of InPartnership, a company providing
collaborative opportunities between non-traditional resources and businesses. Butler is a PhD candidate in the field of transformative learning and
has an expansive background as an entrepreneur, a financial manager,
and a community activist.

17

A Time For Collaboration

Nicholas P. LiVolsi

Being a system of relationships, life on earth must maintain a balance between man-made and natural environments to sustain itself. Underlying this balance are many evolving societal, economic, and ecological shifts such as democracy, ethnic and nationalist fragmentation, open markets, a global economy, and concern for adverse trends such as overpopulation and climate change. Ultimately, long-term preservation of life will depend upon evolving sustainable ways of integrating these social, economic, and ecological systems. This will involve redirecting enormous amounts of resources for creating systems and institutions that support an integrated process of development. For this to happen, a new kind of entrepreneurial spirit and leadership is crucial: a leadership inclusive of everyone in terms of their own lives and agendas, and supported by a new business- and public-spirit toward local and global community, personal responsibility and power, and universal actions needed to sustain societal, economic, and environmental health.

Community

If mankind is to evolve with integrity, we need to focus our energies on integration. This requires envisioning a new life, exploring new consciousness, healing old wounds, and implementing holistic approaches to personal, communal, and global living. The entrepreneurs of the 21st Century will have a very different intention than that of their 20th Century counterparts. As we collectively move into the future, we need to create cohesion in our lives to build a sustainable Community. Community with a capital "C" is defined for our discussion as all who come together in recognition and celebration of diversity but functioning and understanding as one entity. Community with a small "c" is used to identify any group of people that come together based upon common identity, interest, shared geography, backgrounds or experience, skills, etc. Both communities represent the arenas in which we will be able to achieve a sustainable social, economic, and environmental future. As the 21st Century entrepreneurs spring to life they will serve as the visionaries, explorers, healers, and implementors of a new consciousness around Community and communities. Their activities will be designed to expand consciousness and instill a new Community spirit within all areas of human endeavor.

By organizing their activities around Community, entrepreneurs in the 21st Century will be dealing with the most opportunistic arena for social and economic development. By focusing on building Community via collaborative ventures, they will change the relationship dynamics between themselves and the evolving economic system. Authentic collaborations will be the entrepreneurial challenge in the 21st Century.

To define the dynamics of an authentic collaborative relationship I use the definition given in *Collaboration: What Makes it Work, A Review of Research Literature on Factors Influencing Successful Collaborations* by Paul W. Mattessich, PhD and Barbara R. Monsey, MPH (Wilder Research Center/Wilder's Community Collaboration Venture, Amhurst H. Wilder Foundation), which is:

> a mutually beneficial and well-defined relationship
> entered into by two or more organizations (persons) to achieve common goals. The relationship

includes a commitment to: a definition of mutual relationships and goals; a jointly developed structure and shared responsibility; mutual authority and accountability for success; and sharing of resources and rewards.

To achieve a sustainable future, this collaborative dynamic will need to occur in all areas and at all levels of human activity. Bringing collaboration into every aspect of our lives is the basis of the 21st Century entrepreneurial spirit. It is the next step in the human, social, and economic evolutionary process.

Shifting Control

The path to economic integration and sustainability will create new opportunities since it requires shifting the control of business/community enterprises from ownership to collaboration. Ownership will be repositioned as merely the stakeholder group providing the capital investment for an appropriate financial return. The premier power position of ownership within a 20th Century business paradigm is not compatible with creating an integrated economic system in the 21st Century. The buying and merging frenzy of the 1980s witnessed the impact of having ownership control the economic process. The short-term financial benefits received by a few came at too large a cost and with too many long-term structural problems now being borne by many.

United Airlines provides one of the best examples where too much ownership almost proved fatal. During the first half of the 1980s, United purchased a hotel chain, a major car rental company, and other travel businesses in an attempt to become the paramount commercial force within the travel industry. Its publicly stated goal was to provide the fullest range of travel services to its customers. What United did was to take on such a large debt that it almost went into a nose dive. To regain its solvency it quickly sold off its hotel and car rental subsidiaries and began concentrating on its core business. If you talk to any major company in the travel industry today, they will tell you that they are concentrating on their core business. This does not mean they are not forming alliances and new collaborative ventures. United Airlines was able to achieve its 1980 goals through collaborative agreements with its hotel and car rental industry partners. This was only one of the many examples during the 1980s that showed the fallacy of ownership being the most effective and appropriate base for controlling commercial enterprises. The 21st Century entrepreneurs will become essential players for shifting control of commercial ventures to all stakeholders via the collaborative process.

Shifting Consciousness

The process of collaboration is more than just a learned skill. It is a shifting of consciousness. I found this to be true for me in developing and expanding the vision of the World Trust, a non-profit organization established to expand consciousness around Community. In order for the World Trust to achieve its stated mission, it had to become a collaborative process. Collaboration tested our own willingness to share and expand. For my associates and me, it took being aware of our own agendas in order to be clear about creating a shared agenda. Collaboration is like any other consciousness; the more you use it, the more comfortable you are living within it.

One of the basic insights we discovered in developing our own collaborative process is that we are always in collaboration with other individuals and groups within our communities. For the most part, we are unconscious of the ways we affect our communities on a daily basis. By becoming more conscious, we can more effectively begin to build the communities and lives we want. We can consciously integrate our "community-self" within ourselves and collectively build economic systems that serve our common good. We actually have two selves: the individual self, with which we are all too familiar, and our "community-self." The "community-self" can only be experienced in community. These two self-identities are not mutually exclusive. They should be looked at as different aspects of the total person. We can say that the 21st Century entrepreneurs will be integrating their individual and communal selves within the collaborative ventures they manifest.

Therefore, unlike the 20th Century entrepreneurs, the new entrepreneurs will no longer be renegade thinkers or corporate raiders. They will no longer operate privately, protected from public scrutiny. They will be functioning within a public consensus.

The entrepreneurs of the 21st Century will combine the social activism of the 1960s with the spiritual awakening of the 1990s—a combination of spirit and community. These new entrepreneurs will bring a strong sense of ethics along with a vision that transcends the boundaries of ownership and their own personal agendas. They will be creative thinkers who are not as driven by desire for personal success as by their vision to affect something greater than their own domain. They will recognize that to have a thriving venture it must fit into a healthy economic community framework. The focus of the entrepreneurial energy is to foster a safe place for surrendering to a collective process. The new entrepreneurs will create the larger arenas for everyone to participate in the developing economic system that serves both individual and collective agendas. In collaboration, personal agendas are not superseded; they are incorporated. Personal agendas are used to *build* the collaboration. The new entrepreneurs' primary focus will be to facilitate the co-creation of sustainable, ever-expanding arenas via an inclusive and collaborative process. This will require expanding our individual and collective ability to trust.

The new entrepreneurial spirit will be pursued on many paths, all of which will offer personal growth and integration, expanded consciousness, and commensurate financial rewards. The 21st Century entrepreneurs will be balancing both new and old paradigms for business and Community development. They will be the new pioneers, building a new economic system within the new frontier of Community. For me, this frontier represents the greatest challenge to mankind because it requires expanding our consciousness towards integration. What is reassuring about this new entrepreneurial spirit is that it resides in all of us. It is the spirit of survival that seeks to insure that life as we know it will persist on this planet. In order for us to nurture this 21st Century entrepreneurial spirit within, we must gain our own understanding that we are truly interconnected and bear an individual and collective responsibility to the whole. We must know that anything we create has to support the deep healing necessary to promote global and local solutions towards creating global health. The value of vision in creating the collective energy needed for healing our social, economic, and environmental systems cannot take place if we are not witnessing and simultaneously working on our own internal dynamics. If our intention is clear, and we recognize and honor the shifts of consciousness that will inevitably occur from this new entrepreneurial spirit, we will authentically empower ourselves. From a place of willingness to suspend our previously held methodologies and ideas, we can experience the paradigm shifts that will allow us to be more fully engaged in an abundant existence which supports us all.

This shift in consciousness around business begins with a change in our mindset around wealth and the role of money—a shift from wealth based in scarcity to that of one based in abundance; the role of money from being an end in itself to becoming an energy source serving the pursuits of self-knowledge and the collaborative process for building a sustainable future.

Now, and in the future, 21st Century entrepreneurs are an evolving group of people who have undergone their own shift in consciousness around money, business, and community. Business, for them, becomes an economic discipline engaging all members in the community in the process of building Community. For the 21st Century entrepreneurs, this paradigm shift may come quickly through a transformative incident in their life, or gradually over time as they search for a larger life vision. Either way this personal paradigm shift seems to be a prerequisite before it can be collectively manifested.

A personal shift in consciousness can occur from a single incident, as in the case of Franklin A. Reece, III, a friend and a member of the World Trust Board of Directors. Frank heads up a competitive, fast-growing communications company which operates on the leading edge of its field. He is a visionary business thinker, an effective manager, and a leader in the business community. Frank is the quintessential entrepreneur who is creative in his business approach and focused on his quarterly goals which are well planned in advance. As a good corporate citizen, he has always involved himself and his company in a number of community and philanthropic activities. Frank is recognized by his peers and others as a successful business leader, a concerned citizen, and caring family man.

The incident that shifted Frank from a 20th Century to a 21st Century entrepreneur occurred while he was returning home from a business trip. In 1991, Frank experienced a severe chest pain upon landing at Logan Airport in Boston. The pain became so intense that instead of going home he drove directly to the nearest hospital. Arriving at the hospital, things went from bad to worse and by the time his wife arrived, our successful 20th Century entrepreneur's heart had stopped. Somehow Frank was able to hear his wife calling him. Who knows exactly how, but Frank returned to see his loving wife by his side and to finish his life's work. This near-death experience shifted his consciousness. He started looking not only at what got him into the hospital but to what greater purpose he could apply his life. His focus changed from seeing his company and himself as merely being successful in today's competitive arena to being an active force in implementing a new business/community conciousness.

My Own Story

Not everyone needs to have a near-death experience to expand their consciousness. My own transition came slowly over an eight-year period after I left the corporate world and started my own company. After ten years with American Express, I knew staying any longer and moving up the corporate ladder would require sacrificing too much of my own inner creative force. So, I left American Express to start my own business. At first I felt that being a successful entrepreneur and having my own company would satisfy all of my financial and creative needs. In truth, I was looking for a way to put greater meaning into my life and work, though I did not know it. I have always been able to leverage out simple marketing opportunities to connect with larger causes or issues. I had the fortunate experience, while working with American Express, to develop my skills in creating cause-marketing programs. It was natural for me to see how things can be expanded to produce multiple results for the same dollars spent. What I came to appreciate later was that I had a natural desire to expand the vision of whatever I did and to seek collaboration with like-minded people. I had always prided myself on creating a safe place for people to work and allowing them to take the risks needed to create and grow. It was through this desire for even greater connection and greater creative energy that I came to realize that owning my own marketing company was still not satisfying my deeper yearnings.

In 1987, I found myself asking the question: How are strategies created around global issues? This began a two-and-a-half-year inquiry into the strategic thinking around these issues. From this process of inquiry I found myself propelled from within—searching for a way that I, as an individual, could play a part. I had discussions with some of the leading economists, environmentalists, academicians, and business and governmental leaders around the process of evolving global strategies. It quickly became apparent that economics played a key role and that some sort of collective business leadership would be needed. As soon as I grasped the scope of my inquiry I knew it had to involve everyone in some form or another. Strategy around global issues is not something that is going to be done by any one group or groups of people no matter how powerful or well-connected they may be; nor is it going to be resolved by some new technological breakthrough. Technology can assist but it cannot, by itself, lead to solutions.

As I continued exploring ways to participate, I began to see the personal implications being raised for me. The further I ventured into this unknown realm, the more I was forced to look at my personal issues—the issues of trust, control, and my need to know my own agenda. I had to learn to trust my own instincts, to look at how to let go of control (Who can control global issues?), and to decide what I needed or wanted to get out of this effort. Over the course of the last six years these three issues kept coming up in varying forms for me to evaluate. This led me to the realization that, in order to continue being engaged in this pursuit, I must always be in a process of healing myself; evolving my own vision of life and being clear as to how I want to participate. This journey forces me to look at my own fragmentation and how it impacts my life and those around me. It is a continual reminder for me to be in a process of healing myself before I attempt to heal those around me. By breaking through my own fragmentation I am able to expand my consciousness. By expanding my consciousness, I am able to effectively participate in the collective process of integration. This realization did not come easy. My reward is personal growth and evolution. Both Frank and I are discovering the need to validate a new entrepreneurial spirit which fosters an expanded consciousness supporting a vision around social, economic, and environmental integration.

Common Vision

An essential element in the collective process of expanding consciousness is creating common vision. Why vision plays such an important role demands deeper probing.

Modern science is now beginning to confirm that we are not mere observers of a reality that just happens to us. The images we hold, what we choose to think, and how we feel about the future has a great deal to do with the experience we create in the present—the way we imagine possibilities expands or contracts our reality.

Certainly there are two ways we can choose to create our present and our future: unconsciously or consciously, irresponsibly or responsibly, carelessly or lovingly. When we operate unconsciously, we have relinquished our responsibility to forces outside ourselves and we become victims overwhelmed by an environment of diminishing resources and lives that are seen as unfulfilled and subject to stimuli beyond our control. We feel we have no power to affect any sustainable long-term change personally, much less globally. We undermine the power of vision because we use it reactively and not creatively. We undermine our individual impact on global issues when we look externally for solutions before looking internally. We fail to make the connection between our personal vision of physical, emotional, and spiritual health, and our collective global vision of health and integration.

When we create a future from conscious and fully-empowered vision we begin to recognize that we are limited only by our own lack of understanding and self-knowledge. When we tap into and trust our internal resources and processes we begin to create vision which connects us to new ways of living. By allowing inner vision to guide the outer vision, we begin, in the words of Joseph Campbell, "to follow our bliss." Here is were we find greatness, authenticity, and creative abundance. Indeed, nothing external prevents us from living lives that are fulfilling when challenges are recognized as teachings which allow us to fully explore greater and greater alternatives. It's here that we find the tools needed to deepen continued exploration both within and without.

One of the primary roles of the 21st Century entrepreneurs is to create the safe space for creating common vision and managing change. This takes new economic frameworks that support the material needs of community members to develop and implement their own and their community's agendas.

Trust

Here is where the issue of trust comes into play. To be involved with a process of creating common vision and authentic collaborations we must be vulnerable to change. To be vulnerable to change we have to trust ourselves and each other. To do this we must feel and be safe. 21st Century entrepreneurs must value the empowerment of others as their highest goal. They will do this by creating safe places for people to be vulnerable to change, to trust each other and be together in a collaborative dynamic for creating healthy Community and communities.

Twenty-first century entrepreneurs *first apply their skills to empowering themselves.* They begin to look at their own vision and actions. They explore, heal, and implement their own process of integration as the first step to envisioning, exploring, healing, and implementing an external integration.

Trust is the driving force behind change. In today's business climate, trust is losing the battle. Our corporations, one of our most important societal assets, seem to work against people trusting each other. Commercial enterprises are organized around a competitive business paradigm which does not necessarily serve our long-term common good. How do we start trusting ourselves to move from an old business paradigm which has made incredible technological progress and improved our physical well-being but cannot carry us into the future? The technological progress it has produced has altered our perspective on life and is now beginning to work against us. How can we trust ourselves to make the transition to sustainable technology that works on behalf of an integrated social, economic, and environmental development? Not by sacrificing one for the other. This shift will require moving beyond competition as the core business paradigm to that of collaboration.

The real changes in the world will come from all people willing to take risks to find themselves, help their neighbors, and create a safe place to live and work. They will be found in government, the corporate board room, suburbia, the inner city street gang. There are no limits to the places the 21st Century entrepreneurial spirit will emerge. We just have to begin to be aware of what we are looking for and to start empowering ourselves to empower others. The 21st Century entrepreneurs are more powerful because their intentions come from their souls and not their egos. Their endeavors represent more than just an activity or a business. They reflect their personal philosophies and life journeys.

Bill Veltrop

is an "evolutionary agent" in the field of organization design and change. He is convinced that we are in the early stages of a quantum shift in the life-giving potential of our organizing forms. He is the founder of The International Center For Organization Design, a unique network of leading edge change champions passionately committed to supporting this shift.

His work with entrepreneurial initiatives included responsibility for organizational development with Exxon Enterprises' collection of over twenty-five high-tech venture start-up businesses.

A consultant with over twenty years of innovative organization design and change implementation experience in the United States, Canada, Europe, and the Far East, Veltrop has discovered that magic is possible when spirit and heart are evoked.

A hands-on futurist, he is particularly adept as an architect of alliances, designs, change strategies and events that help unfold generative new futures for everyone involved.

The Evolutionary Times: A Fable

Bill Veltrop

Arthur walked down the road to the mailbox in the first rays of the morning sunlight. He loved the way the foliage came to life in the soft light. He breathed deeply of the cool morning air and took inventory of the pockets of fragrance as he walked through them. Douglas fir, his favorite, reminded him of Christmas. Eucalyptus took him back to Vicks Vaporub and his mother's nurturing touch during his bouts of bronchitis as a kid. Poison oak's pungent smell reminded him to wash his hands after playing with the neighbor's dog. It was truly paradise here—just over the mountains from Silicon Valley, thought Arthur, except perhaps for poison oak and the occasional earthquake.

It had been well over a year since Arthur had decided to give himself a sabbatical after almost forty years of service in the world of business. He took another deep breath and counted his blessings.

It was almost eight years since Arthur had left Oldstar, and found this spot in the mountains overlooking Monterey Bay. He was as deeply in love with the area as when he first arrived. Mornings were his favorite time of the day.

In his last twelve years with Oldstar he had been involved with large-scale organizational change and design work. His special interest and expertise had been in the area of innovative work system design. Oldstar itself was a world-class pioneer in this work. Arthur's prior technical and managerial "careers" had been perfect preparation for organizational design work, which soon became his first love. He had had no trouble stepping directly into external consulting work after leaving Oldstar.

The seven years he then spent consulting with high tech firms in "the Valley" had been challenging and rewarding. But something was missing from the equation. This sabbatical was now providing him that missing variable.

He opened the mailbox. Hidden between the bills he noticed a plain business envelope with only his name typed on it. This aroused his curiosity and he opened it on the spot. It contained a copy of what appeared to be a classified ad.

> **Evolutionary Change Architect**
>
> Change is your medium of choice as well as today's inescapable reality. Community change, organizational change, personal change—they all offer unlimited challenge and opportunity for practicing and evolving your special gift. You see these challenges as interconnected and interdependent. You see the potential for a quantum shift at each of these levels. You are a learner-designer. You are a front-line player at all levels of change. You don't identify yourself with any particular "solution." You are able to find and extract the essence from a large variety of different theories and approaches. You are committed to designing elegant, minimalist change strategies that build a capacity for ongoing self-evolution.

That was it. No identification or explanation. No return address on the envelope. Not even a stamp. Arthur scratched his head. "Who could it be from?"

"Joan! It's got to be Joan." The ad certainly captured the essence of their recent explorations together. "She's the only one who knows me this well. But why did she go to all the trouble of hand delivering it to my mailbox? And faking the newspaper ad format?" Arthur was perplexed. Somehow it didn't quite make sense.

Joan had become a deep friend over the last several years. They had met seven years ago when he had first worked with her Omega management team over in the Valley.

Joan was Omega's Marketing VP and generally regarded as one of a handful of outstanding women execs in the Bay Area. They hadn't hit it off instantly. She was hard-driving and outspoken, and less than enthusiastic about the time demands of the work Arthur was doing with the top team.

But Arthur had gradually won her over through his innovative ways of looking at their team and organization, and through his directness and honesty in challenging the group.

Evolutionary or *generative* change had become more and more of a focal point in Arthur's thoughts over recent months. He saw the field of organizational design and change as needing radically new thinking. He and Joan had spent their entire time playing with this challenge the last time they got together for lunch at their customary meeting place.

The "ad" captured the essence of a new "archetype" he and Joan both agreed was needed on the organizational change scene. It had to be her. No one else had been this close to his thinking.

****

He dialed Joan at her home as soon as he got back to his desk.

"Hi," she answered. "What's up? I'm running late and I don't have much time right now."

"I just need a minute. I wanted to express my deep appreciation for the brilliant copy you wrote on my behalf. You do know how to market a concept," he told her.

"I don't have the slightest idea what you're talking about and I really am in a bit of a time crunch," she reiterated.

"Are you telling me you had nothing to do with the ad for Evolutionary Change Architect I received in the mail this morning?" he queried.

"I'm telling you I don't have the vaguest idea what you're talking about and I'm late and I think you've been living up in the mountains by yourself too long. Can't this wait until Friday? We are still on for lunch, aren't we?"

"Yeah, sure. You promise you had nothing to do with this?"

"Goodbye, Arthur."

Joan's tone was convincing. Her impatience suggested he

needed to rethink the situation.

The next morning he was reasonably casual about opening the mailbox. That feeling dissolved the instant he saw a second mystery envelope. He ripped it open and was rewarded with yet another simulated want ad.

Chief Executive Officer

Dreaming the "impossible dream." Has vision of organization as a self-evolving organism based on generative internal and external alliances. Sees advanced communications technologies as nervous system. Sees organizing and learning strategies as essential parts of overall business strategy. Sees R&D investment in this pioneering work as the highest-leverage, lowest-risk investment imaginable. Committed to serve as Chief Learning Officer.

Arthur was perplexed. He reread the ad. He could have written it himself, it was so on-target. One of the reasons he was taking this extended sabbatical was the scarcity of CEOs who were willing and able to take a truly visionary look at the possible organization of the future. He liked the ad. In fact, he'd like to meet the respondents. But he was still bothered by the puzzle of *who* had put it in his mailbox.

The next morning, as Arthur walked to the mailbox, he wondered if there would be another envelope this morning. And indeed, there was a third ad:

Historian

Dissatisfied with historical trends. Ready to write future history with a more generative story line and lots more winners.

This one was short and sweet and provocative. He liked it a lot.

Arthur didn't bother to dress before he went for the mail the next morning. He went in robe and slippers.

And sure enough, there was another of the unmarked envelopes.

Media Magician

Well-connected in radio, television and film. Especially networked with media players who are committed to making a significant and lasting difference through their

work. Close friendship with Ted and Jane would help
a bunch.

Friday: 12:02 pm

"Sorry I'm late, Arthur," Joan said apologetically. "I regret
being so abrupt with you on the phone the other morning. Your
good coaching on how to stay centered while in white water seems
to have eluded me lately."

Joan slid into the booth. "Ah-h-h, it's so good to gaze again on
your warm and smiling countenance. We need you back at Omega.
It's getting more and more like a zoo. Where did all the fun go?"

"And good noon to you, my lovely and beleaguered friend,"
Arthur responded. "Perhaps the fun has been in hiding because it
hasn't yet learned how to play with fear."

"Not so fast, my late-blooming philosopher. I need to decom-
press a bit before you get profound on me. Let's order and just *be* for
a few minutes."

When the waitress came for their orders, Joan decided on the
Lasagna Prima Vera while Arthur remained true to his long-
standing commitment to the Planet Burger.

They were well into their salads before Joan brought up
the subject that had so engaged Arthur all week. "So, what came of
your excitement about receiving an ad for an evolutionary architect?

"Did you track down the mind reader or was this all a product
of your own imagination run amuck?—or do you still harbor the
notion that I, for lack of action in my life, have begun moonlighting
as an alternative style mail person?"

"Well, it did take me a day or two to let you off the hook as a
contender," Arthur said. "Here, let me show you my haul for the
week, and you can tell me what you think."

Joan studied the ads, glancing up at Arthur occasionally to see
if she could pick up a clue. "It's a shame he never got interested
in poker," she thought, "he could clean up." Joan voiced her
reactions. "What a fantasy. Are you sure you haven't been creating
these in your sleep? They all fit with your thinking so perfectly. So,
what do you make of it? Who could be doing this?"

"You know, Joan, I finally decided I was focusing on the

wrong question. I needed to forget about *who* and concentrate on *why*."

"Aren't you curious about who is sending them? Whoever it is sure has your number."

"Sure I'm curious," Arthur replied, "but when I started playing with the ads as pieces of a puzzle I began to get much more interested in solving the puzzle than in finding out who created the pieces."

"So, are you able to make a picture out of the four puzzle pieces?"

Arthur smiled, "It's a bit like sketching a dinosaur when you have only a few fossilized knuckles to go on. However, some ideas are emerging. It was the ad for the historian that got me started. The idea of writing future history hooked me. Maybe that's what's missing. Maybe we need to make a serious attempt at writing the history we want rather than just interpreting the past.

"Maybe we should stand in the future and write about business and the new direction it took during the 1990s. We could describe a revolution in organization design that had an even more profound impact on business than the shift from vacuum tubes to silicon chips. We'd describe how today's thinking about management and organization design got turned upside down—how we shifted from severely limiting assumptions to assumptions designed to serve the common good."

"I'm becoming increasingly convinced that this organizational breakthrough will somehow be pioneered by entrepreneurial initiatives," he continued. "So much of our history has been shaped by the entrepreneur. It makes sense that entrepreneurs will play a major role in leading this global shift."

"Arthur, when you speak of organizational transformation and evolutionary change I know you're not just talking radical change. I know you. You're talking about a profound shift in values as well. I really have a hard time seeing entrepreneurs leading the way in such a shift."

"Why not, Joan? All the true entrepreneurs I know are adventurers and are fired up with the pioneering spirit. Most of them started out being driven more by a commitment to make a difference in the world than to see who could accumulate the most cash and the most toys."

"There's some truth in that," Joan reflected. "We used to have that spirit within Omega. Then as we got successful and grew we seemed to get caught up in the same game as everyone else."

Arthur nodded. "In the world of business, it seems that there's no more effective anesthetic than success."

"So, what's your solution, Arthur? How do we break out of this vicious cycle. It's hard for me to see a band of entrepreneurs on white horses sweeping down into the Valley to save us."

"That seems a little dramatic to me as well. My picture is still unclear but I'm convinced that we're moving toward a magical merging of entrepreneurial and evolutionary spirits.

"But," Arthur added, "I think I'd like to see if there are any more clues forthcoming before I attempt to describe what I'm beginning to see."

"And I do need to return to the zoo," Joan enjoined. "Promise me you'll have a picture of how the world will be saved by a horde of evolutionary entrepreneurs when we meet next Friday."

****

During the week between luncheons with Joan, Arthur received three more ads:

Vision Capitalists

You influence the flow of a large stream of money. You see money as energy. You believe money can become an incredible generative force. You are interested in transforming the role of money in the world and are looking for the most highly leveraged vehicle for exploring this possibility.

Generative Journalists

Willing to conduct an appreciative investigation into the emerging field of evolutionary design; to weave the best possible emerging future from the compelling clues popping up all around and within us. Willing to have Dustin Hoffman, Robert Redford, or equally compelling actress (as appropriate) portray him/her in a screen version of the story.

Story Tellers
Imaginative weavers of enchanting tales. Able to translate
this profound and complex emergence of systemic shifts into
powerful and embraceable metaphors accessible to all.

****

Friday: 12:04 pm

Arthur was already comfortably ensconced in a booth when
Joan arrived.

After they ordered, he laid out the latest ads he had received.

He began, "Seeing these ads as pieces of a puzzle and looking
at them within the context of writing future history was central to
unleashing my imagination. And I did unleash it. I had fun letting
it go wild. It was really difficult to let go of old assumptions and to try
on some new ones. But I did anyway.

"My first new assumption is that we've all been put on earth
to evolve and to create. We've been gifted with exquisite biological
circuitry that we've only begun to utilize. So, you can imagine that
when we spirits are confined to organizing forms that stifle our
natural creative impulse, we get grumpy and turned off.

"My second assumption is that one of our supreme challenges
on earth is to evolve those social organisms that some call organizations to a point where they begin to approach the elegance we see in
nature.

"My third assumption is that there is a small but rapidly
growing collection of players who have excellent experience in
evolving themselves and their work. I'm assuming these players are
scattered all over the place and for the most part don't know each
other.

"My fourth assumption is that the to-be-invented *field of
evolutionary design* represents perhaps the greatest entrepreneurial
opening since the invention of silicon dioxide. Think of the market.
Everywhere in the 'civilized' world there are organizations that
don't work very well and change initiatives that seem to be creating
as many problems as they solve. Seen through these lenses, the field
of evolutionary design offers a market niche of infinite potential."

Joan looked across the table, "I need help here, Arthur. As I
understand your concept of evolutionary design, it would require us

to learn what it takes to redesign our organizations so that they have the infrastructure and capabilities to continuously evolve themselves to higher and higher levels of service. This is a great concept. However, I don't see the entrepreneurial bonanza. I'm missing something here."

"Joan, the business of organizational change is incredibly big business. The total costs of change world-wide are measured in terms of hundreds of billions of dollars. These change initiatives are extraordinarily costly in terms of dollars and pain and they really aren't working very well.

"Joan, I'm convinced the survival of our businesses and of all of our institutions is dependent on our achieving a radical breakthrough in how we approach organizational change and design. I'm also convinced we can design our organizations as self-evolving social organisms that can be ten times as effective as our better traditional organizations."

"Arthur, I love the way you think, but sometimes your claims simply push me over the edge."

"Let me finish, Joan. I'm making the assumption that we have evolved our definition of the bottom line and are now measuring success in terms of net contribution to the *overall well-being* of *all* stakeholders. Financial well-being is essential, but is only a piece of the puzzle. The fact that many of today's businesses are considered successful while the world's condition is steadily worsening suggests we must redefine success."

"So, you're claiming that even our most successful businesses can radically improve their effectiveness in contributing to the well-being of their customers, their employees, their community, etc., in addition to keeping their investors happy."

"That's what I'm claiming, Joan."

"Well I still think you have a terminal case of hyperbole, but I'll let it rest for now. Have you made any more assumptions?"

Arthur continued, "My fifth assumption is that these mysterious ads are laden with clues as to how to sound a note to attract a band of evolutionary entrepreneurs with the requisite variety of skills and resources to begin to shift the entire game of business.

"I've received seven ads—seven puzzle pieces, if you will. The first couple of ads felt to me like someone was reading my mind. The subsequent ads have increasingly been boundary stretchers.

"Picture this, Joan. What if this puzzle had a hundred pieces or more? What if each want ad represented a real living person who is ready to shift to co-creating an entirely new game? What if the picture on the puzzle box is of a new field that's ready to manifest itself—the field of evolutionary design?

Arthur continued: "What if the ads are pieces of a puzzle picturing a new field, a new business ecosystem, an evolutionary business ecosystem? What if our task is to create enough of the rest of the pieces for the prospective players to get a sense of the emerging picture so that they might determine if this is the game for them?"

Joan was still puzzled. "Okay, so you make up more ads that sketch out who you think ought to be involved in your new game. How do you go about finding these birds?"

"I'm glad you asked. I just happen to have an inspired solution. Inspiration struck me when I was standing in line waiting to check out at our local supermarket. I was cheating on my media fast by reading *The National Enquirer* headlines. You know, they've got this newspaper game figured."

Joan grimaced, but Arthur continued, "My impression is that *The National Enquirer* starts by designing its headlines and then creates stories that will fit the headlines. Some might be a trifle put off by their taste and ethics, but the strategy seems quite effective."

"Picture this, Joan. We create an ever-evolving newspaper, drawing inspiration from not only *The National Enquirer* and our ads, but also from Bill Murray's movie, *Groundhog Day*. In the movie, Murray repeated the same day over and over again until he got it 'right.'

"We create the beginnings of a very different newspaper called *The Evolutionary Times*.

"Its classified section would be one of its featured attractions. It would be the puzzle section listing the kind of allies we might imagine to be needed to provide the globe with 'starter dough' that could accelerate the rate of our conscious evolution.

"*The Evolutionary Times* would be unique in many ways. We would start by crafting headlines that speak to the commitments of those budding evolutionary allies we want to attract."

"Let me stop you there," Joan interjected. "What might be examples of such headlines?"

"Hmm . . . Okay, I'll give it a shot.

"How about, **'President's Award Winners For 12 Evolutionary Design Categories To Be Announced Tonight'** or **'Nation Showing Signs Of Recovery From Addiction To Consumerism'** or **'Unemployed Placed On Endangered Species List'**?"

"Why don't you go for something far out?" Joan asked wryly.

"Joan, unless we're able to picture a radically improved, best-case scenario for the future, I don't believe we have *any* chance of getting there. We need uncommon goals and uncommon pathways to those goals.

"We would be out to craft a collection of headlines that would elicit the commitment of an initial collection of allies.

"We would challenge these self-same allies to explore potential generative alliances with each other, to improve on the headlines and to create the stories that will show how their alliances can help bring life to these headlines.

"*The Evolutionary Times* would be like *Groundhog Day* in that we start with a first edition, whatever it might be, and we keep redoing it until we get it right.

"And get this—this could be the best part. There's this book concept, *The New Entrepreneurs*, which is a commitment to develop a new breed of entrepreneurs in a way that nurtures the emerging planetary reality. Many of the evolutionary allies we're talking about will be reading this book. *The New Entrepreneurs* can serve as a high-order incubator for hatching such entrepreneurs."

"What if no one shows up?" Joan asked with some tenderness in her voice.

Arthur looked deep into her eyes and smiled. "Well then, we do it anyway!"

****

This completes my story. Would you like to play a role in the next story?

Michael Ray,
PhD, is the first John G. McCoy-
Banc One Corporation Professor
of Creativity and Innovation and of
Marketing at Stanford University's Graduate School of Business. A social
psychologist, Ray is a Fellow of the World Business Academy and received
that organization's Willis Harman Award in 1991. He has served on ten
public and nonprofit boards, often in the start-up phase.

Among his over one hundred publications are his co-authored books
Creativity in Business (with Rochelle Myers) and *The Path of the Everyday
Hero* (with Lorna Catford) based on his Stanford creativity course that has
generated national and international attention. The course also inspired the
PBS series "The Creative Spirit" for which Ray co-authored (with Daniel
Goleman and Paul Kaufman) the book of the same name. He is also co-
editor (with Alan Rinzler) of *The New Paradigm in Business*. Nearly two
hundred outside visitors, primarily entrepreneurs (including seven authors in
this book), have come to his creativity and new paradigm business courses.

Conclusion

The New Entrepreneurship: A Heroic Path in a Time of Transition

Michael Ray

When one reads this collection of articles there is a sense not of individual knights jousting with dragons for the hand of some fair maiden but rather of real heroes for today, people dealing with the challenges of a world in chaotic transition. These heroes and heroines are operating from a perspective of what they can do in service, competing yet moving more and more into cooperation and co-creation with others.

Because they have been on a personal quest, they know there are dragons out there. They know the difficulty and suffering that is part of this world. But they also have full faith in their inner creativity or spirit with its infinite intuition, will, joy, strength and, most importantly, compassion. They know, as we all must, that the joy and promise of life is taking these inner qualities and bringing them forth into the world to deal with challenges in a constant quest for the highest—for themselves and everyone around them.

What is key, though, is that these are only a handful of the millions around the world who have turned to entrepreneurship as a way of life, a heroic path. We are living in a time of what is perhaps the greatest global mind change in history—this is a paradigm shift

(change in fundamental assumptions) equaling and perhaps surpassing the triumph of Christianity in the 4th Century that moved
the Western world from the classical to the medieval worlds, or the
17th Century Scientific Revolution that gave us the paradigm
under which we are living today.

The Transition

The signs of this current shift are all around us. Every one of
the authors in this book refers to it in some way. The change is so
revolutionary and discontinuous, almost moment to moment, that
we can't depend on the structures of business and society that
seemed to be so long-lasting in the past.

We have to move forward into something new, because it is
apparent that the old paradigm isn't working. Technology and the
scientific view have brought us abundance in many ways. But the
side effects are alienation and despair, hunger, bitter conflict over
what is seen as dwindling resources, and environmental degradation that challenges our very existence. These are forcing us to look
for new ways of being and working together that are represented by
this book.

I'm reminded of Layton Fisher of Imperial Oil, who was
speaking at a symposium of Bill Veltrop's International Center for
Organization Design. He pointed out that if you represented all the
knowledge that had been amassed from the beginning of time to the
year 1980 by one book, you would have to have two such books in
1987, four such books in 1994 and so on. In fact, recent estimates
have it that the mass of cumulative knowledge now is doubling at
twice that rate, every three and a half years.

"Trying to manage your life or your organization in a world
changing that rapidly is like dancing with a gorilla," said Fisher.
"You don't stop when you get tired. You stop when the gorilla gets
tired."

There is no sign that the gorilla is going to stop. As we have
tried to deal with this kind of world, we have seen that momentary
victories change into difficulties and new challenges. Business has
flirted with solutions such as management by objectives, zero-based
budgeting, total quality management, empowerment, self-directed

teams, reengineering, and on and on. Although all of these have some value, none is the Holy Grail.

In fact, within the old ways of business, an intense application of any one of them can lead to great difficulty. As one visitor to our New Paradigm Business course at Stanford said, "If you were doing TQM in the seventies, you were a pioneer. If you were doing it in the eighties, it was probably a good idea. But TQM in the nineties is corporate suicide."

The answer to getting through this time is not to be found in a technique. It is to be found in what this book represents—taking a path with heart, operating from your deepest inner resources in concert with others, seeing a vision and staying with it, dealing with difficulties as challenges but always following the quest in a bigger way.

The Hero's Journey

In short, the answer to getting through this time of transition with exultation rather than misery is to live the life of a hero. But it is to live the heroic life in the new entrepreneurial way, as represented by the authors in this book, bringing out all aspects of your resources—the feminine as well as the masculine, the cooperative as well as the competitive, the creative as well as the destructive, the individual as well as the organizational, the passion as well as the peace, the unstructured as well as the structured—all in the service of something higher, something more functional in today's world of chaos.

In the Introduction of this book, John Renesch refers to probably the most important part of the hero's journey—the "calling." He was referring to entrepreneurship as a vocation, as an individual's meant-to-be, the purpose of their life.

In *The Path of the Everyday Hero*, Lorna Catford and I explore the call in a lifetime way as Renesch does and also look at the process of the hero's journey that we all go through over and over again in our lives. Our depiction is based on myths and stories that span the times and cultures of the globe. Myth is beyond paradigm. The stories of the hero have enriched people in the classical, medieval and modern scientific periods. They will give us sustenance in this period of transition now because, like the lives of the entrepreneurs in this book, they show what is possible, even if the adversary isn't really a physical threat but our own attitudes and outdated assumptions.

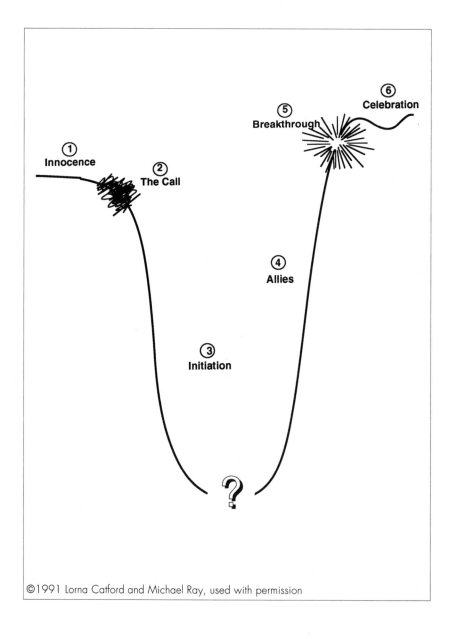

In the heroic myth, the hero goes through tests but always comes out with a breakthrough and celebration in the end. As shown on the previous page, Catford and I represent this repeating journey with a U-curve. At first the hero is in Innocence, a period that is a respite following his or her previous adventure. This is shown by a flat portion on the left side of the figure.

Then there is the Call. Once it is accepted, the journey goes downhill into a Pit, the bottom of the U-curve. Most people, companies and nations try to resist the Call, but their lives are empty and useless until they take it. As Renesch implies in the Introduction, this is not the case with the entrepreneur and the potential entrepreneur in all of us. The entrepreneurial spirit leads to taking the Call and going down into the Pit. This is precisely the kind of spirit that is needed now.

Interesting things happen in the Pit, the bulk of the hero's journey. First, there is Initiation, in which the hero receives a full understanding of the challenge through a difficult situation. Second, there are Allies, people and events that help the hero along. When Paul Hwoschinsky writes about non-financial assets, he is talking about the allies that we all have but often don't recognize. Other entrepreneurs in this book talk about the chance events in their journeys that carried them forward. These too are the Allies.

Finally, due to the experience and validation of Initiation and the help of Allies, the hero achieves a Breakthrough, and our curve moves up to an higher plateau than the Innocence one. And this plateau, on the right side of our diagram, represents Celebration.

Celebration is inevitable, followed by Innocence and the chance to start the cycle all over again. Entrepreneurs, the kind that are needed for the present times, understand this. The entrepreneurial stance to the hero's journey has a constancy about it. Failure is used as a springboard for further advances. There is an understanding of the cyclical nature of the journey.

One entrepreneur told me that he loved the low periods. He likened those times to low tide when you can actually see all the underwater dangers. He said that sailing along at high tide, you don't really know what is going on. This kind of precise observation is exactly what is needed now.

Giving Birth

The same man talked about being in the delivery room with his wife for the birth of their first child. He said he began to realize that giving birth to a business had a lot of similarities to giving birth to a baby. There was contraction and then relaxation and contraction and relaxation—all moving toward birth and the continuing of the process in a different way following that. Again, another hero's journey that entrepreneurs understand so well.

This analogy of the birth process and the process we must now go through in this world should not be taken lightly. You read over and over again in this book how this journey's dramatic course energizes and fulfills entrepreneurs, even as it pushes them on to deal with new levels.

This is strikingly similar to actual experiences of the birth process that have been discovered by the psychotherapist Stanislav Grof. He first used psychoactive substances and later non-drug therapeutic methods to catalyze unconscious memories of their own births in thousands of subjects in Europe and America. His highly reliable and effective findings bear a resemblance to not only the entrepreneurial experience but also the kind of change that we all are going through in this time of transition.

Like the hero's journey, Grof's sequence is painful and causes much discomfort along the way, but it ends in the sort of exultation that can give people a way to move forward with greater humanity.

The first stage of the perinatal (surrounding birth) sequence that Grof found is a state of undifferentiated unity, not unlike the Innocence part of the hero's journey. Then, in the second stage, just as in the Call and Initiation stages, there is constriction, conflict, and contradiction, with an accompanying sense of separation, duality, and alienation. The third stage, somewhat comparable to being in the Pit, is like a death. Subjects talk about it as complete annihilation. Then there is a final stage, like the Allies and Breakthrough steps, that writer Richard Tarnas describes in *The Passion of the Western Mind* as "an unexpected redemptive liberation that both overcame and fulfilled the intervening alienated state—restoring the initial unity but on a new level that preserved the achievement of the whole trajectory."

A Different Kind of Entrepreneur

It is tempting to presume that active entrepreneurs have some better memory of this birth process and are acting it out in a way that most people avoid. Whether or not this is true, it is clear that the kind of entrepreneurship represented in this book is different from the stereotype.

One difference comes from an uncommon level of compassion. The kind of compassion I am talking about here is not the mushiness of "do gooders." It is loving kindness, first for oneself and then for others. It is a deep faith in one's own creativity and goodness and, as a result of that, an ability to see it in others. Over and over in this book you see how the entrepreneurs' own breakthroughs come from and are given as gifts to others.

This connection to others is related to the second difference in the new entrepreneurs, a tendency to move beyond even cooperation to a state that Terry Mollner calls Self-Conscious Consensus or Harmony. In this state, each individual in the group makes decisions that are good for both the individual and the group. Over and over again in this book you read about individuals, contrary to the entrepreneurial stereotype, making moves that benefit others—and that then come back to enrich them a thousandfold. This is the kind of hero that we all need to be in the current times. Entrepreneurs are leading the way in showing that it works.

There is also a new way that the entrepreneurs in this book move and work with others. I remember when I asked Herman Maynard, then a DuPont intrapreneur and now an entrepreneur himself, at a World Business Academy meeting what it would be like if an organization was composed completely of enlightened individuals (having in the back of my mind that one overarching objective for new paradigm business would be the enlightenment of all those within it). I was astounded when he said, "We've talked about that a lot. We think that it would be a situation in which there wouldn't be a need for meetings or even technological communication as much as we see today. People would begin to work together and move together and know what to do without even having to verbally express their needs or their intended actions."

This stimulated me to think about how I had heard of the

Guarneri String Quartet practicing with each other without talking, of basketball great Bill Russell having certain games with the Boston Celtics in which he moved effortlessly with both his teammates and his competitors in the "zone." I also remember the times when I saw dance companies perform incredible individual and group feats of great beauty. This is the sense of the possible nature of work, leadership and organization that I get from reading this book.

Earlier I said that I sensed that these authors know that the present challenge is in taking the inner qualities and applying them in the world of change. One ancient tradition says that there are three obstacles to such a task—a feeling of smallness and inadequacy, a feeling that there are differences and separation between individuals, and a false sense of doing or attachment to the outcomes of actions.

What I have learned from this book is that there are some individuals, perhaps many, who go beyond these obstacles. Without ego, they recognize their own inherent greatness and manifest it in action. They see this same value in others to the point that they feel connected, trusting, and responsible. They act without attachment to the results, but rather for the joy and contribution that action gives.

This is the new "herohood"—the new entrepreneurship that we all need to get us through the present transition.

Recommended Reading and Resources

Barrentine, Pat, ed. *When the Canary Stops Singing: Women's Perspectives on Transforming Business.* San Francisco: Berrett-Koehler, 1993.

Block, Peter. *Stewardship: Choosing Service Over Self-Interest.* San Francisco: Berrett-Koehler, 1993.

Carey, Ken. *Starseed, the Third Millenium: Living in the Posthistoric World.* San Francisco: Harper, 1991.

Catford, Lorna and Michael Ray. *The Path of the Everyday Hero.* Los Angeles: Tarcher, 1991.

Carse, James P. *Finite & Infinite Games: A Vision of Life as Play and Possibility.* New York: Ballentine Books, 1986.

Chappel, Tom. *The Soul of a Business: Managing for Profit and the Common Good.* New York: Bantam Books, 1993.

Covey, Stephen R. *The 7 Habits of Highly Effective People: Powerful Lessons in Personal Change.* New York: Fireside, 1989.

Deming, W. Edwards. *The New Economics.* Cambridge, Massachusetts: MIT, 1993.

Fassel, Diane and Anne W. Schaef. *The Addictive Organization.* New York: HarperCollins, 1988.

Fassel, Diane. *Working Ourselves to Death.* New York: HarperCollins, 1990.

Forrester, Jay, "A New Corporate Design," *Sloan Management Review,* MIT (1965).

Forrester, Jay. "Enterprise Designers Called for by the System Theory Founder." *The New Leaders,* July/Aug 1993.

Frenier, Carol. "Love at Work." *The New Leaders,* Jan/Feb 1994.

Haessly, Jacqueline. *Learning to Live Together.* San Jose, California: Resource Publications, 1989.

Haessly, Jacqueline. *Peacemaking: Family Activities for Justice and Peace.* New York: Paulist Press, 1980.

Haessly, Jacqueline. "Values for the Global Marketplace: A Quest for Quality with Difference." *When the Canary Stops Singing: Women's Perspectives on Transforming Business.* San Francisco: Berrett-Koehler, 1993.

Harman, Willis and John Hormann. *Creative Work: The Constructive*

Role of Business in a Transforming Society. Indianapolis,
Indiana: Knowledge Systems, Inc., 1990.

Harman, Willis. "21st Century Business: A Background for Dialogue." *New Traditions in Business: Spirit and Leadership in the 21st Century.* Ed. John Renesch. San Francisco: Berrett-Koehler, 1992.

Harman, Willis. *Global Mind Change: The Promise of the Last Years of the Twentieth Century.* Indianapolis, Indiana: Knowledge Systems, Inc., 1987.

Harman, Willis. "Sustainable Development: The Modern Challenge for Business." *The New Leaders,* Nov/Dec 1991.

Hawken, Paul. *Ecology of Commerce: A Declaration of Sustainability.* New York: HarperBusiness, 1993.

Hawken, Paul. *Growing a Business.* New York: Simon and Schuster, 1987.

Hwoschinsky, Paul. *True Wealth.* Berkeley: Ten Speed Press, 1990.

Kouzes, James M. and Barry Z. Posner. *Credibility: How Leaders Gain and Lose It, Why People Demand It.* San Francisco: Jossey-Bass, 1993.

Kurtzman, Joel. *The Death of Money: How the Electronic Economy Has Destabilized the World's Markets and Created Financial Chaos.* New York: Simon and Schuster, 1993.

Land, George and Beth Jarman. *Breakpoint and Beyond:Mastering the Future—Today.* San Francisco: HarperBusiness, 1992.

Liebig, James E. *Business Ethics: Profiles in Civic Virtue.* Golden, Colorado: Fulcrum Publishing, 1990.

Liebig, James. *Merchants of Vision: People Bringing New Purpose and Values to Business.* San Francisco: Berrett-Koehler, 1994.

Maynard, Herman and Sue Mehrtens. *The Fourth Wave: Business in the 21st Century.* San Francisco: Berrett-Koehler, 1993.

Miller, William. *The Creative Edge: Fostering Innovation Where You Work.* Reading, Massachusettes: Addison-Wesley, 1986.

Mollner, Terry. "Making Employee Ownership Work," *World Business Academy Perspectives,* Jan. 1990.

Morong, Cyril. "Entrepreneurs, Heros and the New Science." *The New Leaders,* May/June 1993.

Morong, Cyril. "The 'Calling' of the Entrepreneur." *The New Leaders,* Nov/Dec 1992.

Naisbitt, John. *Global Paradox: The Bigger the World Economy the More Powerful Its Smallest Players*. New York: William Morrow and Company, 1994.

Österberg, Rolf. *Corporate Renaissance: Business as an Adventure in Human Development*. Mill Valley, California: Nataraj Publishing, 1993.

"Patagonia CEO Calls for Real Leadership—an End to 'White Noise' and Mediocrity." *The New Leaders*, May/June 1993.

Ray, Michael and Rochelle Myers. *Creativity in Business*. New York: Doubleday, 1986, 1989.

Ray, Michael and Alan Rinzler, eds. *The New Paradigm in Business: Emerging Strategies for Leadership and Organizational Change*. New York: Tarcher/Perigee, 1993.

Renesch, John, ed. *New Traditions in Business: Spirit and Leadership in the 21st Century*. San Francisco: Berrett-Koehler, 1992.

Renesch, John. "Coming Out of the Closet: A Time for Courage in the Workplace." *The New Leaders*. May/June 1991.

Roddick, Anita. *Body and Soul: Profits with Principles—The Amazing Success Story of Anita Roddick and The Body Shop*. New York: Crown Publishers, Inc., 1991.

Russell, Peter. *The White Hole in Time: Our Future Evolution & the Meaning of Now*. San Francisco: Harper, 1992.

Sakaiya, Taichi. *The Knowledge-Value Revolution*. New York: Kodansha America, 1991.

Schmookler, Andrew. *Fools Gold: The Fate of Values in a World of Goods*. San Francisco: Harper, 1993.

Schor, Juliet. *The Overworked American: The Unexpected Decline of Leisure*. New York: Basic Books, 1992.

Senge, Peter M. "The Leader's Work: Building Learning Organizations," *Sloan Management Review*, Fall 1990.

Senge, Peter M. *The Fifth Discipline: The Art and Practice of the Learning Organization*. New York: Doubleday, 1990.

Thompson, John W. *The Human Factor: An Inquiry into Communication and Consciousness*. Farmingdale, NY: Coleman Publishing, 1983.

Wheatley, Margaret J. *Leadership and the New Science: Learning About Organizations from an Orderly Universe*. San Francisco: Berrett-Koehler, 1992.

Business Periodicals*

At Work: Stories of Tomorrow's Workplace
Berrett-Koehler Publishers, Inc.
155 Montgomery St., San Francisco, CA 94104-4109
800/929-2929
Reg. rate: $75/1 year (bimonthly newsletter)

Business Ethics:
The Magazine for Socially Responsible Business
Mavis Publications, Inc.
52 South 10th St., #110, Minneapolis, MN 55403-2001
612/962-4700
Special Rate: $25/1 year (bimonthly magazine)
Free samples available

The New Leaders:
The Business Newsletter for Transformative Leadership
Sterling & Stone, Inc./New Leaders Press
P.O. Box 37, Corte Madera, CA 94976-0037
800/765-4625
Special rate: $89/year, $159/2 years (bimonthly newsletter)

The Systems Thinker
Pegasus Communications, Inc.
P.O. Box 120, Kendall Square, Cambridge, MA 02142
617/576-1231
Special rate: $117/1 year, $197/2 years (10 issues/year newsletter)

World Business Academy Perspectives
Berrett-Koehler Publishers, Inc.
155 Montgomery St., San Francisco, CA 94104-4109
800/929-2929
Reg. rate: $96/1 year (quarterly journal)

*For international orders, check with publishers for extra shipping costs.

Membership Organizations

BUSINESS FOR SOCIAL RESPONSIBILITY
1850 M St. N.W. #750
Washington, D.C. 20036
202/842-5400

BUSINESS FOR SOCIAL RESPONSIBILITY
P.O. Box 280370.
San Francisco, CA 94128
415/931-1795

RENAISSANCE BUSINESS ASSOCIATES
P.O. Box 26510
Colorado Springs, CO 80936-6510
719/495-9616

WORLD BUSINESS ACADEMY
433 Airport Blvd., #416
Burlingame, CA 94010
415/342-2387

How to Contact Authors/Editors

CHERYL ALEXANDER
Alexander Companies
3205 Casco Circle
Wayzata, MN 55391
612/471-0121

RICHARD BLISS BROOKE
Oxyfresh USA, Inc.
P.O. Box 3723
Spokane, WA 99220
509/924-4999
fax 509/924-5322

BETSY BURTON
Supertans
22323 Sherman Way #4
Canoga Park, CA 91303
818/884-8276

SHARON GADBERRY
Transitions Management Group
Suite 1400
220 Sansome Street
San Francisco, CA 94104
415/981-0202

JACQUELINE HAESSLY
Peacemaking Associates
2437 N. Grant Blvd.
Milwaukee, WI 53210
414/444-4747

PAUL HWOSCHINSKY
443 Strawberry Ln.
Ashland, OR 97520-2778
503/482-3277

DAVID JASPER
Quest Management
8900 Birchwood Lane
Bloomington, MN 55438-1362
612/ 944-1111
fax 612/944-1215

MARJORIE KELLY
Business Ethics Magazine
52 S. 10th Street, Suite 110
Minneapolis, MN 55403
612/962-4700

RON KOVACH
Outdoor Enterprises
17911 Portside Circle
Huntington Beach, CA 92649
714/840-6555

NICHOLAS P. LIVOLSI
World Trust
48 Commonwealth Avenue
Boston, MA 02116
617/262-7540

CHRIS MANNING
Manning Advisors
1200 17th Street, Suite 2630
Denver, CO 80202
303/572-6611
fax 303/572-6010

PEGGY PEPPER
First Concept Corporation
5956 Sherry Lane, Suite 1000
Dallas, TX 75225
214/265-1171

MICHAEL RAY
Graduate School of Business
Stanford University
Stanford, CA 94305-5015
415/723-2762
fax 415/725-7979

JOHN RENESCH
New Leaders Press
1000 Chestnut Street #14-C
San Francisco, CA 94109
415/928-1473

ANITA RODDICK
The Body Shop
Watersmead
Littlehampton, West Sussex
BN17-6LS, United Kingdom
011.44.903.731.500
fax 011.44.903.726.250

WILLIAM SECHREST
Winstead Sechrest & Minick
5400 Renaissance Tower
1201 Elm Street
Dallas, TX 75270
214/745-5244
fax 214/745-5390

JEFF SHOLL
6121 Scotin Drive
Edina, MN 55439
612/943-8131

JOHN STEARNS
JHS Enterprises, Inc.
3460 Lythrum Way
Minnetrista, MN 55364
612/472-5737

GREG STELTENPOHL
Odwalla, Inc.
Box O
Davenport, CA 95017
408/425-4557
fax 408/425-1719

BILL VELTROP
International Center
    for Organization Design
1450 Hidden Valley Road
Soquel, CA 95073
408/462-1992
fax 408/474-7256

Index

Additional copies of

THE NEW ENTREPRENEURS

can be purchased from the organizations listed below or their representatives:

CALIFORNIA
Int'l. Center for Organization Design, Soquel 408/462-1992
Odwalla Juices, Davenport 408/425-4557
Supertans, Canoga Park 818/884-8276
Transitions Management Group, San Francisco 415/981-0202

COLORADO
Manning Advisors, Denver 303/572-6611

MASSACHUSETTS
World Trust, Boston 617/262-7540

MINNESOTA
Alexander Companies, Wayzata 612/471-0121
Green Giant Fresh, Edina 612/832-9363
JHS Enterprises, Minnetrista 612/472-6440
Quest Management, Bloomington 612/944-1111

OREGON
Swan•Raven, Newberg 800/366-0264

TEXAS
First Concept Corporation, Dallas 214/265-1171
Winstead, Sechrest & Minick, Dallas 214/745-5244

WASHINGTON
Oxyfresh USA, Inc, Spokane 509/924-4999

WISCONSIN
Peacemaking Associates, Milwaukee 414/445-9736

OTHER BUSINESS ANTHOLOGIES
developed by New Leaders Press

New Traditions in Business: Spirit & Leadership in the 21st Century. Authors include Willis Harman, Michael Ray, Herman Maynard, Jim Channon, William Miller, Peter Senge, Terry Mollner, Robert Rosen, Juanita Brown, Cynthia Barnum, David Gaster, Charles Kiefer, Carol Sanford, John Thompson, and Ken Blanchard; edited by John Renesch.
Available in paperback from Berrett-Koehler Publishing at $17.95 (U.S.); call 1.800.929.2929.

When the Canary Stops Singing: Women's Perspectives on Transforming Business. Author's include Riane Eisler, Carol Frenier, Kathleen Keating, Marie Kerpan, Barbara Shipka, Kim McMillen, Jacqueline Haessly, Jan Nickerson, Anne L. Rarich, Jeanne Borei, Hope Xaviermineo, Cheryl Harrison, Mitani D'Antien, Barbara Fittipaldi, and Sabina Spencer; edited by Pat Barrentine.
Available in hardcover from Berrett-Koehler Publishers at $24.95 (U.S.); call 1.800.929.2929.

FORTHCOMING COLLECTIONS (as of June, 1994):

Leadership in a New Era: Visionary Approaches to the Biggest Crisis of Our Times (est. pub. date August, 1994). Authors include James Autry, Carol Sanford, Barbara Ruth Hauser, Ann Morrison, Ed Oakley, Peter Krembs, Charles Kiefer, Warren Bennis, Kate Steichen, Barbara Shipka, Tina Rasmussen, Larry Spears, Elemer Magaziner, Susan M. Campbell, Rob Rabbin, Margaret Wheatley, John D. Adams, Martha Spice, Carol McCall, Max DePree, Perry Pascarella, and an interview of Norman Lear by Stewart Emery.

Learning Organizations: Developing Cultures for Tomorrow's Workplace (est. pub. date: 1995). Authors include Peter Senge and Fred Kofman, Charles Handy, Rosabeth Moss Kanter, and over thirty other authors.

Community Building: Renewing Spirit & Learning in Business (est. pub. date: 1995).

Rediscovering the Soul of Business: A Renaissance of Values (est. pub. date: 1995).

Corporate Passages: Stories of Personal Transformation Through Business (est. pub. date: 1996).